Jayaprakash Narayan

Jayaprakash Narayan

Series Editor
Dr. M.H. Syed

Editor
M.A. Khan **N.P. Sharma**

Himalaya Books Pvt. Ltd.
'Ramdoot', Dr. Bhalerao Marg, Girgaon, Mumbai - 400 004
Tel : (022) 23863863, Fax : (022) 23877178
Email : himpub@vsnl.com

First Edition : 2011

Published by : H.B.P.L.
"Pooja Apartments", 4-B, Murari Lal Street, Ansari Road,
Darya Ganj, New Delhi-110 002
Phones : 23270392, 23278631 Reliance : 30180392 to 396
Fax : 011-23256286 Email : hphdel@vsnl.com

Sole Distributers : HIMALAYA PUBLISHING HOUSE PVT. LTD.

Branch Offices

Mumbai : "Ramdoot", Dr. Bhalerao Marg, Girgaon, Mumbai-400 004.
Phones : 23860170/23863863 Fax : 022-23877178
Email : himpub@vsnl.com
Website : www.himpub.com

Nagpur : Kundanlal Chandak Industrial Estate, Ghat Road, **Nagpur 440-018.**
Phone: 2738731, 3296733 Telefax : 0712-2721215

Bengaluru : No. 16/1 (Old 12/1), 1st Floor, Next to Hotel Highlands,
Madhava Nagar, Race Course Road, **Bengaluru - 560 001.**
Phone : 22281541, 22385461, Telefax: 080-22286611

Hyderabad : No. 3-4-184, Lingampally, Besides Raghavendra Swamy Matham,
Kachiguda, **Hyderabad - 500 027.** Phone: 040-27560041,
27550139, Mobile:- 09848130433 Telefax: 040-27560041

Chennai : No. 85/50, Bazullah Road, T. Nagar, **Chennai - 600 017.**
Phone: 044-28344020, 32463737, 42124860

Pune : No. 527, "Laksha" Apartment, First Floor, Mehunpura,
Shaniwarpeth, (Near Prabhat Theatre), **Pune - 411 030.**
Phone: 020-24496323/24496333/32326733

Lucknow : Jai Baba Bhawan, Near Dr. Sanjiv Awasthi, Church Road,
Kurshi Road, Aliganj, **Lucknow - 226 024.**
Phone: 9305302158, 9415349385

Ahmedabad : No. 114, "SHAIL", 1st Floor, Opp. Madhu Sudan House, C.G.Road,
Navrang Pura, **Ahmedabad – 380 009.**
Phone: 079-26560126, Mobiles: 09327324149,09314679413

Ernakulam : No. 39/104 A, Lakshmi Apartment, Karikkamuri Cross Rd.,
Ernakulam, **Cochin – 682011**, Kerala.
Phone: 0484-2378012, 2378016, Mob.: 09344199799

Bhubaneswar : 5 Station Square, **Bhubaneswar (Orissa) - 751 001.**
Mobile: 9861046007, E-mail:-orissa@himpub.com

Indore : Kesardeep Avenue Extension, 73, Narayan Bagh, Flat No. 302,
IIIrd Floor, Near Humpty Dumpty School, Narayan Bagh,
Indore (M.P.) 452 007 Mobile: 09301386468

Kolkata : 108/4, Beliaghata, Main Road, Near ID Hospital, Opp. SBI Bank
Kolkata - 700 010. Mobile: 09910440956

Printed at : H.S. Offset Printers, Daryaganj, New Delhi-110 002

Preface

Biography, is now a form of literature, very much in vogue. In fact, biography is a description or account of someone's life and the times, which is usually published in the form of a book. A biography is more than a mention of personal facts (life, education, work, relationships and death), it also portrays the subject's experience of events. Technically speaking, a work is biographical, if it covers, all of a person's life. Biography writing has a long history. A biography is real. Ancient Greeks developed the biographical tradition, which we have inherited, although until the 5th century AD, when the word 'biographia' first appeared, in Damascius' "Life of Isodorus," biographical pieces were called simply "lives". It is quite likely that the Greeks were drawing on a pre-existing eastern tradition. Certainly Herodotus' "Histories" contains more detailed biographical information on Persian kings and subjects. The earliest surviving pieces, which we would identify as biographical are Isocrates' "Life of Evagoras" and Xenophon's "Life of Agesilaos," both from the fifth century BC. "Parallel Lives" by Plutarch, a Greek writing under the Roman empire, is a series of short biographies of eminent men.

The Golden Age of English biography emerged in late eighteenth century, the century in which the terms "biography" and "autobiography" entered English lexicon. The classic works of the period were Samuel Johnson's "Critical Lives of the Poets" and James Boswell's "Massive Life of Johnson". Generally American biography followed English model. By World War I, cheap hardcover reprints had become popular. The decade of the 1920s witnessed a biographical 'boom'. Later, biographical writings developed a lot and today biographies are written and compiled in the finest form of the genre. In India too, biography, as a form of literature has been evolved, cultivated and polished over the years. Here is an effort to promote this tradition further.

This series of biographies of great men, great women and celebrities in all walks of life is an adventurous academic endeavour, in its own right. A team of researchers and compilers has worked for a good period of time to accomplish the project. For this purpose, hundreds of books by eminent authors and editors have been consulted and referred to. We have benefited from various works, liberally, in order to illustrate and enrich this effort of ours. Present book is devoted to the great personality of Jayaprakash Narayan.

Jayaprakash Narayan, widely known as JP, was a great freedom fighter and political leader. He was one of the few leaders of modern India, who fought for its independence and took part in active politics for a long time, after it became independent. He did his higher studies in United States. After returning to India, JP joined Indian National Congress on the invitation of Jawaharlal Nehru in 1929. Mahatma Gandhi was his mentor in Congress. During independence movement, he was arrested, jailed, and tortured, several times by the British. He won particular fame, during Quit India movement. He was one of the founders of the Congress Socialist Party, a left-wing group, within the Congress. Later, he became deeply disillusioned with the practical experience of socialism in Nehru's India. Then, he led a movement against corruption and emergency, which led to the instalment of the first non-congress government at the centre. In 1998, he was posthumously awarded the Bharat Ratna award in recognition to his social service. Other awards included, the Magsaysay award for Public Service. JP is honourably referred to with the august title, Lok Nayak, meaning; 'People's Leader'.

This is a compact and comprehensive account of the above mentioned great life, which is bound to attract the attention of scholars, researchers, students and the general readers alike. Let's hope this humble effort would receive a warm welcome and due applause.

— ***Editors***

Contents

1

An Illustrious Life

Early Life

Jayaprakash Narayan was born in Sitabadiara village in Chhapra District of Bihar, When he was a child, he had many pets. One day, his pigeon died and he did not eat food till two days. His father Harsu Dayal was a junior official in the canal department of the State government and was often touring the region. Jayaprakash, called Baul affectionately, was left with his grandmother to study in Sitabdiara. There was no high school in the village, so Jayaprakash was sent to Patna to study in the Collegiate School. He excelled in school. His essay, "The present state of Hindi in Bihar", won a best essay award. He entered the Patna College on a Government scholarship.

Childhood

When Jayaprakash Narayan, the great revolutionary and the legendary political philosopher was born in village Sitabdaria, which was only 50 miles away from Patna, the capital of Bihar. The city of Pataliputra of King Ashoka fame was later known as Patna. The city was famous in ancient Indian history and was rich in cultural heritage. Patna is situated in the bank of river Ganges, the sacred perennial river of Hindus, that flows down from the great Himalayas. During King Ashoka's regime, Pataliputra or Patna was the capital of India and both politically and culturally ruled over India. But the present day Patna is famous for its involvement in the life and struggle of Jayaprakash. It was the soil of Patna that shaped Jayaprakash into a great revolutionary and legendary figure in the modern history of India. He was a man of sacrifice, dedication, honesty and simplicity. He was a valiant fighter against all injustice and he played a principal role in liberating India from the British subjugation. King Ashoka fought the battle of Kalinga with sword. But after witnessing the blood bath of the war, he lamented and repented and became the follower of great Buddha embracing non-violence for the rest of his life. Jayaprakash too was a great votary of Buddha, as he always acted on non-violence and fought the battle of emergency through the path of non-violence. Thus he followed the heritage of King Ashoka in word and spirit.

The village Sitabdaria stands in the valley between the river Saraju and river Ganges. It was a calm and serene village at the time when Jayaprakash was born. At present it has become a small town standing in the border of the States of Bihar and Uttar Pradesh. You have to cross the river in both sides to reach Sitabdaria as there is no bridge nearby on the river of Ganges. It was a village of Bihar with traditional poverty where people live only on agriculture. Wheat and Bajra are the major produce of the village. Most of the villagers lived under thatched roofs. Since long, Bihar was dominated by feudal lords who controlled its economy.

The maximum land of Sitabdaria belonged to the rich zamindars. The villagers were only tenants who used to pay the zamindars usual rent to cultivate their lands. At present the condition of the villagers are a bit better than it was at the time when Jayaprakash was born. The rich feudal class maintained a life of wealth and luxury at the cost of the poor. The British government leased out the entire village to the feudal agents on certain fixed amount of cess which the zamindar collected from the tenants and paid to the British government. They paid less to the government and enjoyed the rest money for themselves. It was typical parasitic class that became very powerful during the British regime. They behaved with the poor as their rulers and dictators.

They became the head of the society and dictated all social customs and practices to the common people and forced them to obey their verdicts. With the backing of the British government this parasitic class lived on the sweat and toil of the poor. Jayaprakash had the experience of the functioning of feudal system from his childhood as his village Sitabdaria was no exception to that He had seen the plight of the poor and the manner in which they were drastically exploited by their feudal lords Therefore fathers of Jayaprakash were also tenants of the Zamindars who did not cultivate the lands in their own hands. They leased out the lands for cultivation to landless people who gave a share of the produce to them. Those cultivators were known as share croppers. That was the system prevailed during the those days and the society accepted exploitation of the poor as the birth right of the rich.

The father of Jayaprakash, Shri Harsu Dayal was though not rich, belonged to a well-to-do family. He was educated and was an expert in Parsi language. While he was about to complete his graduation, he got a government job and preferred to give up his studies for the sake of his livelihood and was engaged in the PWD department. He took active part in the construction of the great bridge on Son river, the longest river bridge of our country in those days. Being associated with the construction of the Sone Bridge, Harsu Prashad brought glory to his village.

Harsu Babu commanded respect in the area as a dedicated man of service. Phul Rani, his wife gave birth to Jayaprakash on October 11, 1902. Jayaprakash was the fourth child of his parents. The eldest was Hari Prashad followed by two elder sisters Chandrabhanu and Chandramukhi. Harsu Babu and Phul Rani took great care of their children, so that they grew well to become good citizens in future. All the children were intelligent and disciplined. The parents were optimistic that all of them would bring name to the society. The eldest son Hari Prashad joined in high school and was faring well with his lessons. But often Providence did not allow the wishes of the man to be fulfilled. The same happened with the family of Harsu Babu. His family along with other villagers were attacked with epidemic of Cholera and Plague, and the epidemic was the most sorrowful eve of their life. The eldest son Hari Prashad died of Cholera at the age of thirteen along with some other children of the village. In those days of the British regime, medical relief was scanty and poor. It did not reach the suffering people of the remote villages at proper time. So many people had to succumb to these epidemics. The entire family was shocked over this premature demise of Hari Prashad. The grief that was brought to the family was beyond consolation. This made them more conscious towards taking care of the surviving children and they took great care to keep them away from the diseases. They prayed again and again to God to save their children from all epidemic.

Immediately after the cholera casualties, the epidemic of Plague engulfed the village. The shadow of death was hanging over the horizon of the village. There was no treatment available for Plague during that time. People got frightened and being scared, left their homes for distant places and started living in isolated places building small hutments. The family of Harsu Babu was included in this exodus. He migrated to a distant village with his wife and children and other members of his family to save them from the epidemic. But, the epidemic of Plague chased the family mercilessly and grabbed the life of his daughter Chandrabhanu who died at the age of eleven. The shock was unbearable for the parents of Jayaprakash. The children who survived the epidemic were to be taken greater care.

The death of the two children perplexed their parents and they vowed to give full attention to the health and safety of their surviving children. Jayaprakash was brought up in this alarming condition. Another son Rajesh was born during this turmoil to Harsu Babu and Phul Rani. The mother took extreme care of the children including Jayaprakash who was then a small boy. After the sad death of the eldest son, he became the apple of the eyes of the parents. The parents were very careful about the nourishment of Jayaprakash. His mother restricted the movement of Jayaprakash and did not allow him to play with the village children lest he will suffer from the contamination of the disease through the village children. The mother always kept strict watch over Jayaprakash. So Jayaprakash had few play mates in his childhood. The Harsu family had many pet creatures in their house and the child Jayaprakash confined himself in playing with them and gradually developed affection towards the pet creatures. They became the only play mates of his childhood. This helped the boy to learn that all living creatures are same. They are guided by same feelings as human beings. He got this lesson from his childhood days and he upheld this till his last. It so happened that his most loved pet dove died all of a sudden. It was unbelievable for Jayaprakash that his pet dove would part company with him. At the death of the dove he observed mourning and gave up food in grief. It was difficult for the parents to convince him that the death of the dove was a minor event. His affectionate father consoled him by saying *life is transitory and the wise do not repent for death and stick to one's duty*. This was perhaps the first lesson of philosophy which Jayaprakash learnt from his father.

Being encouraged by the affectionate behaviour of the pet creatures he enlarged his family of pets in his house. Be built up his world of pet creatures comprising horses, rabbits, swans and dogs. He learnt to communicate with them in their language and treated them as their own friends. The friendship was very intense. He was able to exchange feelings with his pets. He learnt to understand the language of their heart. From these pets he learnt to respect and know the sentiments of others and the art of communicating with the people through the language of heart.

In his later life he became the master of studying the emotions of the people and responding them with affection. His deep affection towards his pet at times turned into suffering. Once his pet horse gave birth to a pony. Jayaprakash was excited at this scene and ran up to the mother horse who was his pet. But the horse behaved astonishingly and gave a hard kick to Jayaprakash. He was seriously wounded and was hospitalised for few months to recover. He learnt to resist the physical suffering with calm and patience. Later on he underwent and resisted severe physical tortures with unusual calmness while participating in Indian Liberation movement. He developed a spirit of rebellion in himself and trained himself to cope with all physical tortures which were imposed on him during the British regime. He also resisted several physical tortures during the period of Emergency in his own country. To tolerate and resist all physical tortures in complete calmness is the ethics of Gandhi's concept of satyagraha.

Harsu Babu's family moved from place to place as his job was transferable. It was difficult for the family to carry all the children with them to all places. So, Jayaprakash was kept in the custody of his grandmother in the village. Jayaprakash grew with the affectionate care of his grandmother. Both of his elder sister were staying with the parents. Therefore, he did not get any opportunity to live and enjoy the company of his sisters and brother. Nor did he develop any intimacy with them in his childhood. He became intimately attached to his school, his home, the trees and orchards, the vast paddy fields and beasts and birds. They became their childhood friends.

Jayaprakash enjoyed their company to full extent. He enjoyed the sight of looking to herds of dears grazing in the fields, small brooks originated from heavy showers, the ripples of flowing Ganges, the charming scenery of river Saraju and other bounties of nature available in the vicinity of the village. With this Jayaparakah developed his poetic genius from his childhood. He also developed friendship with the pet elephants of the Zamindars who were staying in the village. The home of the family was situated in the flood affected area. Each year the flood washes away the house and each time the house is rebuilt by Harsu Babu. It was a mud-packed house where the family used to live. Jayaprakash had the exciting experience of flood every year. He enjoyed the scene of vast stretch of water of Ganges and Saraju. The waters were dear to him for he loved to swim and row over them on boats.

The boatmen were his friends. They gladly pick up the charming boy on their during the flood and used to take him on a long trip. His boatmen friends took great care of him and taught him the lesson of rowing over water. Often they were inviting Jayaprakash when they used to take their boat to cross Ganges. This cultivated intrepidness in Jayaprakash to cross over the vast stretch of water which helped him to be a fearless man in future. He was never afraid of the unfathomable depth of the water and always enjoyed the boat ride with his sailor-friends. Fearlessness, courage and valour were the ornaments of his life which he did put on throughout his life. These ornaments adorned him from his child hood and were preserved by him throughout his life time. He was never afraid of anything, not even death. He knew that "Death will come when it comes". It cannot touch him even a second earlier or later than its schedule moment. So, he displayed to the world the strength of his courage in his revolutionary life. In the suffering moments of his life he did not care for death, though he knew that death is the mile stone of all lives.

Alike all children, Jayaprakash grew with his environments. He became a courageous philosopher with a wide vision which the vastness of water had taught him. It helped him broaden his own heart and lift it above the self. He knew that life should be viewed beyond one's ownself. The aspiration of self should merge with the aspirations of others. Once this concept of living is established in heart, man would obtain the vision of life alone with the purpose of living. The vastness of vision would help the man to rise above the shallowness of mind. Jayaprakash was extremely fortunate to get this vision in his childhood which helped him to build himself as a selfless man caring for the self of his fellowmen. He got the vision before he entered the school. The boy Jayaprakash was wise before he was literate. His literacy followed his wisdom.

Beginning of the Career

Jayaprakash Narayan joined Bihar Vidyapeeth founded by Dr. Rajendra Prasad for motivating young meritorious youths and was among the first students of eminent Gandhian Dr. Anugrah Narayan Sinha , a close colleague of M. K. Gandhi who later became first Deputy Chief Minister cum Finance Minister of Bihar. In October, 1920 Jayaprakash married Prabhavati Devi, a independence activist in her own right and a staunch disciple of Kasturba Gandhi. Prabhavati was the daughter of lawyer and nationalist Brij Kishore Prasad, one of the first Gandhians in Bihar and one who played a major role in Gandhi's campaign in Champaran. She often held opinions which were not in agreement with J. P.'s views, but Narayan respected her independence. On Gandhiji's invitation, she stayed at his Sabarmati Ashram while Jayaprakash continued his studies.

In 1922, Narayan went to the United States, where he worked to support his studies in political science, sociology and economics at the University of California, Berkeley, University of Iowa, University of Wisconsin–Madison and Ohio State University. He adopted Marxism while studying at the University of Wisconsin–Madison under sociologist Edward A. Ross; he was also deeply influenced by the writings of M. N. Roy. Financial constraints and his mother's health forced him to abandon his wish of earning a PhD. He became acquainted with Rajani Palme Dutt and other revolutionaries in London on his way back to India.

After returning to India, Narayan joined the Indian National Congress on the invitation of Jawaharlal Nehru in 1929; M. K. Gandhi became his mentor in the Congress. He shared the same house at kadam kuan in Patna with his close friend and nationalist Ganga Sharan Singh (Sinha) with whom he shared the most cordial and lasting friendship. During the Indian independence movement he was arrested, jailed, and tortured several times by the British. He won particular fame during the Quit India movement.

After being jailed in 1932 for civil disobedience against British rule, Narayan was imprisoned in Nasik Jail, where he met Ram Manohar Lohia, Minoo Masani, Achyut Patwardhan, Ashok Mehta, Yusuf Desai and other national leaders. After his release, the Congress Socialist Party, or (CSP), a left-wing group within the Congress, was formed with Acharya Narendra Deva as President and Narayan as General secretary.

During the Quit India Movement of 1942, when senior Congress leaders were arrested in the early stages, J. P., Lohia and Basawon Singh (Sinha) were at the forefront of the agitations. Leaders such as Jayaprakash Narayan and Aruna Asaf Ali were described as "the political children of Gandhi but recent students of Karl Marx." He was also a great advocate of correlation "SAHJEEVAN"

Initially a defender of physical force, Narayan was won over to Gandhi's position on nonviolence and advocated the use of satyagrahas to achieve the ideals of democratic socialism. Furthermore, he became deeply disillusioned with the practical experience of socialism in Nehru's India.

After independence and the death of Mahatma Gandhi, Narayan, Acharya Narendra Dev and Basawon Singh (Sinha) led the CSP out of Congress to become the opposition Socialist Party, which later took the name Praja Socialist Party. Basawon Singh (Sinha) became the first leader of the opposition in the state and assembly of Bihar and Acharya Narendra Deva became the first leader of opposition in the state and assembly of U.P. His party is the first national party who distributed tickets on caste line.

Marriage with Prabhavati

Jayaprakash came in contact with the leaders of Champaran Satyagraha. Shri Braja Kishore Prashad was one of them It was on his invitation Mahatma Gandhi went to Bihar to lead the Champaran movement. Braja Kishore was a distinguished pleader and was a widely respected person of Bihar. He was a powerful Congress leader of the time. He was related to Dr. Rajendra Prashad, the first President of India. Originally he was a resident of village Sri Nagar in Sarang district. But later he moved to Darbhanga town and established there.

Braja Kishore was a very rich person with lucrative legal practice. He maintained luxuriant living style. But after coming into contact with Mahatma Gandhi he changed his course of life. He gave up legal practice and accepted simple living style. His esteemed wife Phuljharia Devi followed her husband with simplicity and dedication. She was religious and extremely devoted to God... Prabhabati was the eldest child of Braja Kishore and Phuljharia. Mahatma Gandhi infused a spirit of renunciation in thousands of families in India. Braja Kishore and Phuljharia were no exception. Their eldest daughter Prabhabati followed that ideal of her parent from the childhood. She was also leading an austere life. From the mother she leant to be truthful, compassionate and religious. The parents loved their eldest daughter very much and did not object to her practising austerity and simplicity in her life. She was never allowed to do any household work by her parent. Specially her father Braja Kishore was very fond of his daughter and never wanted his daughter to do any physical work of the household as there were lots of servants in his house. But Prabhavati rebelled against the practice of extracting services of the servants for those house which those she could do by herself.

It was natural for Prabhavati to be attracted towards Mahatma Gandhi from her childhood as her father had intimate relation with Gandhi. Prabhavati was very influenced by the personality of Gandhi. Gandhi was also moved at the simplicity and affected dealings of child Prabhavati whenever he happened to see her. Mahatma Gandhi was so much impressed with the behaviour of the little girl that he expressed his desire before Braja Kishore to take Prabhavati to his ashram as he had no daughter of his own. The parents did not take it seriously, rather they treated this as an affectionate gesture of Mahatma Gandhi. But Gandhi was serious. He was influenced by the dedication and perseverance of the small girl. He could visualise the talents lying hidden in the character of the small girl Prabhavati. The father Braja Kishore took it to be a great fortune that his daughter would go to the Ashram and would stay at the affectionate care of Mahatma Gandhi. Gandhi must have discovered some talents in her. The father was overwhelmed with joy. But Prabhavati's mother Phulijharia did not want to part with the tender girl. It would be difficult for her to live without her in the family. And the deal of Mahatma Gandhi was dropped. Later on the family completely forgot it. But Gandhi has always been a serious person. Even in his jokes, there were lessons for others to learn. It was difficult for all to make a difference between the joke and seriousness of Mahatma Gandhi. But he was serious of taking away Prabhavati from the parents. When he used to get the opportunity, he used to remind Braja Kishore about his intention about Prabhavati.

During those days, the age of fourteen was taken as the marriageable age for the girls. Accordingly, when Prabhavati reached the age of fourteen, Braja Kishore started searching a bridegroom for his daughter. Though he was a wealthy person, he did not want to conduct the marriage in pomp and luxury as he was devoted to Mahatma Gandhi. The family was already leading a austere life. He was also searching for a bridegroom for his daughter who would not demand any dowry. Dowry system is still a most uncultured system of the present society. We are still experiencing many deaths of the innocent brides whose parents fail to comply with the conditions of the dowry. The dowry system was rampant in Bihar society during those times. And Braja Kishore wanted a groom who would not love his wealth but love his daughter. It was difficult in those days to get a groom of that character, as dowry was then a common practice in the society.

Braja Kishore had also in mind that if a suitable groom was not found for Prabhavati, then he would send her to the Ashram of Mahatma Gandhi. At this moment, a friend of Braja Kishore came forward with the proposal of college student Jayaprakash for Prabhavati. The friend strongly recommended that he would be a suitable partner for his daughter. The boy bore a charming personality with good character and good academic record in the college. Braja Kishore was moved by the appearance, dealings, conversation and manners of young Jayaprakash. He agreed to the proposal of the marriage of his daughter with this boy. The knot was tied between Jayaprakash and Prabhavati in the October, 1920. At the time of marriage Jayaprakash was 18 and Prabhavati was 14 year old.

After marriage Prabhavati came to stay at her in-law's house. She stayed in Sitabdaria with Braja Kishore and Phuljharia who showered there love on her. The mother-in-law was dealing with her daughter-in-law with utmost affection. Both of them remained as mother and daughter...Though Prabhavati came from a very wealthy family, she did her best to accept the living style of Sitabdaria to the full satisfaction of their in-laws. After staying for a month in her in-laws house, she returned to her father's house. It was not possible on part of Prabhavati to stay with her husband as Jayaprakash was reading in the college at Patna. It was also not possible for her to stay in Sitabdaria permanently as the family of Harsu Babu moved from place to place as his job was transferable. Prabhavati's parents were disturbed at this situation. The antique custom does not allow the married daughter to stay with her parents for along time. The proposal of Mahatma Gandhi to take Prabhavati to his Ashram was still open. This pending proposal of Mahatma Gandhi struck to the mind of Braja Kishore. He consulted his wife and she gave a nod. Braja Kishore wrote to Mahatma Gandhi reminding of his earlier proposal to take Prabhavati to the Ashram and Gandhi promptly gave a green signal and Prabhavati was taken by his father to the Ashram of Gandhi. She became an inmate of the Ashram.

The Gathering Storm

That was the time when the whole nation was charged with the emotion of liberating India. The British government was taking all cruel and inhuman steps to check this movement. Oppressive methods like torturing and shooting the Satyagrahis was a common method adopted by the government. The fire of patriotism was burning in the heart of every Indian. The climax of British cruelty was exhibited in Jalianawala Bagh near Amritsar in Punjab. The British soldiers shot at a crowd of innocent and unarmed men, women and children killing about 300 people at an instance. This happened in the month of April in 1919.

This inhuman and cruel act was condemned by the whole world. The key player of this inhuman act was General Dyer who was spat upon even by the British civilians. The blood bath of Jalianawala Bagh added fire to the revolution. Young anarchists were ready for retaliation. The British officers in India did not move out without police protection. Thousands of legal practitioners in India gave up their legal practice stating that they would not bow down their heads before the British magistrates nor did they seek justice from the White judges. Thousands of students gave up their studies in schools and colleges and jumped into the fray. These events shook the heart of young Jayaprakash who though married was continuing his education. He was eager to take active part in the freedom movement. He was looking forward to grab an opportunity for that.

At that time Mahatma Gandhi visited Patna, he appealed to the people of Bihar to non-cooperate with the British government at all levels. Those included discarding the use of foreign goods, discarding the British educational system by boycotting the schools and colleges., giving up legal practice, resigning from all government posts, throwing away of mill-made clothes. Jayaprakash was very much moved by the appeal of Mahatma Gandhi. He was reading in second year Science in Patna college...In response to the appeal of non-cooperation by Mahatma Gandhi, Jayaprakash threw away his books to the pond and vowed not to read in any college managed by British educational system and gave up studies in 1920. The parents were unhappy at the decision of Jayaprakash. All these days they wished Jayaprakash to be a great scholar and a wise and great man. The decision of Jayaprakash shattered the dreams of the parents. He was advised to join in the Banaras Hindu University founded by Pandit Madan Mohan

Malviya. But Jayaprakash rejected the proposal for Banaras Hindu University which was getting huge money from the government. At last he joined in Bihar Vidyapith founded by Bihar Congress. The parents of Jayaprakash heaved a sigh of relief that their son did not give up college education.

Mahatma Gandhi gave a clarion call to the people of India that if the people became true Satygrahis in body and spirit and vigorously implement his non-violent and non-cooperation programme with full dedication and determination, then India would be independent within one year. But his promise was not fulfilled. Instead of giving independence to India, the British brought forth some administrative reforms. These reforms did not satisfy the people of India for they needed complete independence. They could know that they were cheated by the government. At this Mahatma Gandhi decided to start Satyagraha again.

The British government decided to suppress the movement with double repression. But Mahatma Gandhi was not a man to be cowed down by the government. Young Jayaprakash was moving inside the college as a chained tiger. He wanted to come out of the college and join the movement. Mahatma Gandhi had infused the flame of patriotism in the hearts of every Indian. And Jayaprakash was one among them. After Jalianawala Bagh, another violent incident of Chauri Choura in Gorakhpur rocked the country. Police fired at the unarmed mob of Chauri Choura in which few people were killed.

The procession which was peaceful suddenly lost temper when they found some of the innocent people died of police bullets. The mob grew violent forgetting the tenets of non-violence given to them by Mahatma Gandhi. The mob surrounded Chauri Choura police station and set fire to it. Some police men who were firing at the mob ran into the police station for protection. When the entire police station was ignited the police came out of it praying for help. But the mob was furious at the sight of their murdered companions. They caught hold of them and threw them into the burning fire where they were charred to death. The revengeful ghastly act of violence displayed by the mob of Chauri Chaura pained Mahatma Gandhi very much. He took all the blame on himself. He repented by saying he could not properly teach the people for offering a non-violent fight. It was owing to his own failings that violence erupted at Chauri Chaura. Amidst great repentance Mahatma Gandhi declared that the Indian mass was not yet prepared for non-violent battle. He withdrew the movement immediately. He rejected the persuasions of leaders like Jawaharlal Nehru that for the violent behaviour of few people the entire Indian Masses could not be blamed or disqualified. But the Mahatma was not prepared to accept any plea overcoming the human values. He withdrew the movement from all over the country. On the other hand the government had put all the blame on Gandhi alleging that he incited the people of Chauri Chaura for violence and he should be punished. He was tried for this offence by the government and was declared guilty and was imprisoned. Gandhi accepted the punishment with calm and marched into the prison. He was a brave man and had never cared for the consequences for defending truth and justice.

The withdrawal of the movement pained many leaders, but they had no courage to defy Gandhi and walk on their own. The Mahatma could not tolerate any violence and cruelty of the Indian masses. The Indian masses must behave as non-violent soldiers without any malice and attitude of revenge towards the opponents. He contended that the Indian masses could not win the freedom struggle unless they were completely serminised by non-violence The entire nation was in a grip of sorrow at the withdrawal of the freedom movement. But Mahatma Gandhi was of the opinion that the battle would be war if the Indian masses will reorganise themselves with full vigour of non-violent action.

Alike all revolutionaries who participated in the freedom movement, young Jayaprakash too aggrieved at the withdrawal of the movement. He could not do anything as he could not come out of college. His parents wanted him to continue his studies and he could not defy them. But at the same time he was not satisfied with the education of Bihar Vidyapith as it did not offer any scope for higher education. He had two missions in his life. One was to be academically proficient with higher education, and the other was to participate in the freedom movement of India under the leadership of Mahatma Gandhi. He felt that both of these could not be done at a time. So he decided to go for higher education.

First he thought to go to Oxford University. But he dissuaded himself from it thinking that it is a university managed by the British people who were oppressing the Indians. One of his friend who was in America was insisting Jayaprakash to come over there for higher education. He also wrote to him that he could earn and read and thereby meet the expenses of his study. The family of Jayaprakash was incapable of providing his expenses in America. So, he had to find out means to support his study expenses at America. Jayaprakash approved the idea of his friend to go to America for higher studies. He collected his passport and made all the preparations for it.

Jayaprakash wanted his young wife Prabhavati to accompany him to America. Accordingly he wrote to Prabhavati who was then staying in the Ashram of Mahatma Gandhi. But Prabhavati did not agree with the proposal. She had already involved her in the activities of the Ashram and Kasturba Gandhi who was treating her as her own daughter did not want to part with her. Her training as a social worker was going on there with full swing. She was doing all household work of the Ashram, beside she was looking after Kasturba Gandhi and was also learning Gujarati. She gave up all these responsibilities once at a time and joined her husband in his trip to America. There was also resentment in the mind of his mother who was not keeping in good health. She wanted her son to be near her all the time. But other family members of Jayaprakash convinced his mother that Jayaprakash should go to America and complete higher studies and return back as a respected man of the society. That would enhance the prestige of the family. He at last gave his consent.

On to America

Jayaprakash was so eager to go to America that he left Patna on May 16, 1922 and reached Calcutta. He boarded a ship to America forthwith and after a long voyage reached San Fransisco on October 22, 1922. Though he was desirous of taking admission into California University of Barkley, but by the time he reached America the admission period was over. He had to wait for the starting of next academic session. Some Indian students who were reading in the same University advised Jayaprakash to earn in the period of waiting and so he would meet the expenses of his studies easily. He also found that many Indian students were working in Morrisville. He decided to take a chance there. With great hope, he went to Morrisville and roamed hither and thither for a job, but did not get any. He was disheartened and tired. The next day was Sunday. He was standing by the side of the road. At that moment a Pathan gentleman of North-West frontier of India greeted him and enquired about him. Being pleased with his personality and manners he promised Jayaprakash to find out a job for him and asked him to accompany him. Jayaprakash followed him.

His passion for going for higher studies imposed numerous physical labour on him. From the childhood he had no experience of doing any physical labour. He was the most beloved of the entire family. And the family members did not allow their affectionate child to do anything except laying and reading. But in this foreign land, he resolved to do any job to support his expenses in America. He made no differentiation between a so called white collared job and job of the menial. Both were equal and dignified for him.

The Pathan gentleman took him to a fruit orchard owned by a gentleman and found out a menial job for him. His work was to pluck the grapes and dry them in the sun. His wage was $ 21 in a week. He gladly did his job with great sincerity. He discovered the ethics of dignity of labour and practised it in his daily life. By that time Mahatma Gandhi had already translated John Ruskin's book "Unto this last" into "Sarvodaya". The book expounded the theory of both equality and dignity of labour. But by physical labour to earn his bread Jayaprakash experienced the plight of millions of labourers who are toiling hard for their daily bread. He was drawn to assess the conditions of the labourers Perhaps his direct involvement with physical labour had made him drawn towards Marxism.

He continued to struggle hard to earn through any kind of job that came to him. After working for one month in fruit orchard, he moved on the Berkley and stayed in a small hotel. The problem of getting job there was also difficult. There was no question of finding a suitable job for him. In those days America was not so prosperous as it is today. There was poverty, unemployment and hunger for the common man. The rich were prospering at the cost of poor and the poor were struggling under the clutches of poverty and hunger. Conventional capitalist attitude played a great role in America to foster inequality among its people. So Jayaprakash did not get any suitable job for him. He got a job in a restaurant for cleaning the dining table and cleaning the dishes.

These jobs in the modem society were considered indignified. But to Jayaprakash, it was his training to divest himself to join the working class. He became a labourer and a worker in the strict sense of the term. He did this so called indignified job with great pleasure. He loved to earn in this way to fulfil his passion for higher education. The experience as a labourer had made him one of the most dignified and seasoned Socialist in the world. He had never thought of earning his bread through 'white-collar' profession. He had shown to the world that mere education would not be accepted as a base of dignity and prestige. He had established that human dignity is never degraded by doing physical labour for one's living.

That was his greatest achievement in America. He not only gained experience in the field of various types of labour oriented jobs, but by that he had upheld the dignity of labour before the world as he was never hesitant in doing that. He gave a fitting reply to the members of the sophisticated society who despise those who survive by doing labour. There has been a false notion among the intellectuals that doing hard labour affects the intelligence which is bogus concept. Gandhi, Vinoba who were masters in doing hard physical labour could not be said to have less intellectual capability. Vinoba who qualified himself by doing hard labour for eight hours a day, lived upon the wages that a common labour labourer earns. He survived with his intellectual brilliance. Jayaprakash had at last collected the funds required for his admission into the University.

He preferred to take admission into California University though it was an expensive affair. The academic standard of the California University was better in comparison to other American University. But a friend of his Bhola Panth, who was reading in Iowa University, was requesting him to come over to Iowa

University where expense were bit less. At last Jayaprakash shifted to Iowa University at the request of his friend and took admission in science faculty. At Iowa he prepared a routine of his life. In his leisure, he continued to earn for his living and for his reading. In holidays he was doing various kinds of jobs. For his living he worked in motor garages, factories and hotels. In a long vacation he worked in a meat factory at Chicago where beef was processed in shape of fast food.

The cruelty towards animal displayed by the industrial civilization created a hatred towards industrial civilization in the minds of Jayaprakash. The senseless butchering of cattle in large scale and the processing of the meat and packing them for human consumption all brought pain and grief to Jayaprakash. He could not tolerate the magnitude of cruelty practised in these factories whose products were used by the civilized people. "Were these people really civilized who live upon the butchering of innocent animals?" Jayaprakash asked to himself. Why did not we call them civilized cannibals? His mind went back to the ancient age where naked men and women were living upon human flesh. He could see this primitive cruelty and brutality in the modern industrial civilization. In a society where cruelty towards animals has been a vital part of civilization, there we could not expect human values to be flourished. However Jayaprakash had to swallow all the evils of industrial civilization as he was forced under circumstances to work in the meat-processing factory for his living.

No doubt America was a rich and prosperous country in comparison to the other countries of the world, yet Jayaprakash could find himself amidst the poverty stricken people of America. He had completed one year of staying in America and he had already realised that inside the so called prosperous America, there existed acute poverty where basic human wants were not provided to huge section of the people. He also felt that the hatred of White People towards the Black Negroes was very severe. He had come across many organisations of America whose objective was to eliminate Negroes from American soil. Those organisations were very active during the time of his stay in America. He himself faced humiliations from white people and their organisations as he was of Indian origin. Young white fellow students of Jayaprakash would often say to him that

> "You Indians are cowards as a herd of sheep, therefore a small country like England is ruling over your vast country having such a vast population. You don't have any sense of dignity."

Young Jayaprakash would hang his head in shame. He was helpless at that moment. He was shocked to know about the invisible disease of hatred towards human beings in America society, he was seriously thinking to find a way out of this disease economic inequality and human hatred. Accordingly he was drawn to Karl Marx whose revolutionary literature in support of the weak and oppressed people of the world shook the heads and hearts of many intellectuals who were eager to establish economic equality among the people. Through his concept he established that 'poverty' is man-made and can be eliminated by man. The changes in economic structures can eradicate the difference between rich and the poor, high and low. No man would be allowed to exploit another man for the betterment of his own self. In the 1848, both Karl Marx and his colleague Federic Engels jointly prepared a manifesto hereafter known as "Communist Manifesto." Marx developed his own theory of Socialism appealing to all workers of the world. It said:

> "Workers of the world, unite. You have nothing to lose but your chains, and have a world to win".

The crisis of European capitalism gave birth to communism. Marx appealed to the workers of Europe to take full advantage of the economic crisis. He narrated in his socialistic theory that the capitalistic system is bound to face crisis of its own and it would surrender before the proletariat. Though his dreams about the European revolution did not materialise; yet his Workers' Theory gained momentum all over the world. In 1867, Marx greatest Book "Das Capital" was published in German. In that Book he has condemned the existing economic theories and explained his own socialist theories. He dealt with the conflict of classes in human society. He said class conflict is unavoidable. Marx died in 1883. By that time his ideas and theories had already been implanted in the minds of many young intellectuals of the world who needed to put an end to the exploitation of the poor by the rich. There was an awakening of the working class in England even after the death of Marx. The great exponent of Marxism was Lenin who led the proletariat revolution of Russia and established a Socialist government in Russia. The Czar, the ruler of Russia was thrown away. The ideology of communism was fresh and the working people worked upon it with great enthusiasm. The history of the oppressive world took a turn. The poor were the masters of their own fate.

The mind of young Jayaprakash was deeply engrossed in Marx. He read all the books of Marx and was encouraged by the glorious achievement of Russian Revolution. He was convinced that 'each should get according to his needs' and then only the class would vanish. He was also eager to dream about a classless society where all people would enjoy equal economic and social status. He also read the literatures of M. N. Roy, a friend of Lenin and a good interpreter of Russian communism. He was impartial in dealing with the theories of Marx and suggested some modifications. Jayaprakash also appreciated M. N. Roy's comments. Jayaprakash was so much influenced by theories of Marx that he treated him as the greater philosopher and the greatest liberator of the world. He was still a student pursuing his studies but he was totally inclined to Communism. He was regularly participating in the communist study circles whenever he found time. There he enjoyed the thread bare discussion on communism.. But he did not join the Communist Party. He was hypnotised by the slogan of the Communist the "Poor should be governed by the Poor". He was giving this slogan even after he returned to India.

On seeing his craving for communism, one of his friends suggested him to go to Moscow and join Oriental University established in Moscow. He was also inclined to go to Soviet Union. He wanted to have a clear picture of the functioning of the proletariat government of Russia. He was informed by his friends that if he could only arrange passage money for Moscow, then his expenses of study and maintenance would be borne by the Soviet government. But there was no money with him. He also wrote to his father to send him passage money for Russia which his father could not afford at that time. Accordingly his proposal to go to Moscow was dropped. The parents were distressed to learn that Jayaprakash was going to be a Communist. They were afraid for the government puts the communists in jail. The government of India put communists and Anarchists behind the bar. They did not want him to face the same treatment when he returns to India. They were perturbed and went to Dr. Rajendra Prashad requesting him to dissuade Jayaprakash from communism. Dr. Rajendra Prashad complied with the request of the parents and wrote a long letter to Jayaprakash to get involved in the freedom struggle of India going on under the leadership of Mahatma Gandhi which according to him was a more radical revolution based on mass non-violent action. It was, too a revolutionary movement for a befitting cause. Rajendra Babu suggested that he need not go to Russia to gain revolutionary experience. The dreams which he was looking forward to visit a country where the State was run by the working class for their own upliftment, could not be materialised.

The only source of income for Jayaprakash was to do a job and arrange money for his maintenance. There was no other source of income for him to meet the expenses of his studies. But, it so happened that he did not get any job for a long time. This made him to face severe hardship. He suffered from tonsillitis in the winter of 1926 at the time when he was almost penniless. However he was admitted in the hospital and got his tonsillitis operated. Unfortunately the operation was not successful and he had to lie in the hospital for three months.

The little money that he had was exhausted. A Hospital bill of $900 was due on him. He was at a fix. He wrote to his father to send money for clearing the Hospital Bill. Harsu Babu sold some of his lands and sent money to Jayaprakash and he temporarily rescued from his pecuniary situations. His father wanted him to be an engineer by reading Science. But this did not happen as Jayaprakash, at the advice of his friend changed over to the curriculum of Arts. He got his Bachelor's degree in Arts in 1928 and in the year following he passed his M. A. with distinction. The Paper he submitted during his M. A. examination was of high order and was adjudged the best in the whole University. He emphasised in his Paper that social change could be brought about only changing the system of producing wealth. His views expressed in his Paper was influenced by the philosophy expounded by Marx. His result in M. A. encouraged him to go for Ph. D. and he was mentally preparing for the same. But his desire remained unfulfilled. News came that his mother was not keeping in good health and she wanted him to be at her bed side. His devotion and affection for his mother was so high that he decided to return to his home. The ailment of his mother shocked him. He wanted to rush to her immediately. He felt like all devoted sons that his career was not more valuable than the life of his mother. So he returned to his home after spending seven years in America.

Returning Home

By the time Jayaprakash landed in his home his wife Prabhavati had entered into 23rd years and was a young and charming lady. He was nourished by Mahatma Gandhi and Kasturbaji in the Ashram as their foster daughter. She was taught and trained in many things in the Ashram so that she could accommodate without her husband in his life. The Gandhi's taught her not only household matter, but certain manners and customs that would fit in to the conjugal life. Gandhi too taught her some English so that she could be able to help in some ways his America-returned husband. The Mahatma had already known about the devotion and deep faith of Jayaprakash in Socialism. He thought the wife should be fully acquainted with the attitude of the husband and should be fit to subscribe to the ideas which the husband cherish. Accordingly Mahatma Gandhi gave some basic lessons of Socialism to Prabhavati and gave her to read some books on socialism. There lied the greatness of Mahatma. He had never approved the concept of Marxian socialism, but he helped Prabhavati to be acquainted about the thoughts on socialism. It would help Prabhavati to communicate and discuss about socialism with her husband. There was basic difference between the outlook of Mahatma Gandhi and Jayaprakash so far as Socialism is concerned. He wanted Prabhavati to develop her own ideas without any imposition. Let she follow her husband with her independent views. She could build up her own ideas and could be competent to carry on dialogue with her husband. Gandhiji wanted Prabhavati to put forward her own views of social life without any reluctance. Jayaprakash should convince her to participate in their ideological path. Prabahabati was equally grown and matured in social action and thoughts. She was no longer a small uneducated village girl. In the mean time she had learned many things about India's freedom movement and the course of action prepared by Mahatma Gandhi's leadership. Through Mahatma Gandhi, she had been already known to all great leaders of India's national movement Jayaprakash built up his wisdom in America where as Prabhavati built up her wisdom in Gandhi's Ashram. She had grown equally wise and accomplished so that she could be engaged as a volunteer in the freedom movement. She had completed all the preparation needed for that.

When Jayaprakash arrived at Patna, his young wife along with some members of the family rendered him a hearty welcome. Seven years of separation between a young husband and a wife was not a minor affair. Both of them were astute followers of their ideologies and both of them bravely faced this long separation without an iota of regret in their minds. Their devotion towards each other helped them to gladly accept this long separation. For both knew that the relation between a husband and wife was emotional and devotional than physical. So the meeting was full of joy for both. In the village Sitabdaria also a great ovation was given to Jayaprakash by the villagers. His mother could not check her emotions embracing her son after seven years of separation. The meeting scene of the mother and son was a picture of affection, love and emotion.

During that time the Bihar Congress session was going on in Mungyr. Many national leaders including Sardar Patel were attending the session. Dr. Rajendra Prashad and the father-in-law of Jayaprakash Sri Braja Kishore attended the session. The Gandhi of Bordoli, Sardar Ballabh Bhai Patel was the chief guest of the session. He led the peasant movement of Bordoli in 1928 and achieved unique success. The British imposed an illegal tax on the peasants to enhance its own exchequer. The peasants of Bordoli protested against this injustice and decided not to pay the portion of the enhanced tax. The peasants of Bardoli rallied around Mahatma Gandhi, who was the main architect of Bardoli Satyagraha. The peasants and the volunteers displayed unique courage of non-violence and patience. And Sardar Patel led the peasants to victory. The British government withdrew the imposed tax and accepted the subsidiary demands of the peasants. Jayaprakash who attended the Congress session was greatly influenced by the deliberations of the meeting and he was ready to jump into the freedom movement Being encouraged by the attitude of her husband Prabhavati wanted to take Jayaprakash to Mahatma Gandhi to solemnise him to work as a freedom fighter. But Jayaprakash had yet to take decision about joining Gandhi. He had earlier decided to work as a lecturer in Banaras Hindu University. But Mahatma Gandhi's appeal created conflict in his mind. Besides, he had already been influenced by the Marxian interpretation of M. N. Roy. So he could choose his path immediately.

Prabhavati was very optimistic about Jayaprakash joining the freedom movement under the guidance of Mahatma Gandhi. So, she took Jayaprakash to Gandhi's Ashram at Wardha. But by the time they reached. Mahatma Gandhi was completely preoccupied with the meeting of the Working Committee. He had no time to talk to both of them. After the meeting Jawaharlal Nehru who came out of the meeting met Jayaprakash and talked with him about his future plan. Jayaprakash said he had not decided yet. Pundit Nehru invited him to come to Allahabad and said he had work for Jayaprakash. Jayaprakash agreed to go to Allahabad. Nehru was also impressed with Jayaprakash at the first sight. His personality was charming that rested on his simplicity of heart He never spoke with words those could not come out of his heart.

At last Prabhavati and Jayaprakash met Mahatma Gandhi. They talked with open heart. Both of them exchanged their view points. Jayaprakash did not agree with all the view points of Gandhi, but he was amazed to see his personality and simplicity and the powerful conviction on his ideas. He talked to him as his own friend and showed deep affection towards Jayaprakash. Gandhiji treated him as his son-in-law and proclaimed before him that Prabhavati was a daughter to him. There ended the conversation. They again met during the historical congress session of Lahore held on 31 December, 1928. Jawaharlal Nehru presided over the session., It went on for two days. The session demanded for "Complete Independence". By that time the whole Nehru family was involved in the freedom movement The Congress office was opened in the old house of Nehru. Jayaprakash could not keep out of the freedom movement. He did not want to waste more time and joined the movement He was appointed a Secretary of the Labour Cell of the Congress. He and Prabahabati lived in the same room where Motilal Nehru was staying. Intimacy grew between Jawaharlal and Jayaprakash and they became close friends.

In the same year the health condition of Phul Rani deteriorated and Jayaprakash and Prabhavati rushed to the village Sitabdaria. Prabhavati stayed at Sitabdaria and nourished her mother-in-law with great care. But she became serious and was brought to Patna for better treatment, but she breathed her last. There was sorrow all over the family. Some time after, the grandmother of Jayaprakash also died. The child Jayaprakash got all care, love and affection from his mother and grandmother in a short time. He reminded the advice of his father when he left food at the death of his pet swan. His father had said not to grieve for those who are gone but look to the future to perform one's duty. So Jayaprakash tried to digest the grief and concentrated on the problems of the labourers and pursued them to participate in the freedom movement.

In 1930 Mahatma Gandhi started the Salt Satyagraha. He appealed to the people to break the Salt Law and violate the Salt Tax imposed upon the people by the British government. Mahatma Gandhi himself led the people to Dandi, a place at seashore of Gujarat where he violated the Salt Act along with thousands of Satyagra—his by preparing salt of their own. He declared that to consume salt is the birth right of every individual. It is a product of Nature and no one could claim ownership on it. No government would intervene with this fundamental right of the people to prepare their own salt and market it according to their will. The preparation of salt and violation of Salt Act was carried on in many parts of the country with thousands of people participating in it Mahatma Gandhi's call to boycott foreign goods and schools and colleges was another landmark of the freedom movement.

Bonfire was carried on at different places by burning foreign clothes. This non-cooperaration of the British goods and the British system of education charged the nation with the passion to liberate India from the fetters of British. Though the government took many repressive measures to suppress the movement and imprisoned thousands of people without any warrant or trial, yet Gandhi succeeded in keeping the national spirit intact.

The government was mad at this own failure and banned Indian National Congress and confiscated properties of the organisation. It was impossible for Jayaprakash to confine himself in the Allahabad office. He jumped into fray and took leadership in organising the people to paralyse the British government. When warrant was issued in his name he did not surrender but went "under ground" to keep the torch of movement burning. He published clandestine papers and appealed the people to keep the movement live without caring a fig for the repression of British government. He advised people to display commitment to non-violent action of Mahatma Gandhi.

After staying away from Allahabad, he returned there to take part in the movement still by staying in "under ground". His wife Prabhavati was imprisoned from a protest rally of women along with Kamala Nehru. Both of them were good friends. They participated in the freedom movement together at Allahabad. The oppression of the British government on unarmed men and women of India was condemned by the whole world. Those were the days when Lord Irwin was the Viceroy of India. He too felt that one sort of reconciliation must be made between the Congress and the government. He communicated his intention to the British government at London.

Accordingly the British government at London invited representatives from India for negotiating with them. The Congress formally did not participate in it. But nothing substantial was attained. The impact on the government of the people of India through non-violent non-cooperation was so effective that the government was forced to release Mahatma Gandhi and withdrew all the repressive measures. The government also released about one lakh prisoners from different jails of India. Prabhavati was one of the prisoners who was released in this occasion. In this way, Prabhavati became acquainted with jail life. He never hesitated to face arrest whenever the same was needed by the circumstances.

The young leaders of Congress like Jawaharlal and Jayaprakash and many other did not approve withdrawing of the movement by Mahatma Gandhi. They were not happy about it. Jawaharlal wrote a long letter to Gandhiji expressing his discontent that such huge mass movement in which millions of people were involved so intensely should not have been withdrawn simply because insignificant few violated the ethics of non-violence while conducting Satyagraha. Jawaharlal, the most popular of the young Congress leaders, was satisfied with the performances of the majority of masses. They were fully non-violently charged to face the oppressions of the British government as and when required. But Gandhi wished to see the masses hundred per cent committed to non-violent non-cooperation without any motive of vengeance for the adversary.

Gandhi was a hard task master and he warned those leaders who objected to his withdrawal that in no way violence would be allowed to creep in any form while offering non-violent resistance. Gandhi would not tolerate a Satyagrahi to think ill about the oppressor. The spirit of the Satyagrahi should be completely non-violent. Subhash Chandra Bose, who later on hailed by the nation as Netaji, was one of the close associate of Mahatma Gandhi was so much dissatisfied with the withdrawal of the movement by Gandhiji that he left the people of India in the middle of the ocean from which they could not swim ashore. But in spite of all differences between Gandhiji and the young leaders, the Congress supported Mahatma Gandhi's strategy of non-violence in the freedom struggle.

Instead of this, the turmoil continued in the minds of young and dedicated people of India. Jayaprakash never surrendered to the police, but preferred to stay behind the scene and actively helped those who were participating in the movement. He carried all the information and instructions of the Congress to the people who were engaged in the struggle. He was publishing leaflets and magazines explaining the various strategies of the freedom movement and the messages of the imprisoned leaders who could not come out of the prison. Young patriots like Sahid Bhagat Singh, Sukhdev and Rajguru revolted against the British oppression and shot dead the British Office Sanders. He beat Lala Lajpat Rai of Punjab in a process. Lalaji was severely wounded and hospitalised and ultimately died. Bhagat Singh and his two companions threw bombs and pamphlets into the Central Hall of the Legislative Assembly at Delhi. They were arrested, tried and ultimately hanged, because the British government wanted to get rid of the revolutionaries But Gandhiji did not approve this act of violence and continued to train his volunteers in non-violence and peaceful resistance. He was even ready to negotiate with the British government demanding Independence for India. And in this connection, he agreed to lead a delegation of the Congress to the Second Round Table Conference at London.

Gandhiji attended the Second Round Table Conference at London, but nothing came out of it. Britain was not convinced by the logic of giving freedom to India. Mahatma Gandhi returned empty handed. Both the leaders and the Indian masses were disheartened. It was felt that as if the battle so sacredly conducted under the guidance of Mahatma Gandhi was going to be lost. Alike many others, Jayaprakash was extremely frustrated.

Every one was thinking that Gandhiji drove the nation on a wrong path. It seemed as if strategy of non-violence and peaceful persuasion of the freedom movement did not influence the leaders of the British. Some young leaders along with Jayaprakash were exploring new avenues to conduct the freedom struggle. But Gandhiji was not a man to accept defeat of his ethics. He continued to keep the momentum of the movement by his great personality and gigantic political farsight. He again gave the call to the people to recharge themselves. The British started the oppression again. Gandhiji was arrested on 4th January, 1932. Many leaders were also arrested.

As usual Jayaprakash did not want to surrender to police. He felt that he could be able to do more work by remaining outside the prison. He went 'under ground' and went to Bombay. He started a secret Congress office there and became its secretary. He convened a secret meeting of Congress Working Committee at Bombay and appraised them of the political situation of the country.

During this time, a British Parliamentary delegation visited India to study the political and economic situation. Jayaprakash welcomed them and placed the political problems of India before them. He insisted that British should give up their domination over India and accept terms and conditions expounded by Congress under the leadership of Mahatma Gandhi.

Jayaprakash accompanied the British Parliamentary delegation to Madras. While returning to Bombay and after bidding farewell to the Delegation, he was arrested by the police on the way and was sent to Nasik Jail. He was delighted to see Morarji Desai and socialist leaders like Ashok Mehta, Minoo Masani and Ram Manohar Lohia in the Nasik Jail. He enjoyed their company. All of them discussed about the future of the country and about the independence movement. They were not very much satisfied with the strategy of Gandhiji. They did not approve his soft approach towards the capitalists and his sticking to non-violence in the freedom struggle. They did not agree to the Trusteeship theory of Gandhiji as they had no faith on the characters of the capitalists that they would behave as trustees of the society. They held that capitalist's greed for wealth could not be eliminated by Gandhiji's approach of peaceful pursuasion.

They were, in a way, revolting against Gandhiji's approach of social change. Though Jayaprakash was not advocating the Russian pattern of Communism, yet he believed in the theory of Communism. He was a communist in the strict sense of Marxism. He did not approve the role of the Indian communists who went against the Freedom struggle of India and described it as a movement to establish Capitalism.

So Jayaprakash was not ready to believe that the independence movement headed by Mahatma Gandhi was aimed for protecting capitalists of India. In spite of his reservations, he was confident that the independent movement led by Gandhi was a mass movement. It was the only movement in India working for attaining independence. He advised his young friends to take part in the movement of Gandhiji irrespective of their strategic differences. He thought it better to stay within the Congress and shape the organisation in a socialist pattern so that more people could be involved in the Socialist movement. The socialists inside the

Congress were very active in this matter. But it was extremely difficult for them to supersede the leadership of Mahatma Gandhi, who had indomitable support of Indian masses. It was also difficult for those young socialists to ignore Gandhiji.

So after the release of Jayaprakash from jail, he came over to Patna and formed Bihar Socialist Party in 1934. Other Socialist friends of Jayaprakash like Minoo Masani of Bombay and Shrimati Kamala Devi Chattopadhayay of Maharastra joined with him and were engaged in spreading the Socialist movement in India staying inside the Congress. His wife Prabhavati was staying in Gandhiji's ashram while Jayaprakash was in jail. She came over to Patna to join Jayaprakash but she did not show any interest in the socialist movement of Jayaprakash as she was fully dedicated to Gandhian ideology of non-violent resistance and non-violent non-cooperation. But, as a wife, she was fully dedicated to her husband and was looking towards his comforts so that Jayaprakash could smoothly grow with his own vision of life. The Socialists inside the Congress were incessantly working to shape the Congress as a socialist organisation. They were yet to agree with Gandhian pattern of Socialism. They had their own ideal of forming a Socialist State. They were growing impatient.

Jayaprakash suggested to his socialist friends to discuss among them regarding the prospect of working for Socialism inside the Congress. And accordingly he convened a meeting of the Congress socialists during the General Session of the Congress. The response was good. They formed Congress Socialist Party with separate identity. The Party took decision to fight against all types of exploitations, to fight against the profit extracting motive of the capitalists in the country, to enforce the distribution of national wealth equally among the people of India.

The Party resolved to work for the welfare of all people of the country irrespective of caste, creed, religion and gender. It would not allow communalism to pollute the minds of the masses. It declared its policy of "Lands to the tillers". All those who cultivate lands must have a ownership right over it The "absentee land lord-system" should be abolished. Tillers should be the owners of the lands which they cultivate. The Socialist Party announced that it would thrive for the nationalisation of industries, large scale Trading Corporations and Life Insurance Companies and Banks. It wanted a total change of the prevalent economic system. It resolved to abolish Zamindari system and the Kings and Nawabs without giving any compensations to them. The established government should take over their properties and distribute them among the poor. The Congress Socialist Party in its session decided to fight against the economic, political and social inequalities in all fronts.

In the mean time intimacy had grown between Nehru and Jayaprakash. Nehru had great inclination towards socialism. He subscribed to the socialist thoughts in many ways. The Congress Socialist Party wanted to bring Nehru to their fold. In 1936, Jawaharlal Nehru became the President of the Congress, and Jayaprakash was made Secretary of the Congress at the initiation of Nehru. It was the opportune moment for the Congress Socialist to push their agenda into the Congress. Taking this opportunity Jayaprakash requested Nehru to join Congress Socialist Party as he was of the same political ideal.

But he did not join Congress Socialist Party. In 1936, the Congress Working Committee decided to take part in the Provincial election conducted by British government. Candidates of the Congress were set up to contest Provincial election. The Congress Socialists did not appreciate the contesting of Congress candidates in the election. They thought this to be a plea of the British government to delay independence.

Congress won the election and Congress governments were formed in 18 Provinces in 1937. But they were functioning under the framework of the policies laid down by the British government. The Congress Socialists including Jayaprakash were not satisfied with the performances of these Provincial governments. Jayaprakash felt that these Provincial governments were safeguarding the interests of the capitalists and were working against the interests of poor peasants and workers. He wanted a complete change of the policies of the British government in respect of the democratic process. Jayaprakash was terribly dissatisfied with this decision of Congress and tendered his resignation from Congress Working committee. He thought it would be difficult for him to compromise with the ideology of the

Socialism. With him, many more young people who were dedicated towards the cause of Socialism left Congress Party. He also appealed to the Indian communists to join hands with the Socialists and carry on independent movement jointly. But he did not succeed. The Communists did not oblige him. Then he tirelessly worked to strengthen the socialist movement in India single handedly to lay the foundation of Socialism in India.

But it was not a easy venture to mould the Indian masses to socialism. But Jayaprakash toiled hard keeping hope against hope. In spite of his deep love of Gandhiji towards him, Gandhiji did not accept his suggestions in toto. Some Congress leaders like Sardar Ballabh Bhai Patel were very critical about Jayaprakash. Sardar patel openly criticised him in the open session of the Congress in 1938. During this time Jayaprakash wrote letters to Mahatma Gandhi expressing his view points regarding the policies adopted by Congress Working Committee.

He expressed his dissent over them. Jayaprakash also discussed this matter with Gandhiji personally. Gandhiji wanted to pacify Jayaprakash and advised him to be calm. But Jayaprakash was the last man to digest the insults thrown out to him by Sardar Patel. He stuck to his resignation. Though Nehru and Jayaprakash subscribed to the same ideological bent of mind, Nehru remained silent in this turmoil. He did not intervene in the matter. Still then Jayaprakash had great regard and affection towards Nehru till the last.

Taste of Revolution

Jayaprakash turned out to be a revolutionary from the moment he resigned from the Congress humbly putting this vice of descent before Mahatma Gandhi. Even he did not know then that he was revolting against so many social deprivations. He thought, that he would rather walk alone, but he could not go against his conscience. When he found that friends who subscribed to his socialist ideology stayed behind, he decided to walk alone with his own ideal with some like-minded colleagues. Even during that time he harboured no animosity towards any Congress leaders. He was against the decision of the Congress, not against its leaders and workers. That was his greatness.

In 1939, Britain declared war against Germany and that war became the Second World War. Many European nations were involved in this war. Britain sought help from all her colonial countries to help her in the War. Germany massacred millions of Jews in Gas Chambers during this war. The Second World War continued for long eight years and ended in 1945. India as the colony of the British was drawn to the War.

The colonial government of India too declared war against the Axis Powers. But the Congress opposed the war because the decisions about war was taken by Britain without taking the referendum of the Indian people. Taking the advantage of War, the Congress suggested that the people of India would support the war if the British grants independence to India. But the British did not comply with the suggestion of the Congress. So Congress opposed the war and asked its Provincial governments to resign. The Congress asked the people to oppose war at all fronts and non-cooperate with the war-fund raising campaign carried on by the British government.

The anti-war campaign boosted the spirit of Jayaprakash and he took leadership in propagating anti-war campaign boosted the spirit of Jayaprakash and he took leadership in propagating anti-war ideas among the people in various ways. He told the people that the way in which Britain is opposed to Fascism of Hitler, in the same way we are opposed to British imperialism and colonialism in India. We could only help the British in their fight against Fascism on one condition, and that condition is India's complete Independence.

It was a bargain of give and take and there was nothing immoral about it. Jayaprakash turned out to be a revolutionary against all war efforts in India. Tirelessly he moved from place to place to propagate against helping war efforts of the government. He went to Jamshedpur and raised his voice against war. He organised rallies of Steel factory workers at Jamsedpur who revolted with him against the Second World War. He appealed to the workers that under no condition they would lend support to British government in conducting war. The workers of Jamshedpur responded him with great zeal. The British government could not tolerate the mass popularity of Jayaprakash and he was at last arrested by the police accompanied by magistrate and journalists. He was produced before the court and was sentenced to nine years imprisonment. Jail to Jayaprakash was a place to practice devotions to strengthen the cause of fight. For him, it was a place of renewal of his zeal and to sharpen his commitment Jayaprakash was always optimistic and never had the sentiment of frustration to weaken his moral. In the month of December, 1940 Jayaprakash was released from Jail.

The army of Hitler was on their road to victory. Congress has already started movement against the war. Mahatma Gandhi thought it to be a fit occasion to give a call for "Individual Saryagraha". Individual Satyagraha meant that the Satyagrahi or the volunteer of the Freedom Movement should roam from place to place with message that no body would cooperate with the government in all war arrangements and would ask the masses to desist from paying any money to the 'War Fund' that the government was collecting from the people to meet the expenses of War. The volunteers would address the meetings individually declaring the protest against war and court arrest. In this way volunteers were arrested one after another by offering Satygraha. Acharaya Vinoba Bhave was the first volunteer selected by Gandhiji as first Individual Satyagrahi. He was the first to give a speech opposing the War and courted arrest later on Jawaharlal Nehru was arrested for delivering speeches against Britain and was imprisoned for four years.

The anti-war opinion was created throughout the country and the atmosphere was charged against British imperialism. The Indian masses were ready to overthrow the government at any moment. There was contempt towards British administration from all quarters in India. Jayaprakash took this moment to be the appropriate moment to launch a Revolution against the British regime. His craving for a Socialist Revolution in India was taking shape in his mind. He could not suppress his passion for building up a Socialist India. With this objective in view he travelled all corners of the country appealing to the masses to keep themselves ready to participate in the Socialist Revolution which was getting nearer day by day. In some parts of the country people responded to the call of Socialist Revolution. He was arrested while popagating for the Socialist Revolution in 1942 and was imprisoned without any trial. He was confined to jail as a under-trial prisoner. But he was not allowed to face trial of his crimes. He was first sent to Bombay jail and then was shifted to Delhi Camp Jail. The British government was treating Communists and Socialists of India as Violent revolutionaries.—And they were kept under the cordon of Armed Police. The government even did not offer any treatment to them when they became ill. The British government wanted them to suffer and die in the prison without any treatment. A companion of Jayaprakash who was kept as a detainee went mad with his illness but was refused treatment by the authority. The fellow prisoners raised a heavy protest against this attitude of the government, but the government was determined to kill him by negligence. It did not pay any attention to the protests. Jayaprakash and his fellow prisoners fasted indefinitely to press their demand for the treatment of their companion.

Ultimately, the British surrendered before their demands of the prisoners and sent the ailing companion for treatment Inside the prison, Jayaprakash was eager to contact their under ground friends who were engaged in preparing the nation for a Socialist Revolution.

During the time an unfortunate incident happened. Learning about the precarious and unhealthy conditions of Delhi Jail, wife Prabhavati, who was outside the bars, came to visit him. She observed the conditions in which her husband and other prisoners were kept in custody and was very much pained. She came to visit him again. Jayaprakash was ready with a letter addressed to his socialists friends who were out side the prison.

Jayaprakash handed over the letter secretly to his wife Prabhavati to be delivered to his friends. But this act did not escape the attention of the police who were guarding around. Prabhavati was taken before the Jail authority and the letter was forcibly taken away from her as a seized document. The British government made public the contents of the letter which according to the government agency, was written against the non-violent strategy of the freedom movement pioneered by Gandhiji. He gibed at the individual Satyagraha as false pretension and requested his socialist friends to carry on violent struggle to overthrow the British government. But real truth about the contents of the letter created controversy throughout the country. Gandhiji was himself pained at this type of observations of Jayaprakash. But the real truth of the contents was yet to come to light as the letter was disclosed by the government who was bent upon to create difference between Jayaprakash and Gandhiji. On the basis of the letter the British government brought charges of conspiracy against Jayaprakash. But Mahatma Gandhi defended Jayaprakash by saying the "Clive and Warren Hastings were involved in conspiracy for their own country and killed many, but Britain worshipped them as dignified heroes. Then how could be the patriotic activities of a man like Jayaprakash who spent so many years in foreign land, interpreted as conspiracy? Gandhiji asked this question to the government.

In the Jail, Jayaprakash and his companions were not given the status of the political prisoners. And so they did not enjoy the facilities of political prisoners. They were treated as ordinary criminals in the Jail. When the government did not listen to their demand to be treated as them as political prisoners, Jayaprakash started hunger strike in protest. After some days of fasting his health deteriorated and caused concern for everybody. Mahatma Gandhi appealed to Jayaprakash to break the fast when his demands are met by the government. But Jayaprakash stuck to his fasting. Gandhiji along with many Indian leaders were worried about him. Gandhiji did not give up the hope. He sent his secretary Mahadev Desai to meet him in the Jail and requested on behalf of Gandhiji to break the fast. At last the government conceded to the demands and he broke the fast. Jayaprakash fasted for thirty one days in the jail.

Jayaprakash was shifted to Hazaribag jail which was situated inside a forest. By this time the World War had taken a new turn. Britain was getting frustrated. She realised that it was impossible for her to win the war without the support of the people of India. So he started to appease Congress. Britain declared to constitute a Constitution for India. Accordingly she sent a parliamentary delegation headed by Sir Strafford Cripps to India to review the situation and give a report to British government. The Congress and the people of India were well acquainted with this delaying tactics of the Government. They had already lost all faith on the British diplomacy. The British bureaucrats were experts in cheating the people with their time to time false promises. The Congress felt this nerve of deceit of the British and demanded complete independence for India.

The Congress did not give any importance to the fake promises of the government and asked the British government to give India the freedom. In the All India Congress Committee session at Bombay on 8th August, 1942, the Congress demanded absolute and immediate independence of India. Mahatma Gandhi himself gave the clarion call of revolt against the British regime and paralysed the government. Gandhiji called the people to fight for freedom or die in the process.

It was a heroic day in the Indian History when the people of India asked the British imperialists to 'quit India'. With this announcement the British government arrested Gandhiji, Sardar Patel, Maulana Azad, Jawaharlal Nehru and Harekrishna Mahatab. The British rounded up all Congress leaders from all parts of the country. The movement went on without any leadership. The people took up the movement into their hands and gave the freedom movement a violent shape. They were agitated against the British and they destroyed many government properties, set fire to government offices and police stations. There was nobody to control the violent mob. The movement went on in full swing. It was felt as if this fight was the last fight for the Indian freedom as they poured all their energies of sacrifice into the movement. It reminded the lines from English poet Browning:

> I was never a fighter, So, one fight more The last and the best.

The nation was fighting the last battle against the British with full vigour dedication and sacrifice. It was difficult for the British government to control the masses. The whole nation was charged with the spirit of sacrifice. Every Indian was ready to face severe oppressions and even death for the cause of freedom. Gandhiji's "do or die" declaration shook the sleeping hearts of thousands of Indians.

Jayaprakash was still rotting in the jail. He was no exception. He greeted the "do and die" call of Mahatma Gandhi with full enthusiasm inside the jail. He was impatient to come out and take active part in the revolution going on outside the jail wall. He learnt in the jail that this was the final and last fight of non-violence against the British and the British imperialism had to be thrown out. He wanted to work with the enthusiasm of the people and offer them the leadership. Dr. Mukherjee of Calcutta was staying with Jayaprakash in the same cell. He was a good doctor of repute and great freedom loving man. In the day time, he treated the ailing patients as the jail doctor and in the night he was engaged in the revolutionary work inside the prison.

But the police was able to know this and Dr. Mukherjea was arrested and was kept in the same cell where Jayaprakash was imprisoned. They became good friends. He was the chief architect of the escaping mission of Jayaprakash and his friends. Dr. Mukherjea laid down the plan of 'escape' before the fellow prisoners. It was decided that at the first attempt Jayaprakash and his five co-prisoners would be sent outside as per the plan. The place and the date was selected. A small isolated place in the corner of the jail was selected to carry out the programme of escape. The place was dark in the night.

The wall of the jail was twenty feet high that had to be jumped over. The night guards used to march on by the side of the wall once in every eight operation. The day was 8th August, 1942 and night was pitch dark. The celebration of Diwali was going on with songs, dances and beating of drums in the jail. The guards as well as the prisoners were merrymaking. Most of the Hindu guards of the jails had gone on leave.

The atmosphere in the jail was noisy with music, songs shouting of chorus songs. There were only four guards nearby, who were allured by the prisoners with jokes and humours At this moment six prisoners planned for escape. It was 10 pm at night. It was a no moon night with darkness outside. A table was placed at the corner of the scheduled place. The young prisoners rode on the shoulders of one another. The first one climbed on the wall and he used his Dhoti as rope and helped his companion to come up to the wall. In this way all the six prisoners jumped over the twenty feet wall and landed in the darkness they and breathed the air of freedom. But the shoes, warm clothes and their wallets of those escaped could not be thrown beyond the wall owing to shortage of time. Only the friends were able to remove the table from the escaping spot. It was the time for the guards for their round. They continued to dance and sing after the 'escape operation' in order to avoid suspicion of the guards on duty. The celebration went on with full swing.

The jail authority could only know about it in the next morning Jayaprakash and his five friends ran all night in the jungle on thorns to save themselves from the police. They trotted throughout the night and covered as many distance as they could. They had not brought anything except their clothes that they put on. There were no money, except a hundred rupee note which a friend was carrying with him. It was difficult for them to buy anything in exchange of that in the village, as the villagers were poor. There was rare circulation of hundred rupee notes into the villages. The small shops of the village did not exchange it for any commodity.

Further, the villagers might suspect them with the hundred rupee note. So they preferred to move forward suppressing their hunger. One of the friend had four anna coin. They purchased some roasted rice and met their hunger. Jayaprakash was having severe pain in his legs and waist lie was not able to walk any more. He was carried on the shoulders of their friends. It was also difficult for them to walk with his load. They found a bullock cart on the way and requested the cart driver to carry Jayaprakash.

The cart driver demanded three rupees for the journey. But they had no money to pay the fare. Jayaprakash offered his watch to the cart driver in exchange of the fare, but he did not agree. So all of them walked for three days limping and by dragging their feet After three days they entered into Gaya District. They reached a village where the people were very kind and hospitable. They gave them food, shelter, clothes and money and bade them fare well. It was not always safe for them to move in a group. People might suspect them as thieves or robbers. They might inform the police regarding their movement. So, they decided to part company and moved away to different directions. After undergoing great difficulties and overcoming many hurdles, Jayaprakash reached Varanasi and stayed with a professor friend. From there, he moved on to Delhi. He reached Delhi and established secret relationship with the office of the Socialist Party. His old socialist friends were keeping contact with them.

Jayaprakash sent messages to the freedom fighters that they should not be cowards. Bravery and violence is far superior to cowardice, so they must come forward to put on a brave fight to oust the British from the soil of India. He supported violent action against the British regime. He appealed that the British government was bent upon crushing the freedom movement of India and therefore it was continuing its oppressive measures against the people of India. He appealed them to disrupt all communications by cutting the telegraph and telephone wires.

According to him this could be taken as a violent action. He did not even hesitate to the policies and strategies of Gandhiji. He said the people of India had the right to choose their line of action to attain independence. In the meanwhile one year had passed Subhash Chandra Bose, one of the dynamic leaders of the Congress, left the Party and escaped somewhere outside India by befooling the police. He went to Japan and established contact with them and asked them to help him in his fight in India. He established Indian National Army by recruiting patriotic army personnel from Indian Army. He led the Indian National Army to Delhi to liberate India. Jayaprakash supported Subhash Chandra Bose in his violent fight against the British. But he did not believe that collaboration with Japan would be fruitful in respect of attaining Indian independence.

The underground hero became a terror to the British government He was taking active part in the struggle in his state of hiding the government which exhausted all its energies to capture Jayaprakash. The devastating Bengal Famine occurred in 1943. About a million people in Bengal and North Orissa died of hunger. It was man made famine. People starved while the hoarders were hording million tones of food stuffs. The British government remained unconcerned about the poverty and hunger of the people. Jayaprakash could not tolerate the plight of the hungry masses. He issued instructions to Congress workers asking them to break open all food godowns and distribute food stuffs to the starving millions. To him, this was not at all an act of violence. The British government declared Jayaprakash as a terrorist and declared ten thousand rupees on his head.

Jayaprakash slipped away to Nepal for safe shelter. He was giving training in warfare to freedom fighters who deserted British Army for the cause of Indian freedom. He was secretly doing all these to boost the morale of freedom fighters. The British government when informed about this put pressure on the Nepal government to arrest Jayaprakash and hand over him to Indian police. The Nepal government succumbed to the pressure of the British government and arrested Jayaprakash and his colleagues. While they were led to India under police custody, the guerilla fighters came to know about it and fought with the police. There was fierce battle between the guerilla army and the Nepal police.

Taking advantage of the fight Jayaprakash and his friends escaped. They trekked several miles on foot for a safe shelter, but it was difficult for them to get one. At last they crossed Nepal border and reached India. But the hurdles were chasing him. While crossing a river on boat, the sailor saw the guns which they snatched them from the Nepal Police and suspected them as a gang of dacoits. He raised a cry and the villagers surrounded them. The guns were all empty.

Jayaprakash and three friends tried to convince the villagers that they were not dacoits but freedom fighters. But the people did not believe their words. They wanted to capture them and hand over them to the police. There was no other way to escape. So, they threatened the villagers with empty guns and came away. Then he hanged his name to Mehta and roamed throughout the country. Again he reached Delhi to contact his co-workers. He was fully engaged in his movement for freedom. He was still conducting his activities remaining underground. Once, while he was travelling by train from Delhi to Rawalpindi, one old police officer who knew and saw him earlier traced him. Jayaprakash repeatedly told the officer that he was not Jayaprakash, but Mehta. But the officer did not believe it. He was confident about his identity and arrested him. Jayaprakash was sent to Lahore Jail in 1944. He was put inside a dark cell with no light. He was tortured physically severely. He was not allowed to sleep at night. After spending 16 months in the dark cell of Lahore Jail, he was brought to Agra Jail. Mahatma Gandhi was released from jail on grounds of health in the month of May, 1944. The British started negotiating with Indian leaders regarding independence. Gandhiji did not approve the violent method that Jayaprakash adopted in the freedom struggle. He did not take into account the magnitude of sacrifice Jayaprakash did for not the cause of freedom. Jayaprakash was pained at the attitude of Gandhiji towards him. Prior to that both Gandhiji and Kasturba Bai were imprisoned in Aga Khan Palace. Kasturba was severely ill in 1943 in the month of December. At that time Prabhavati was in Darabhanga jail. Gandhiji requested Viceroy to sent Prabhavati to Aga Khan Place to attend to Kasturba Bai. Prabhavati was brought to nurse Kasturba from Darbhanga Jail. But the condition of Kasturba Bai deteriorated. She died on 22th February, 1944 and Prabhavati was again taken back to Darbhanaga jail to continue her prison term.

In the same years Jayaprakash was transferred from Agra Jail to Lal Qila at Delhi. The political situation of India was fluid. The government was tired of oppressing the people. So it desired to negotiate with the leaders about granting independence to India. To create an atmosphere of peace the government released Mahatma Gandhi in May, 1944. Both the government and the leaders were aspiring for coming to a settlement. At last a settlement was reached and it was decided that the power should be transferred to India. The negotiators demanded to release other Congress leaders including the socialist leader Dr. Ram Manohar Lohia. As a result, most of the leaders were released on April 12, 1946. Prabhavati was also released during the same time. The same year her father died.

When it was decided that independence would be granted to India shortly, the Congress workers felt no further necessity for continuing the struggle. But Jayaprakash and other Socialists did not believe in it. They wanted to change Congress into a Socialist organisation. But there were some matured Congress leaders who wanted to prevent Socialists to dominate Congress organisation. That faction of the Congress was very powerful. The British prepared a programme of transfer of power. Accordingly, a Constituent Assembly was formed to prepare the Constitution of India. During that time, Nehru was the President of the Congress. He invited Jayaprakash to be a member of Congress Working Committee. But Jayaprakash refused it. He was still hopeful about transforming the Congress into Socialist organisation. Congress was a powerful Party of its own win the soul backing of Mahatma Gandhi. It won all seats in the Central and Assembly election of 1945. It was during that time Muslim League leader Muhammad Ali Jinnah raised the point of formation of Pakistan in areas of majority Muslim population. He and his followers did not agree to remain in the Indian Union. They wanted a separate Muslim nation. Jinnah's proposal was suicidal in character as India had to be divided into two nations. Mahatma Gandhi was shocked at this and tried to pacify Jinnah. But Jinnah insisted upon his deal. The British government wanted to divide India and supported the cause of Pakistan.

The Muslim Leaders advised Muslims to place their demands by raising revolt. As a result, Hindu-Muslim riots started and blood bath occurred in many parts of India. Thousands of Hindus became homeless and refugees in East Bengal and Punjab. People in thousands were killed in the riots. The Interim Government, headed by Jawaharlal Nehru, failed to control the riots, communal crimes and robber)'. The whole of India was in turmoil. At the request of Gandhiji and Nehru, Jayaprakash agreed to be a member of congress Working committee. But no change was brought about in the attitude of the Muslims. India was bathing with communal frenzy. The British openly supported the demand of a separate Muslim Country to teach fighting Indians a lesson. The British diplomats were active in spreading communal hatred among Hindus and Muslims. The situation forced the congress leaders to concede to the demand for a separate Muslim country. Accordingly, India was divided as two nations. Pakistan was formed on 14th August, 1947, a day before India became independent. India got independence on 15th august, 1947.

The crisis of Jayaprakash did not end there. Sardar Patel initiated an amendment to the Constitution of Congress that members of other political parties could not remain inside the congress organisation. It was difficult for the members of the Congress socialist party to digest the insult. Jayaprakash protested against this move of Sardar Patel but nothing happened. As a result the Socialists had to sever all relations with the Congress. A separate Socialist Party was born. The most painful incident of

Indian history took place on 30th January, 1948 Mahatma Gandhi, the Father of Nation was shot dead by a mad communalist Nathuram Godse by name. The whole nation was perturbed and shocked. Jayaprakash lost his mentor, the man who loved him the most. His grief was fathomless. He was furious against the functioning of the Indian Government and demanded resignation of Nehru and his government as he could not provide proper security and failed to protect the life of Gandhiji. From that time he severed all connection with Congress.

A Rebel Socialist

The Indian Constitution was carefully introduced. India was declared as a Sovereign Democratic Republic on 26th January, 1952 and the first General Election was conducted in 1952. The Socialists under the guidance of Jayaprakash participated in the General Election with the objective of establishing Socialism in India, but they could not get effective response. Jayaprakash who was the key policy-maker of the socialist movement in India did not contest election. He wanted to lay a strong foundation of Socialism in India by remaining outside the power. Congress won the election with majority and formed government both in Centre and in the Provinces.

The election result shattered the dreams of the Socialists who wanted to build up Socialist state. Jayaprakash too was very much disheartened But he was a staunch revolutionary. He did not know to bend his knees before adverse circumstances. He explored other avenues to infuse socialist ideology amongst the masses without going to the power. He was more concerned for the people's power than the power of the parties.

Thus he became the most famous socialist of our county. He continued to give the leadership to the socialist workers. Branches of Socialist were established almost in all provinces. As a true revolutionary, he believed in building up people's power, not Party-power. The political Parties will just play coordinating roles in delegating power to the people. Jayaprakash had his own concept of Socialism. Socialism means to uplift and uphold the dignity, security even to the lowliest man of the society. Jayaprakash accepted the socialist ideology only to derive benefit for the poor.

He was a man who cultivated a capacity to identify with the poor throughout his life. His concept of socialism aims at creating human equality and integrity. The poor and underprivileged must be brought to the forefront of the society where they could join their terms to the functioning of the society. There was a time when young Jayaprakash gave the slogan "Poor Should be Governed by the Poor". He conceived of a socialist society where rich and the privileged should not be allowed to rule over the poor. He wanted to change the whole social structure of the present society by overhauling the value system.

The so-called intellectuals, according to him, are parasites and thus, they grab the lion share of the national wealth. In a true socialist state, there should not be any difference between the wages of the 'intellectuals and labourers as the basic needs are same to both. There should not be any discrimination in their remunerations as remunerations are given to satisfy the essential requirements of the individuals. Jayaprakash wanted to induct these radical concepts into socialism so that socialist revolution can take place involving common people. A socialist must associate himself with the problems of the have-nots and must try to solve them by changing the fundamental social structure of the society. Jayaprakash established socialist units in various parts of the country and engaged in preparing and teaching the masses for a socialist revolution.

He had often said:

> "Socialism is not a mere jargon. Socialism does not mean a political or economic structure. Socialism is related to Socialist culture and Socialist man. I am confident in my mind that we have to build up a Socialist culture. We have to build up a Socialist man. This cannot be done by promulgating laws. It cannot be done simply by taking power into the hands and through administrative methods. The Socialist society cannot be established through these measures. This had never happened in past nor it will happen in future. The history of the past and various evolutions of the present are proclaiming repeatedly that social change cannot be brought about through power."

Jayaprakash held that whether the government wants or does not want, revolution can be brought about in the society by pursuing the people to adopt socialism in their own life and then bring revolution to the society. Socialism was dear to his heart that he visualised in all revolutionary programmes of his life. Socialism cannot function without democracy. One cannot flourish without the other. The path of autocracy is antagonistic to Socialism. It cannot lead to socialism at any time. Autocracy kills the freedom of expression and freedom of action of the individual. His incentive is suppressed from all angles.

For any social change the voice of people is the primary instrument. That instrument can be available only through democratic behaviour and democratic conduct of the people. The people are accustomed to individual freedom and democratic behaviour. They never wilfully accept autocracy unless they are provoked by compulsion. Jayaprakash wanted to utilise this individual freedom to protect them from the oppression of autocracy. He held that when the people will learn to uphold their 'individual freedom, then only they can be able to utilise their power of 'collective freedom. It is the collective creed of thought, word and deed that will boost the spirit of Socialism among the masses. To him Socialism was not simply a philosophy, but a way of life. Each individual must build up the proper outlook within himself so that he could embark upon socialist revolution.

While he was a student in America, he was inclined towards Russian communism. He was a great votary Russian communism. He was very much impressed with the performance the Russian government in the initial stage. The government of proletariat that had been a dream to him in his student days had come true. And he had great illusion about the Russia. But after few years he was disillusioned. He had sad experience of the performance of the Russian government during the days of Stalin, where individual freedom and individual initiatives were suppressed by violence. State violence was rampant. Authoritarianism was not the only alternative to Capitalism. It was not possible to eradicate Capitalism simply by nationalising Banks and "industries, trade and marketing and agriculture'. Socialism would still be too far. Even it may not lead us to our goal. By robbing individual freedom and by performing state violence, perfect socialist state cannot be established. Jayaprakash was exploring the avenues for an alternative to State dominated socialism. He was 'in search for a process through which the Socialism can be established ignoring State power. He was eagerly moving towards the process through which people with their voluntary efforts people would come forward to lead a Socialist life preserving the spirit of Socialism.

The ethics of the socialism is based on three cardinal concept of Liberty, Equality and Fraternity. These three concepts are full of rich human values that have to be cultivated by us. These values are not only be appreciated as a theory, but should be adopted as a way of thinking and living. Throughout his life he as a rebel, he cherished these values as cynosure of Socialism. To quote Jayaprakash in this regard:

> "I have been always in quest of the path of 'human welfare 'till now and reached this stage. The light of Liberty, Equality and Fraternity has been showing me path till now. The same light has dragged me to my goal of Sarvodaya. I always keep this Pole Star in front of me to decide my path. I regret very much that I could not reach this stage while Gandhiji was living among us."

He had digested Socialism in his life and became its pioneer, He was not only a critique of non-violence method of revolution adopted by Gandhiji, but when Gandhiji succeeded in attaining freedom through the process of non-violence, he was drawn to the process. And he was fully convinced with the ethics of the application non-violence in a mass scale, when Gandhiji was gone. He linked Socialism with democracy and non-violence. He was convinced with the 'change of heart' process of Gandhiji. He was amazed to see the performance of Gandhiji in using non-violence as an alternative of violence while fighting the battle of Freedom with the British. That made him to follow the path of non-violence in all types of mass struggle. He was fully confident that the role of non-violence in bringing about social changes cannot be ruled out. The technique of adopting non-violence in mass scale in solving the problems of the masses was Mahatma Gandhiji's was great revolutionary invention by which Jayaprakash was influenced intensely.

As a rebel, he revolted against all deprivations of the society. May it be political, economic or social. The deprivations in the functioning of democracy had pained him. He wanted to overhaul the democratic system so that people should play a participatory role in its functioning and move into its decision-making process. He thrived to work out ethics of democracy in his life. In democracy, people are the power house and it is they who have to generate power. The function of the political parties to catch hold of the power and utilise it to lift the conditions of the people. The more important thing for those who capture power is to exercise the power properly for human welfare. This is the paramount objective of the role of power in democracy. Jayaprakash was very keen to modify the functioning of democracy. He held that mere establishing the democratic structure of government would not produce any result. The mass must accept democracy as a way of life. Faith in human values, tolerance, respect for the sentiment of the adversary, surrendering one's self for the well-being of the community, are the basic values of democracy those have to practised 'in the society. Democratic values cannot be preserved simply by changing the structure of the government.

He held similar views about Socialism. It cannot be established by bringing outward changes in the society. It is a pattern of life to be practised by all members of the society. It can only be achieved by changing the existing values of life. But the Socialist movement has only worked to make progressive laws. It has not worked for changing the individual. The individual cannot be rebuilt nor changed by enacting laws. So, Socialism can be established outwardly by the government in power, but it cannot establish the socialist values in the society. The power-oriented government is capable to erect an outward economic and social pattern, but it cannot build up socialist culture. So, genuine socialism cannot be established by taking the lever power in hands, but through the process of training of the people. Once new values are digested, they are spontaneously active in our lives. The modern Socialist States are giving more importance for erecting the power structure than to changing the outlook of the people of society. That is the reason why the capitalist ideas are entering the structure through back door. Jayaprakash had drawn the inferences from the functioning of the present Socialist governments of the world that the establishment of new values in the society cannot be done either through power or through methods of violence. Both have failed to carry the mission infusing new ideas into human mind. We are looking forward to a third power.

This third power is the power of love-non-violence-compassion; He observed that the functioning of this third power is not new to our country. Our saints and seers have pioneered the process of transformation of human hearts through this process. Christ, Buddha and Mahavir have also applied it in social sector. It is time to explore the process more deeply with scientific approach. To quote Jayaprakash:

> "Christ has thought and accordingly advised to spread the power of love to the neighbour. The broad meaning of neighbour can be extended to whole human society. But there is hardly any attempt made by the followers of Christ to apply the Religion of Love in their social life. It cannot be expressed that the present Christian society is based on the commandments of love-non-violence-compassion. Mahavir and Buddha have established religion on the base of non-violence and compassion. But this religion was confined to their followers and some people. King Ashoka was the only Emperor, who after repenting for the blood bath of Kalinga war, adopted Buddhism and vowed not to indulge in any war in future. Still then, it was never felt that society under Ashoka's regime the Indian society was a non-violent and compassionate society. It would be a great blunder to believe that absence of physical violence is non-violence Exploitation, oppression, inequality along with various types social and economic injustices those Junction under the strength of State power; are definitely violence though sometime in a concealed manner. In this way Christ, Buddha and Mahavir had applied the Third Power in the social field but the followers of these three religions based on the foundation of love-non-

violence-compassion could not build up their society on the basis of this foundation. Today we want to make the experiment of this third power in the social sector."

Jayaprakash is optimistic about the success of the third power in delivering a non-violent, affectionate and compassionate human society. We must carry forward the experiments initiated by Christ, Buddha and Mahavir till the entire human society is not absorbed in the heart of the people. Mahatma Gandhi had to do up to half way as he was grabbed by death all of a sudden. That made his Mission unfulfilled. Jayaprakash inducted the "Third Power" endorsed by him from Mahatma Gandhi and inducted the same into his concept of Socialism. Gandhiji had paved the way for the application of this Third Power of love-non-violence-compassion through his successful application 'in both at South Africa and in India.' So, Jayaprakash had to accept the inferences of the experiments done by Gandhiji without any hesitation. Through Gandhiji's successful experiments, he wanted to change the entire concept of Socialism and carry it to the common man. That made him critical about the present functioning of the Socialist Parties.

Each leader of the Socialist claims to be perfect in working out the concept of Socialism. Capitalists like Birlas say that the Congress can establish Socialism if they want. The people of Jana Sangh speak about Indian Socialism. Therefore, everybody is claiming to be Socialist. We propose to nationalise the Banks, Key Industries and Mines. It has to be done. But does that mean that the Socialist venture is complete without paying attention to the problems of agriculture and that of small farmers and agricultural labours. Our country is the country of poor agriculturalists. They have to be benefited by Socialism. Socialism cannot come shouting slogans, nor it would come by imitating the Socialism of Europe. The European people have a different background than that of Asia. Most of the common people there are industrial workers where as in Asia most are agricultural workers. So the Asian Socialism cannot adopt the same model of European Socialism. We have to think in different way for establishing socialism in Asia. Here, we have to apply it in our own life. We have to conduct different experiments, different types of thinking, to implement Socialism in India.

Explaining about he pattern of Socialism required for the Asian countries, Jayaprakash said:

> "The main problem is what is the meaning of Socialism in a Agricultural oriented country. The little knowledge that I have on Socialism, I can say this much on the basis of it that I have one answer to it. The answer is that it is not Socialism to abolish Zamindari, promulgation of land ceiling Act, or the policy of "Land to the tiller" or consolidation of holding or Agricultural insurance, or similar enactments of land reform. The only meaning for agriculture-based socialism, is to establish community ownership of land and its management. What happened to Zamindari abolition? That was not a programme of Socialism. In America there was no Zamindari, nor Royatiwa in the past, nor it is today. But through this one cannot say there is Socialism in America. Similarly we have promulgated Land Reforms Act by fixing land ceiling in our country. It had nothing to with socialism In Japan, General Mc. Arthur fixed land ceiling to three acres. We cannot dream of it here. Namboodripad in Kerala had fixed land ceiling up to Ac. 16. Does that mean Mc. Arthur was a greater revolutionary than Namboodripad? The Socialists place the demand to wave the revenue of the peasants. But is it really the revolution? I declare that the pattern of Socialism in India has taken shape through Gram Dan. I am confident that the new Socialist society about which we have been dreaming of can be achieved by laying the foundation of Gram Dan. A great revolutionary step has been taken by surrendering the individual ownership of land in Gram Dan."

His strong conviction on Socialism has taken Jayaprakash to cultivate basic humanism through that. He was not a doctorian, instead he was a humanist incessantly searching for humanism inside Socialism. He was always on the lookout to find the application of his Socialist ideal. In that sphere, he made several new discoveries in modifying the approach of his ideal. He has gone to the extent of modifying even the basic concept of socialism. In socialism, instruments of production should be owned by the society and all the wealth produced out should be spent for the welfare of the society. But he said, these cannot be done through state power, as has been expounded in the Socialist theory. Because we cannot change the attitude of the people by enactments. We cannot force the people to produce and spend for the welfare of the society. We can do this only through peaceful persuasion.

In most of the countries Socialism has been established generally through State power. If there is democracy in the country, Socialism is established through electoral process. Predominately, the help of Law is taken for that. Communism adopts the method of violence for establishing socialism. Jayaprakash suggests three interpretation of Socialism:

- Socialism that is established through the methods of violence is fake Socialism, it is Communism, functioning of the government some times and express discontent with the government far various situations, but still they believe that if at all any solution to any problems has to be done, they look forward to the government to solve them. This faith has already been founded in the minds of most of the people. Even some of the big persons believe that the government is the only instrument through which all problems can be solved This anti-democratic faith can only be wiped off when the people are infused with enlightenment. Democracy cannot function properly unless the leadership of the people grows out of themselves. We do not find a single example in the world where we can find the all-round upliftment of a country is done by the State government. A country can only lift herself through people's power. The people's power of country cannot be built up through coercive process of the government. Jayaprakash held that we are yet to understand the fundamental truth about democracy. That is why we mentally depend upon the government to solve our problems and that we have no responsibility of our own in dealing with our own problem.

We have not yet understood the true meaning of Democracy. The true meaning of Democracy is that the people should be capable of upholding their right to solve their problems of the society. But it seems everywhere that people are neither interested nor prepared to take on their democratic responsibility. As a result, the huge manpower is lying in slumber and is being treated as a burden instead of being treated as wealth of the nation. This irresponsible mentality of the masses is harmful and also suicidal to the people's power or to democracy.

This effortless attitude of the people is due to faulty policies of the government too. It squeezes the initiatives from the people and leaves them without aspiration and keeps them mentally idle. So, in a democracy, the government plays a great role in building the power of the people and enhances their capability of participation through their own initiatives. But today's democratic governments have failed to create the power of initiative in the people to work for the society. This needs special and sincere initiatives on the part of government to allow the people to taste the fruits of Democracy, also he did not subscribe to the methods of violence in bringing about social change.

The technique adopted by Gandhiji in his struggle against British power had influenced him a lot. It was not the stereotype technique of revolution adopted by the earlier revolutionists. It was a revolutionary departure from that old technique of revolution. Such a technique was never witnessed before in the history of revolution. J. P. was convinced that the revolutionaries should change their methods. They must use the weapons of love and suffering and instead of preaching violence and hatred that Gandhiji used and succeeded.

True revolutionary must be an expert in inviting self-suffering without any malice in his heart, so that he could be able to establish noble ideals of socialism that includes equality, freedom and fellowship, peace and international brotherhood. The ideals of the Socialists could not be fulfilled simply by socialist power. We have experienced that the ideal often gets a back seat when attempted to be used by power. In the hoard of material development they are often forgotten. So, the ideals must be attended to and from the beginning by diverting all programmes accordingly. To quote from the report from the Book Twentieth Century socialism:

> "The ultimate source of confusion and division which afflicts socialism today is that the true ends are being forgotten. The doctrinaires have defied the means that were once thought to bring certain salvations, into ends in themselves. For them socialism is measured in terms of more public enterprise, more planning, more money spent on social services—irrespective of the results. The empiricists, on the other hand, in becoming more realistic about the choice of means, have scaled down their ends to nothing more than the immediately acceptable. In neither viewpoint is there any room for the ideals which have been the one enduring foundation of the socialist faith?"

J. P. had enough experience of the functioning of the Communist countries who wanted to implement their ideals through their programmes. They used typical jargons to justify the working of their ideas. They claimed democracy functioning, under dictatorship, socialism under state capitalism and world revolution with colonialism and national expansion. Equality and freedom, two most cherished values of socialism could not be established even after 40 years of revolution. So J. P. held that we cannot establish socialism according to its ideal simply by destroying feudalism and nascent capitalism. Socialism cannot be equated with mere economic growth. There is wrong 'in calling economic growth as socialist achievement. But J. P. reminds us that even rapid economic growth have occurred under capitalism and fascism. So, more economic development cannot be treated as a measure of socialism. The socialists must be conscious about the fact that establishment of socialist values is more important than the economic growth. And in no way socialist values be sacrificed in the alter of economic development. A powerful State machinery can initiate rapid economy growth, but cannot establish values of socialism.

Most of us who are committed to socialism or communism must discover new roads to establish the ideals that they hold.

The progressive political workers and thinkers were caught in theories, institutions and organisations. The old framework of socialist thinking will no longer bring about any result. We should not push more power into the State and do everything through State power. Instead through revolution we should make people make more powerful than the State. We have to evolve a new process for that. And the process expounded by Gandhi and Vinoba can replace the old process. It is the process of self-transformation and self-suffering.

The noble values of equality, freedom, fellowship and international brotherhood could be established through the above process. Socialist society cannot be established if each individual of the society craves and hankers after acquire more and more for himself. All individuals of a socialist society must believe in the act of self-control and adopts a way of life to foster the spirit of voluntary surrendering for the welfare of the community. Such a life of self-control and self-renunciation would remove the strife between man and man, man and groups and classes and between nations. Though Science has created possibilities for universal happiness, yet owing to man's covetousness and greed, all prospects of universal happiness are transformed into universal miseries. So long man would be craving more for himself, ideal of socialism would remain as a far cry. Hence, desire for craving more have to be subdued.

The moral development of man must coincide with the technological development Revolution theories expounded by earlier revolutionaries based on conflict of interests, has become non-operative 'in the present age of reason'. We have no right to interfere in the interest of others. The values we want to create would work only under the new way of life. Instead of conflict, we have safeguarded the self-interest of others. The future revolution will be conducted in Gandhian technique where we would not hanker after power, instead but learn to live according the ideal we cherish. Any value that we want to establish must be practised in our own life. The noble Marxian ideal "From each according to his capacity and to each according to his needs". This ideal cannot be imposed by the State being initiated by the change of outlook, rather can be practised by each individual from the very day when accepts the ideal. To quote J. P. 'in this regard:

> "Therefore, let those who believe in equality proceed to live accordingly. Equality does not consist in taking from the rich and distributing to the poor. If the poor tiles to establish equality by merely distributing the wealth of the wealthy among themselves, without accepting the philosophy behind it, they would soon recreate different forms inequality amongst themselves. And if the poor accepted the new philosophy and practised it in their own lives, and if they did it in mass scale, the rich would not remain behind. Likewise with other ideals and values of Socialism."
>
> *(Bhoodan, Nov. 14, 1956)*

Mahatma Gandhi was successful in building up a mass movement by bringing about internal changes in man. It could be called as a moral mass revolution. The sane people are eagerly waiting to experiment this new technique of Mahatma Gandhi in every comer of the world. They expect India to give them a lead. But after Mahatma Gandhi, the people of India and their leaders too have disrobed themselves of the Gandhian techniques. The lust for power has entered into every fibre of the leaders. They have forgotten about the moral mass power and the people's power displayed by Mahatma Gandhi. To quote J. P. again:

> "Rut I am sorry to say that while Gandhiji's name is on the lips of everyone here, our eyes are turned eagerly to others. The lure of power is too great, and everyone who wants to do anything for his country wants to get to the seats of power. The only exception, as you probably know, is Vinoba Bhave and the small group of workers around him. His Bhoodan movement, of which you might have heard something, is an experiment of the new social dynamics, of which I have been speaking. He is trying to develop a mass movement... and he has largely succeeded in it—for persuading people to live a life sharing and to denounce the notion of individual ownership of property. Wealth can be distributed by law, but shared

only voluntarily. Distribution of wealth may be an uncertain step towards Socialism, and sharing of wealth is real and full Socialism.

(Bhoodan, Nov. 14, 1956)

The ideal of Sarvodaya is a magnified ideal of Socialism. It depends solely upon human reconstruction. Political reconstruction may play a role in arranging the administrative network, but it can do little for human reconstruction. It is only through moral mass movement, that ideals are settled in the hearts of the masses. The movement of mass reconstruction cannot be a political movement in the sense, as its aim is not to capture power. The movement of remaking the man has nothing to do about the supremacy of the State. The Socialist movement should drive towards that.

Gandhi's Disciple

Like Gandhiji. Jayaprakash too wanted a Socialist revolution through peaceful persuasion. This is to be done by convincing each individual as well as the society at large, to accept and act upon Socialism in social life. Otherwise Socialism would be left out only as a word of jargon. From the beginning, Jayaprakash was against capturing of power for himself. He held that power should generate from the people and should be the nucleus of the power structure of any country.

True democracy or true socialism can operate through people's power, not from any outward sources. If violence is allowed to function as a lever of power, then the will and the initiative of the people should be crushed. They will only remain as an instrument of emasculation of the human society. Jayaprakash endorsed this consciousness from Gandhiji. He felt that even in a Socialist State, the state power may rest on dedicated people with the promulgation of progressive policies, but it has been observed from experiences that the people at below are not benefited out of it properly. The People will be only benefited when they would feel that it is they who depute power to various sectors.

A great many revolutions have been made in this world. Revolts were done for establishing new social values in the country like. The French Revolution. The American War of Independence. The Russian Revolution, The Chinese Revolution. No doubt, those were all successful revolutions. But what happened after that? Irrespective of the revolutionary goal of the revolution, post revolution era of most countries were gloomy. We have seen in the post revolution periods that all the leaders who pioneered the revolutions were seated on the citadel of power of their countries and handled power in their own hands. No doubt there was logic in that. They had to take power 'in their hands for the sake of establishing new values in the society, to establish a new structure of the Society and to fulfil the objective of the revolution'. George Washington did it in America. France changed power from one hand to another. Lenin also took power into his own hands in Russia. The same happened in China, Turkey, Algeria, Cuba and in many other nations.

The post revolutionary history went on like that. But Gandhiji was an exception to that. He kept himself away from the citadel of power. Perhaps the only mass leader of the world who handled the masses with full political authority at the time of political struggle, but when the political goal was achieved he declined to handle power. Because he knew that no purpose of the welfare of the nation could be served by that. He wanted the people to be politically powerful, so that they could be able to handle power by delegating the same to their genuine representatives. Gandhiji was not a small or a mediocre political leader.

The world knows that he kept the entire nation at this command for 25 years. But yet he preferred to keep himself aloof of power. Jayaprakash observed and learnt from Gandhiji to keep himself away from power politics. He was a typical politician. In his socialist days he distributed tickets to his party candidates, he conducted elections and propagated for his party, he never stood as a candidate in any election. Because he did not want to handle power in his own hands. He closely watched the political performance of Gandhiji and observed that Gandhiji was involved in different kind of politics. It was not just power politics. It was politics of the people. His objective was to create political consciousness among the people by going to them not through legislatures or Parliament, but through voluntary efforts. The

Indian independence movement was not a political movement alone, it was mass movement aimed at changing the characters and attitudes of the masses. So, though Jayaprakash was directly involved in party politics, he did not contest election ever in his life. Alike Gandhiji he too believed that people's power could not be built up by passing progressive laws and promulgate progressive regulations in assemblies and Parliaments. We must work voluntarily with the people and make them conscious of their powers and their rights in a democratic country.

That was why Gandhiji wanted to dissolve Congress and shape into voluntary organisation Lok Sevak Sangh by name. He prepared an amendment for Congress Constitution just one day before his death. He wrote it in his own hands. But God willed otherwise. He wrote:

> "The Congress has done a great deed by giving independence to the country. But now it has to do a more difficult work. The country has achieved political independence, but it is yet to achieve economic, social and moral independence specially in the villages. The more India moves forward in the direction of democracy, there is more possibility of a tussle between people's power and army power. Therefore, army power should be kept under the subjugation of Peoples power. We have to built up this type of social structure."

Jayaprakash got himself indoctrinated with this powerful attitude of Gandhiji, which he materialised later in his life. He learned the technique of dissuading himself from power politics while keeping himself engaged in all political activity. He built up a strange personality of revolting against political autocracy at all moments, but at the same time, keeping himself directly involved in party and power politics. He was also engaged in doing "People's Politics' named by his mentor Vinobaji as "Lok Neeti". Jayaprakash believed that People's power cannot emanate from any government authority including State power. According to him, there must be some other organisations other than political parties who will do the work. The volunteers of such organisation would roam from village to village and not only arouse political consciousness, but arouse consciousness for a fundamental change in the social structure appealing them to change their social behaviour. He held, people must change their ideas of self-indulgence and greed and to build up the attitude of equality and brotherhood to accommodate themselves into the new structure of the society. To implement these ideas 'of social change, people have to take their own initiative for decentralisation of power. According to him all powers must rest with Gram Panchayats or in the long run with village councils. He wanted to revolutionise the Punchayat Raj system of India. Unless the system is changed, according to him, the Panchayats will continue to function as a unit of the government than as an unit of the people. So Jayaprakash wanted to revolutionise the Panchayati Raj system.

Jayaprakash did not jump into the ideas of Gandhiji all of a sudden. He had been watching his miraculous personality and his powerful performance while leading the independent movement of India. Even if he believed in Marxian concept of social change, yet he joined Gandhiji's movement of liberating India, which Gandhiji conducted through non-violent and peaceful means. He did not believe then in violent method, but he participated in the National Liberation movement. He participated and suffered in the independent movement but he maintained his inner attitude of rage and violence against the Britisher.

No doubt he was participating with the non-violent strategy of Gandhiji, but he did not accept non-violence as a way of life or a basic philosophy of life like Gandhiji. Even at the peak hour of the independence movement, Gandhiji had expressed many times that most of the Congress leaders accepted "nonviolence" simply as a strategy, not as an ethic. And hence, Gandhiji said "non-violence has been delayed. Had the Congress workers adopted 'Non-violence as a cardinal principle in their lives, the liberation of India would nave been attained much earlier. Jayaprakash was one among them who could not rule out non-violence completely not could he accept it completely. He had still doubt regarding the non-violent application in bringing about social change. According to Socialist Jayaprakash the exploiters and the oppressors are so immune to torturing and exploiting the poor and the underprivileged, that it is difficult for them to give up the practice through peaceful persuasion. So the oppressors have to be dealt with severely. The Socialist Party which was formed by Jayaprakash after he left Congress was resolved to give the strategy of physical violence. They were yet to be convinced about the impropriety of 'violence in spirit' or 'the violence of soul'. The Socialist Leader held for some time that 'destroying of material objects that has no life' does not amount to violence. Violence was confined to them of doing harm to any living being which was antagonistic to the interpretation of violence by Mahatma Gandhi. But the humanist Jayaprakash was pondering over this matter and very often disagreeing with his colleagues. He was gradually being occupied with the ideas of truth and non-violence of Mahatma Gandhi. He felt these two concepts were the basic human values and had to be preserved in all aspects of human life. To quote Jayaprakash in this regard:

> During Gandhiji's life time, in spite of the fact that I was gradually drawing close to him, as I have recounted above I have read no doubt Gandhi's writings through change of heart. As I have indicated above, Gandhiji, soon after independence, was evolving in his mind a national programme of launching upon the second and greater phase of his unique carver. His proposal to transform organisation which he has fashioned as a non-violent army of freedom into Lok Sevak Sangh.

But he was completely transformed after getting the shock of Mahatma's abrupt assassination. He suddenly felt that Gandhiji was completely right in his approach to life and to society at large. The long turmoil that was going on within him was subsided and he preferred to surrender to the concept of Mahatma Gandhi. Not only that, Jayaprakash discovered his spiritual power within the concept of Gandhi. Spiritualism does not only mean to lead a life of a mendicant, but to enrich one's life by accepting and applying human values as the mean of survival. This made him a great worshipper of human values. He tuned his life in such a way that the whole of Gandhi penetrated into his thoughts. He had many rebirths. While a student he became a Marxist, from Marxist he became a revolutionary, from a revolutionary he became a freedom fighter, from a freedom fighter he became a Socialist, and from a socialist he became a political spiritualist. He expounded a different type of spiritualism in his political life. His main objective was to induce human values into the sphere of politics. A complete change in his political attitude was displayed in his life. The application of spiritual values into politics was not a new thing in our country. Shri Aurobindo and Balgangadhar Tilak and Gokhle were the devotees of building People's Power through Politics. It was they who first identified that independence of India could only be achieved through the untied power of the common masses. They felt that under the existing circumstances it was not possible to go for violent revolution. Therefore, they explored the alternative and decided to go for non-violent revolution for the liberation of their motherland.

Shri Aurobindo and Balgangadhar Tilak also discovered the method of violent revolution and experimented on it. All of them made commendable contributions to India's liberation movement Shri Gokhle founded Servants of India Society during the period. He declared that the Society would thrive for applying spiritual values into the process of politics. With this objective The Servants of Society was founded. Mahatma Gandhi inherited this spirit from them, but he was not a disciple.

It was not necessary for an inheritor to blindly follow the process. Keeping the founding spirit intact, the inheritor modifies the instruments of application and widen the path of application. Mahatma Gandhi purified the path shown by these apostles and made it result-oriented. It was Gandhiji's invaluable genius by which he transformed non-violent resistance into Satyagraha, which was absolutely his own discovery. He applied Satyagraha as a weapon of doing good to all.

It was a typical instrument to fight out evil but at the same time doing no evil to the evil-doer. The astute revolutionary Jayaprakash withdrew himself from the cult of violence in the same way as being done by Aurobindo, Tilak and Gokhle and accepted into the Gandhian method of 'spiritual' politics. That was why he had not participated either in Power politics or in Party politics. He endorsed political jargon of Vinoba known as "politics of the people" or "Lok Neeti". He tried hard to bring people to the forefront of the political arena of the country. It is not the Parties, but the people who are to be oriented to control the Parties who claim themselves as Political Masters till now. He wanted that the Parties would follow the will of the people instead people following the Parties. He admitted that this change of the political concept was discovered by Gandhiji through his concept of Ram Rajya where people would be ruled by themselves and also look after for each other for their common welfare. That was his concept of Lok Neeti.

Accordingly he was gradually drawn towards humanism leaving behind popular political activities and attempted to dive into the hearts of the people of our country. He had become fully armed with the ideas of Mahatma Gandhi and had already applied them for his personal purification and for the society. Though outwardly he did not seem like a man treading over the path of 'salvation' or any sort of personal spiritual achievement, yet inwardly, he cultivated habits of both purification of deeds and purification of soul. He learnt from Gandhiji that purity of personal conduct and transparency in political life is the foundation on which humanism revolves. He was a compassionate man with divine qualities of truthfulness and love, He believed in tolerance towards his adversaries.

He believed in universal brotherhood of mankind He was a celibate throughout his life. His wife was an ashramite in Gandhiji's Ashram since her young days and was fully engrossed in practising celibacy and was successful in dedicating her body to the service of the country as being advised by Mahatma Gandhi. When Jayaprakash returned from America after seven years, she asked her husband to accept the ethics of separation of body for the rest of their lives and yet remain as devoted husband and wife. Jayaprakash had never been a coward. He compiled with the request of his young wife and joined hands with his wife in the endeavour of purification of body. In spite of their bodily separation, Jayaprakash and Prabhavati remained as an ideal partner till their last breath. In this way Gandhiji's influence was acting on him. Through that he enhanced his inner power and spiritual strength that helped to keep command over many people of the country. He developed his will power to dedicate himself totally to the welfare of the society with full conviction. His integrity helped him to grow over other leaders of the country. It also helped him to acquire wisdom that always moved in a positive trend. The association of Gandhiji and his participation in the revolutionary process had made him fit to keep command over his body and soul. He was moving deep into his own soul and was visualising a new vision of total well being of all people with the magnetic power of attracting and convincing the people of our country. He started behaving not as a political leader but as a humanist having love and faith for every human being. To quote Jayaprakash from his Total Revolution:

> Disciplining the body appetites is essential for a moral life and growth of human personality and blossoming of all human qualities and values. This is true particularly of socialist values. The socialist way of the is a way of sharing together the good things that common endeavour may make available. The more willingly this sharing is practised the less tension and coercion in society and the more socialism. I believe that unless members of society learn to keep their wants under control, willing sharing of things may be difficult, if not impossible, and society would be bound to split into two divisions.

He had never minimised the need for the material prosperity for the poor. But in itself this did not close the chapters of Total Human Welfare. He was against preserving material happiness and encourage an outlook on life that feeds an insatiable hunger for material goods. He proclaimed many times that there cannot be peace of minds and hearts of men nor peace amongst men, if this hunger chases them constantly. Preserving the basic values and adopting them in our social life amounts to spiritualism. Constantly striving for economic and social equality amounts to spiritualism. To be engaged in the competition of surpassing our neighbour in material prosperity to Jayaprakash, was against the ethics of humanism and hence against spiritualism. To go against the self-interest of our neighbour for our own prosperity had never been considered by him as a process of human development.

To him, it was an act of violence and immorality. In this way he had digested all material and spiritual values expounded by Mahatma Gandhi and acted upon them in his own life. In the later life he moved on the path of Gandhiji with close watch.

Dedicated to Vinoba Bhave

Jayaprakash was closely watching the Bhoodan movement of Vinoba since 1952. His emotions and aspirations were searching for an outlet. He wanted to move out of the purview of the Party politics. Even he was not able to convince his own comrades about a partyless revolution in which only the people would participate with their own identity. He was not at all satisfied with the performance of the Socialist movement in India. He was in constant quest of a programme that would fulfil the real Socialist ideal. He saw a beacon of light in Vinoba's Bhoodan-Gramdan movement. To quote his own words in this regard:

> I am afraid this process of original enquiry has been halted for the past few years in the Indian socialist movement. It is time that the thread of enquiry has been picked up again. The process should be facilitated by two different trends of development: one unfolding the Gandhian technique of social Revolution and reconstruction as exemplified in Bhoodan and Gramdan and Gramswaraj movement.

He was astonished to observe the events great significance that happened in a remote village of Telengana on 18th April, 1951. The day the Bhoodan was born, his first reaction to this event was not very much encouraging. But it created a great impression on him, He pondered over the happenings of Bhoodan. The event provoked him to look back to Gandhiji through Vinoba. Jayaprakash was not at all unknown to Vinoba. He was well acquainted with the background of Vinoba. Speaking about Vinoba he said:

> I had known Vinoba for years and often when I had the occasion to visit Wardha I went specially to see him. I always found him unusually stimulating, and original. Some of his writings I had read had an-

> exhilarating freshness. I recalled how Gandhiji had selected him as the first Satyagrahi in 1941. I remembered again his clear-sighted lead at the conference of the political and constructive workers after Gandhiji's death.

So after Gandhiji, Jayaprakash looked to Vinoba as the first associate who could represent Gandhiji's thought and action. Vinoba to him was the only man who could fill up the vacuum of Gandhiji. So, when he saw a person, like him who started a non-violent campaign to solve the land problem of the country. He attributed towards it with full seriousness. He was watching that the movement was gaining momentum all over the country with powerful mass response. The method of non-violence and peaceful persuasion which was applied seeking lands for the landless by Vinoba impressed Jayaprakash. It was a type of Satyagraha based on compassion that revealed the Gandhian character of Vinoba. Though a lot of political leaders ruled out Bhoodan movement as 'impractical', but Jayaprakash could not ignore the movement, instead he discovered a political process of social transformation inside the Bhoodan movement. He predicted that the results of Vinoba movement would be far quicker and faster than movements launched by various political parties of India. About this time, the old Socialist Party had already adopted a course of action under the initiative of Jayaprakash to give full support to Bhoodan movement. He was convinced about the revolutionary outlook of the Bhoodan movement. To put in his own words:

> I went to see Vinoba when he was in the Banda district of U.P. to discuss the question of land distribution. I saw he was serious about the problem and his economic outlook was revolutionary in a basic way. I decided to join Vinoba's Bhoodan movement.

He never had this type of thrilling experience of getting immediate result in the process of the movement. He did not believe on his own efforts when he received gifts of seven thousand acres of land within a week simply by appealing to the people. He was extremely excited to see that most of these donors were small holders. He thought he was gathering sanction of the people for land redistribution. He was very much impressed by the process of Bhoodan movement. It touched the heart of the people and at the same time demonstrated the spirit of sacrifice of the small land holders for the landless of the village. Vinoba initiated a revolution of human heart including the heart of Jayaprakash. He plunged into the movement at Gaya of Bihar and dedicated himself to Vinoba. In a plenary session of All India Sarvodaya Conference at Bodh Gaya he declared that "I am dedicating my life to Vinoba's Bhoodan Garamdan movement." His declaration moved the entire audience of Sarvodaya Workers and Vinoba was so emotional that tears of pleasure rolled from his eyes. It was a great victory of his and for his movement to attract such a gigantic political personality like Jayaprakash. Since then he worked untiringly for the success of the Bhoodan-Gramdan movement.

Another historical event took Jayaprakash by storm. The Bhoodan movement of Vinoba disclosed a massive political ideal concealed in the Sarvodaya movement. The Bhoodan had evolved itself into Gramdan, which meant voluntary surrendering of individual ownership of land to the village. In 1952, the first Gramdan was declared by the people of Mangroth village of Hamirpur district of U.P. The people for the first time in India surrendered their individual ownership to the village community so that the land could be kept in a pool and redistributed among all the villagers in an equitable way. To put the definition of Gramdan in his own words:

> Vinoba has a talent for coining words and investing old words with new meanings. Thus DAN in his vocabulary does not mean gift, but "sharing together". That is the rendering of Shankar's definition. Danam Sam Vibhagah. Gramdan was equitable sharing together of the lands of the village by the people of the village. Bhoodan signifies distribution of land to the landless, Gramdan on the other hand, meant communalisation of the land: institution of community in place of individual ownership of land.' It became evident that Bhoodan had within it the germ of agrarian revolution. And how beautiful a revolution, how different from all others.

The history of revolutions taken place in the world had been linked with physical violence, bitterness and hatred, misery and tyranny and concentration of power in few hands. Those who were opposed to revolutions or denied to participate in it, were physically expropriated. They were not granted any opportunity to defend their opinions on it. In past, the violent revolutions gave birth to dictatorship and a powerful bureaucracy.

Ownership were abolished through violence or through other kind of force. But, in the beautiful revolution of Gramdan of Vinoba, ownership was not abolished by force of any kind, but freely and voluntarily surrendered to the community. In this non-violent revolution of Vinoba, the outward social change was accompanied by the inward human change. This was otherwise termed as Sarvodaya revolution. In that unique type of revolution, social tensions, conflicts and tyrannies were replaced by individual freedom, mutual good will, and brotherhood.

Jayaprakash apprehended that the Bhoodan-Gramdan -Gram Swaraj movement was creating such a social consciousness and an enlightened soul, about which all governments, may it belong to any political party, would be afraid of. In Western democracy the administrators become afraid of the public opinion till the end of election. Once, the election is over, they ignore the voice of the people in all respects. The people were too accustomed of it. They did not hesitate to tolerate the misconducts of their elected representatives and the administrators. But in India, there was a different type of political system.

The warriors were controlled by Brahmins. It otherwise meant that neutral people had control over the administrators. Mahatma Gandhi and Vinoba too wanted this type of political system, in which state power would be controlled by moral power or by power of service. He felt the intensity of this new political system evolving out of the Bhoodan-Gramdan movement which would ultimately reach a stage where people would hold the lever of power in their hands. The State authority would be bound to bow down before them. He joined Vinoba's movement to organise the people to exercise their power and to make the public opinion a most powerful instrument of politics. To quote Jayaprakash in this regard:

> Though I have taken leave from Party politics, it did not at all mean that I would remain silent when injustices occur in the country. It is my birth right as a citizen to raise my voice against any injustice. I have some responsibility to perform being as a citizen. When I would feel that I have to speak as a citizen, I must speak definitely. On the basis of my recent speeches, some people think that Jayaprakash wants to return to politics again. But I can assure them that I have no desire to return again to Politics. Moreover Bhoodan itself is a deep rooted politics. How can the movement which is thriving at changing the whole society, be kept aloof from politic? But definitely, it is different than party politics and now, I have no faith on party politics.

The non-violent social revolution of Bhoodan-Gramdan-Sarvodaya was creating an atmosphere of genuine political change in the country and Jayaprakash was convinced that it was not just a movement to initiate land reform but a movement to change entire political structure of the country. The function of State would be modified through this movement through decentralisation of power. With the establishment of small village councils and village banks in Gramdan will shift the base of power from State to the people. It would amend the relations between the Sate and the human society by making the state powerless. The ideal of Stateless society conceived by the Socialists can be achieved through this movement of Vinoba. He advocated throughout his life that human society must play a key role in controlling State power, otherwise the objects of the democracy will be jeopardised. To quote Jayaprakash:

> I continued to feel strongly that human freedom could be fully and wholly realised only in Stateless society. I was, and am, not sure if the State would ever wither completely. But I am sure that it is one of the noblest goals of social endeavour to ensure that the power and functions and spheres of the State are reduced as far as—possible. I became at this time, and still am, an ardent believer, like Gandhiji, in the maxim that

that government was the best that govern the least. The test of human evolution for me because man's ability, justice and cooperation with his fellowmen without outward restraint of any kind. That is why I have considered human and social problem to be at bottom of moral problem.

The Gramdan movement had brought about the possibility of forming small societies, which is very important for the evolution of human nature to be a perfect human being. Man cannot grow in a big society which is complex in character. We have had enough experience of the functioning of big society which is heaven for parasites, namely of bureaucrats, managers, technocrats. They contribute less but enjoy more and accelerate human suffering. Jayaprakash was convinced that unless the nature, conduct and outlook of the human beings are changed, social change cannot be brought about.

This change is needed for both Socialism and Sarvodaya. It is only 'in small communities man can establish healthy relation with his fellowmen and get scope to practice human values in the society. Self-government, self-management, mutual cooperation and sharing, equality, freedom and brotherhood—all could be practised and developed 'in far better way, if man lived in a small community. Man must grow in cultural and spiritual way. Genuine human development completely rests on these factors. Otherwise would behave in a society exactly like "social animal", not as a human being.

He was confident that Gramdan movement of Vinoba would create such a atmosphere in the country that a Revolution would take place as quickly as possible. J. P. contemplated that land revolution would place by 1957 and the individual ownership of land would go forever. Vinoba had assigned five years time for and revolution. More than 44 lakhs of Acres of land had been collected in five years in India and in Bihar 23 lakhs Acres of land was collected. One could not ignore the response of the people for this non-violent revolution. The foundation of land revolution had already been laid down by Bhoodan-Gramdan movement The foundation of land revolution had already been laid down by Bhoodan-Gramdan movement. The Bhoodan-Gramdan movement was in its peak in 1956-57. J. P. was very optimistic about the success of the movement. To quote J. P. in this regard:

> Before the end of 1957, all villages in India must have undergone a land revolution i.e., landlessness must be eradicated through land distribution. This our declared aim and our work derives its hope and enthusiasm from it. Five years of time allotted to this work have been past. And 44 lakhs of Acres of lands have been collected. Much thought and discussion is being given to the question of finishing the remainder of the work within the allotted time. A friend told us how many felt some what down hearted at the thought that the proposed task will not be accomplished; this is one way of evaluating the work which has been done so far My late friend Yusuf Mehrally often told us how a glass containing some water would be described as half full by an optimistic, to a pessimistic it would be half empty. It depends on how you look at the same thing. It is obvious that if we consider the total target in relation to land acquired in five years, the proportion of achievement does not seem meagre If you review the growth of the movement you will see new developments at each stage; new aspects of movement were accepted and established.

J. P. was virtually moved by the Gramdans in Orissa. In 1956, there were 800 Gramdans in Orissa. He could sec the prospect of land revolution in those Gramdan villages. It created a new political and economic situation that demanded analysis of all sensible citizens who wanted for total change of the existing social order. The Bhoodan movement had through this situation climbed a ladder living behind only land gifts and land distribution of plots of land. To J. P., it was the process of ending ownership of land. He thought if the villagers would boldly come forward with 'village gift' in Orissa, then why it could not be done in other parts of the country? He appealed to the Bhoodan workers to concentrate in obtaining Gramdan from all over the country, and spread these new ideas, experiments and new vision regarding the dissolution of ownership of land and plant its roots everywhere. He also appealed to political leaders and other important people to take responsibility in bringing about this non-violent revolution. This revolution was as important as our national struggle in which Indian masses whole heartedly participated. He welcomed the efforts of changing the attitude of ownership in Gramdan villages all over the countries and went on spreading the message of land revolution through Vinoba's movement. He also asked the government and public administration and those are in public life to come forward to share their responsibility in changing the society.

During those days the Indian government and many state governments were supporting Bhoodan movement of Vinobaji. But it was just leap sympathy and nothing more than that. J. P. as critical about their role. The administration and the government were not lending legal support to put an end to the land ownership nor they could promulgate regulations to materialise the objective of "land to the tiller' policy.

This was because, the government personnels themselves belonged to the groups of vested interests who did not want any change 'in the economic structure. J. P. was critical about their role. They did not play any role to make the movement more successful by using their influence and skill. Simply land distribution was not enough to help Vinobaji's movement. They must come forward with the efforts to establish the idea of 'collective ownership' and Gram Swaraj J. P. was confident that the devotion and dedication of Sarvodaya workers could make land revolution a success. He appealed to those who expressed sympathy with the movement to share some of his work and time, so that the movement will reach its goal. We all have to devote our full time to make the land revolution a success. To quote J. P. in this regard:

> I do not think anyone except Vinobaji could honestly say that he has directed his entire energy into Bhoodan. I have withdrawn myself from other activities and concentrated in this work; but I cannot honestly say that my entire energy was devoted to Bhoodan. I feel

> that I could have done twice the quantity of the work. This is an occasion for searching our hearts... our real strength is not in plans and programmes but in the inner purity of heart. When I take note of my own faults and shortcomings, I often feel that very little good could be brought about through me. But introspection is the only way we can purify and strengthen ourselves It is only when we have full faith in this movement as a means for purifying our lives that we shall be to devote our full energies into it. We have not done all that we could: until then we cannot ask for new methods of work.

J. P. was a rebellious politician. He revolted against the present politics of the parties, he had openly said many times that you cannot attract masses simply through your pedagogy. You need to purify your heart. Any non-violent evolution is a heart to heart dialogue. The heart gets purified through this dialogue. He insisted that any Bhoodan or Gramdan obtained from the landlord or from the peasant should be made out of pure love and sympathy. The speciality of the movement was that the landlord should be taught to love the landless and vice versa. It is quite natural for the landless to harbour hatred and anger towards the landlord because of the sustained poverty' and exploitation imposed on him by the landlord since generations. This ill-feeling is a threat to non-violent revolution. The Bhoodan movement does not want to exert pressure on the landlord taking the advantage of the ill-feeling of the landless. It is purely a movement of change of attitude by peaceful persuasion. Any gesture of direct or indirect violence is strictly forbidden in non-violent revolution. J. P. was very particular about this aspect of the movement. He said:

> Some people ask why we do not start an organisation of landless persons which could he used for exerting pressure. Popular strength does not come by mere aggregation of people. 'Jana Shakti' can only he regarded as the moral strength of the men in it. It is only when the dispossessed follow the path of truth and morality that they will generate real strength... Leftists often ask me whether I really believe that the

> rich will give up their lights of ownership only if the ideas of Bhoodan are explained to them. Will the factory-owners declare that their capital belongs to society? Perhaps they give away their part of wealth to get some publicity Even there is some change of heart, what are the prospects that ownership will itself go? My answer is when I go too rich man I do not expect him to give up everything or even one-sixth. It is a wonder that people give everything at all, when we observe the values, behaviour and condition of our society. Even partial gifts seem to be coming only because of the cultural background of our country and the work of men like Buddha, Gandhi and Vinobaji.

The success of non-violent revolution depends on the joint surrendering of their respective wealth to the society. Both the rich and the poor would behave 'in the same manner and display their change' in the attitude of individuals ownership. The poor grabs his earning of Rs. 25/- exactly as the rich grabs his wealth of 25 Crores. J.P. held that exploitation cannot be ended and equality cannot be established unless every one talks in the same language about ownership. Both of them have to practice what they preach to other.

When thousands and thousands of lives of the people are transformed, Sarvodaya society will be established. The Bhoodan movement teaches millions of the people to declare that what they get does not belong to them, but to the society. J. P. had already taken lesson from the outcome of Russian Revolution and those revolution occurred prior to that. According to him, they failed to achieve their goal. The changes that took place by those revolutions fell far short of their ideals, which our young men are dreaming to day. In China and Russia, the landlords and the capitalists were liquidated and their lands and properties were redistributed. Collective farming and centralised economy were introduced to keep control of the State over the distribution. All these were done to establish equality. But there were discrepancy in remunerations. An ordinary labourer of Russia got 400 Rubles where as a senior executive got 2,500 Rubles. The greatest Dictator

Stalin had to bend his knees before the acquisitive 'instinct' and the 'instinct of greed of man. He had receded a step backward from 'equality', this was because he did not pay any attention to pursue the individuals to change the 'established instinct of acquisitiveness'. J. P. held that one cannot establish equality simply by eliminating rent, interest and profit which were the three major causes of economic equality. That was done in Russia but total economic equality was not established. The executives, the engineers, the managers refused to work on the same income as the labourers. They did not accept Stalin's concept of equality in spite of severe persecution and massacre. They demanded extra pay for their talents and wisdom. Hence establishing equality among the people of different profession were hampered. So, our problems cannot be solved simply by distributing the wealth of the rich to the poor. The experience of the world showed that no revolution comes out of distribution of lands and property by force. It would be just change of hands with the attitude of ownership intact. It would be the initiative of the poor that can create the atmosphere of equality in the minds of the privileged. For that they have to eschew the greed from their own hearts. Bhoodan had been doing that through its process of persuasion.

It would be consistent here to quote Aldous Huxley from his book Science, Liberty and Peace:

> "Now it seems pretty obvious that man psychological, to say nothing about his spiritual, cannot be fulfilled unless first, he has a fair measure of personal independence, and personal responsibly within and towards a self-government group, unless, secondly, his work possesses a certain aesthetic value and human significance, and unless, in the third place, he is related to his natural environment in some organic, rooted and symbiotic way."

Jayaprakash believed that Gramdan—Sarvodaya movement was the only path to establish small, enlightened efficient, accomplished human society with the object of human welfare. Even the material developments could be carried on smoothly by small societies. The benefit of technology will reach every individual discarding top-heavy developments in which the needy man is being left out. Science can operate freely and efficiently in small units of production and other developments. The present trend of applying science to large scale production backed by centralised economy has led to immense miseries of the common man. So small decentralised units of productions are the only way out. Jayaprakash divided science into two categories—(1) pure science and 2) applied science. He termed applied science as technology. Application is an important function of science. It largely depends upon the character of the society. The money-makers, who are a powerful class of the society force the technology to follow their path. Sarvodaya stands for application of science in small societies and political power is naturally concentrated in their hands. Even in those countries who had progressive revolutionised did not escape concentration of power in their countries. Thus it is evident, large industrial establishment is followed by concentration of power. It would be in the fitness of things to quote here few lines from Aldous Huxley, the great philosopher of the modern times.

The Demise

He died in October 1979; but a few months before that, in March 1979, his death was erroneously announced by the Indian Prime Minister to the Parliament as he lay fighting for his life in Jaslok Hospital, causing a brief wave of national mourning, including the suspension of Parliament and regular radio broadcasting, and closure of schools and shops. When he was told about the gaffe a few weeks later, he smiled.

2

An Eventful Career

As it is evident from several sources, young J. P. felt unhappy to see the Indian subcontinent under the colonial rule. During his college days at Patna he attended political meetings, studied deeply about the political system specially the repercussions of a foreign rule in any country. In his early years, he was impressed by the political philosophy of Mahatma Gandhi and he watched his socio-economic and political programme with meticulous calculations. He felt unhappy at the ghastly tragedy of Jallianwala Bagh at Amritsar and, thereafter, he made up his mind to devote his whole energy to attain Swaraj. After one year, when Gandhi launched the first Non-Cooperation Movement, he showed his complete faith in the Gandhian ideology and shared his feelings for the achievement of Swaraj. At this point of time, he was fairly young as well as married to Prabhavati. His plans to go abroad for higher education were finalised by the members of his family and his in-laws. This became essential to make himself well-equipped for the political struggle after 1920.

In the long-drawn political struggle against functioning of the Raj in the subcontinent, the role of Jayaprakash Narayan is unique in the annals of our history. Throughout his long career which was exclusively devoted for the upliftment of the economically and socially weaker sections of the Indian society, he struggled consistently for the achievement of complete independence. During this struggle, he was jailed several times and suffered both physically and economically. However his urge for the grand mission of life was consistent for the solution of numerous ills in our society and he always dreamt to remove them as far as possible. He was greatly influenced by the writings of Bankim Chandra Chatterjee, Garibaldi and de Valera.

He was born on 11 October 1902 in the family home at Sitabdiara village on the confluence of the Ganges and the Ghagra rivers situated on the borders of Bihar, undoubtedly he was a promising student from his early years in the school at Patna where he was admitted at the age of eleven. He got high marks in English, Hindi and Mathematics, passed his Matriculation Examination in the first division and received the government scholarship of Rs. 15 a month. Thereafter he joined the prestigious Patna College.

During his stay in the USA, young Jayaprakash Narayan struggle hard to meet his expenses for education. To achieve this aim he did not hesitate to undertake any kind of small manual work offered to him. He worked at the farms, orchards, restaurants and other places from where he could earn some money. Probably he realised that he belonged to a middle class family and if he did not work hard it would be impossible for him to achieve the aim of his life. Another consideration in his mind was that he was a married youngman, he should therefore work as much as he could in foreign land so that when he reached his homeland, he should be well-prepared to cam his livelihood. Last but not the least, he had the consideration in his mind that he should achieve something unique after completing his academic career from the States. After reading Marx, Lenin and the philosophy of Socialist thinkers, he became restless and this restlessness enkindled in him the new spirit with new ideas and ideology.

With the passage of time, his financial difficulties were over and he could continue his studies with the amount he had earned with much labour. He passed his M. A. in sociology and was to keen to seek admission for the doctorate degree. But he was informed that his mother was seriously ill. He, therefore, had to come back to his village to meet his ailing mother.

"Jayaprakashji's sojourn in the United States of America for full seven years in quest of knowledge was indeed a saga of patience, perseverance, hardships and hard work. When he had set foot on the soil of the great American continent in 1922, he was a callow youth of only twenty years of age, fresh from his feudal surroundings in Bihar. When he returned to India in 1929, he was a well-experienced, wise.

Later in a letter to an American friend, he is reported to have written the following words of gratitude:

> "I spent the best part of my youth in your great country and seven of my happiest years. I went there as a student and learned much, not only from its universities, but also from its factories and farms..."

When he came back to India in November 1929, he found much political awakening in all the regions of the subcontinent under the leadership of Mahatma Gandhi. The national upsurge had become a glaring phenomenon with the appointment and visit to India of the Simon Commission which was opposed tooth and nail by a combination of all the political parties. The Nehru Report and the Congress programme for Dominion Status were a common talk in late 1920s. The left wing of the Congress had taken the shape under the leadership of Subhas Chandra Bose. Gandhi was busy in giving a new orientation to his political programme and was agreeable to the new ideology enunciated by young Jawaharlal Nehru whom he saddled with the responsibility of the presidentship of the Indian National Congress in 1929. At this point of time, when the Congress was more than four decades old, it was thought politically an appreciable step to change its strategy and gear up the resources of the masses towards complete independence. J.P. met Mahatma Gandhi and Jawaharlal Nehru and exchanged his political views with them. Both Gandhi and Nehru liked young J.P. and invited him to work for the cause of Swaraj.

Soon the opportunity came at the Lahore Congress in 1929, J.P. also attended this session along with his wife Prabhavati. In fact Gandhi, Nehru, J.P. and his wife travelled together to Lahore to attend the session of the Congress. Young J.P. was introduced to several prominent leaders assembled at Lahore. His personal links with Congress specially with Gandhi were strengthened through his wife's father. Brajkishore Prasad, a prominent Congress leader of Bihar. Moreover Gandhi and Kasturba treated Prabhavati as their adopted daughter. The decision of complete independence at the Lahore Congress had much impact on the mind of young J.P.

At this point of time, when J.P. was unemployed, he received an offer of an academic assignment from the Banaras Hindus University. But Nehru intervened and persuaded him to join as head of the newly created Department of Labour Research in the office of the All India Congress Committee at Allahabad. This led to J.P.'s attachment with Nehru and both began to consult each other on several socio-economic and political issues facing the masses of our country. So far so, Kamala Nehru and Prabhavati became close friends and shared their feelings regarding the upliftment of the status of women in our society.

The Lahore Congress presided over by Jawaharlal Nehru gave a clear warning to the Raj regarding the complete independence. All the delegates representing various regions scattered with one aim in their minds, i.e. the attainment of Swaraj. Gandhi, took as usual, took the lead and tried to negotiate with the Viceroy, Lord Irwin. He wrote him a lengthy letter in which he apprised him of the political situation in India as well as the bad socio-economic plight of a common man. It was a letter of warning to the Viceroy in a usual style of Gandhi who did not believe in any kind of secrecy in his political struggle.

Great Personal Charm

In the Words of a Close Watcher

Jayaprakash Narayan is a man of great personal charm and moral integrity who has been a commanding figure in Indian public life for almost two generations. In build he has always been slender and taller than most of his political contemporaries; but it is in his bearing and not his size that he possesses the pride and dignity of a statesman.

His features are remarkably handsome, perhaps not so much for a high forehead and the long upper lip and delicately chiselled bow of mouth over a square chin as for his sensitive, youthful - seeming vitality. In his thirties he wore the brooding expression of the revolutionary; in his sixties, his fine brown hair had receded a little and his brown eyes, full of movement behind thin-rimmed spectacles, had worry, gentleness, impatience and vision written in them. His flesh was slowly drawing closer about his high cheekbones and wide jaw structure, making him resemble more nearly the exaggerations newspaper cartoonists have made of his appearance. But he still possessed the fluent movements of his eloquent hands, the fine looks, the manner of a sage and the compulsive work capacity of youth which had made him a leader of men.

He has possessed an immense ability to influence others through a combination of personal fearlessness, physical and moral daring, scrupulous intellectual honesty, and a love for his fellow countrymen which has extended to the whole human family. He has always granted his contemporaries the right to criticise him for shortcomings in his practical philosophy of social reconstruction or to demand from him public explanations of the motives for his political conduct.

The real strength and depth of his capacity lay in a purpose that was always honest and high principled, and in a total unselfishness. Much of the admiration and reverence paid him by his country, he has won because in his public character he has refused to seek honour or public position, and in his private life he has renounced material comfort. His voice has a light, pleasant quality, precise in its articulation of both Hindustani and English. He possesses both erudition and simplicity, addressing with equal facility a group of ill-clad, illiterate village farmers in Bihar and the well-to-do members of the Bombay Merchants' Chamber.

He has the affection of the masses for his championship of their welfare, the recognition of scholars for his original social thinking, and the distinction of successfully mediating in disputes between India and some of her neighbours. He has been a foremost critic of India's foreign affairs policies, a founder of one of India's most important political parties, and president of India's largest trades unions.

He may claim a large share in the achievement of his country's freedom from foreign rule and a great part in her moral advancement towards a more just, peaceful, egalitarian community. He may claim a major share in saving millions of lives during famines for his appeals aroused worldwide assistance. His reproaches against the complacency or inefficiency of a number of his people made him respected as 'the conscience of the nation'.

His influence has tended to conserve what is good in man; to shame that which is self-seeking, destructive or evil. His life has been an inspiration towards a more noble and elevated attitude in a world full of social injustice, violence and thirst for power.

While we have done our best to check the temptation to write a book of personal memoirs about him instead of a biography, we would like, however, to include a description of those private aspects of his life that we remember with affection from the time of our first meeting with him in 1958 in Bombay, when we were in our twenties and he was fifty-six. Like thousands of others, we were captivated by his warmth and singular charm and by the sense of youthful idealism that permeated the early days of the Bhoodan (Land Gift) Movement.

When we first met Jayaprakash we were shy and gauche. We had been in India only a few days and her poverty had overthrown our comfortable sense of security and accepted place in the world. As a consequence we were particularly vulnerable to any unresponsiveness or lack of sympathy in others, and we awaited our interview nervously. All we had to recommend us was a brief letter of introduction from a London businessman.

It had been arranged that we should meet him at his younger brother's flat on Marine Drive. The room we entered that hot Sunday morning seemed full of people. We realised quickly that we had interrupted the family's breakfast, and this added to our sense of confusion. We were deeply relieved when Jayaprakash immediately came to us, introduced himself, drew us apart to chairs in a corner of the room and had tea and fruit brought for us.

But it was more than his formal politeness or his swift response to our embarrassment which captivated us. It was his charm, the unique quality that had made him a public leader and a national hero. All who have known him, even fleetingly, have been aware of this quality, whilst being, nevertheless, unable to define it. Mrs. J. J. Singh—who with her husband extends whatever hospitality Jayaprakash requires during his visits to Delhi—narrated to us a 'little incident' that was typical of J. P.:

> He was staying with us a few weeks ago and went out during one afternoon to some appointments. About six o'clock there was a ring at the door and I went. The gentleman there introduced himself and said he had come to see J. P. I explained that he was not in, doubtless delayed, and asked the visitor to wait in the library.

About half-an-hour later another ring brought me to the door and another gentleman claimed that he had come to see J. P. I invited him in also. Do you know, within the next hour I had five guests in the library and eventually it became clear to me that J. P. had invited them all to the evening meal and forgotten to tell me. As you know we do not have Indian-style food at night, and Western-style food is served in set portions. It can't really be made to go round. I rushed out to the kitchen and told the cook to do what he could. And then J. P. arrived. The contrition on his face was quite delightful. He took me aside. 'My God, Malati/he said, 'all these people. I forgot to tell you. All the way home in the taxi I thought to myself, What am I going to do? Where am I going to buy some dinner from? I thought of stopping the taxi-driver at some market but didn't know what to buy.' Well, we managed of course.

Jayaprakash expresses great warmth in his personal relationships. Throughout India friends and admirers vie with each other in what might be termed 'J. P.-manship'. Susceptible to his warmth and unselfishness, imprisoned by his capacity to make them feel loved and needed they rarely escape this delightful bondage. Even old friends who have parted from him in major political battles still like to dwell on the times when Jayaprakash loved them.

Many spend their days in his service. They meet his friends and acquaintances who have arrived by train or plane, from other parts; they obtain his railway tickets; they provide him with transport; they bring his papers from one office to another; they hover at night, wrapped to the ears in large shawls or blankets, on cold railway stations, waiting for his train to arrive so that they may greet him. They reluctantly give place to some other disciple he must see, and wait with a mixture of anxiety and resentment for the few words of personal affection that so drew them in the beginning.

'J. P. has called me' is an accepted reason for leaving a home, a wife, a day's or a week's work; and sufficient cause for travelling perhaps hundreds of miles to some remote village where Jayaprakash has his 'camp'.

We found ourselves particularly susceptible to this devotional aura that surrounded Jayaprakash, and without giving it conscious critical thought, we became involved in it. Thus we were simply charmed when a small, bearded man, who sat on a pouffe near us, apologised humbly for intervening in our conversation: 'I am sorry to take Jayaprakash from you, but I asked him to come to our meeting today. I should not take J. P.'s time, I know, but I love him too much.'

When Jayaprakash then asked us with a certain diffidence if we would also like to accompany him to the meeting, we accepted eagerly and were further warmed by the feeling of acceptance when he took us in his car, leaving the others to follow.

The car stopped outside another block of flats, and a group of people wearing white hand-spun cotton clothes received Jayaprakash. He went up the front steps and through the double doors ahead of us. There were dozens of pairs of sandals on the steps, and as we added ours, we looked into a small hall which overflowed with people. Men were standing in the doorway, but, inside, the audience was seated on a blue cotton carpet spread across the floor. Women occupied one side of the hall; the men filled the other half and the balcony upstairs.

We joined the audience. Immediately in front of us were three low tables, drawn together, covered by spreads and backed by bolsters, and on this dais four priests sat cross-legged, one of them speaking into a microphone. To the left of the dais were three chairs and Jayaprakash was shown to the middle one.

The cool austerity of the hall and the fragrance from the garlands of flowers, that lay under the dais, added to the atmosphere of religious devotion so that we readily accepted the ethical terms of Jayaprakash's speech.

Had we been socialist friends who had known him for years we would have seen him as a familiar, earthy figure preaching an almost identical doctrine with his past interpretation of socialism. We might almost have felt some impatience that a former interpretation of history, which had relied upon a historical study of man's development, had now been usurped by a theory which placed man's affairs in the hands of God. For it had only been a year earlier that he had made a final break with the political party he had founded. But we had had no experience or knowledge of a former Jayaprakash Narayan and we accepted him in terms of what he was that day. In one sense ours was a truer understanding because we trailed behind us no previous expectations, and we assessed him purely in terms of his undoubted sincerity and the new moral premises from which he had come to judge the affairs and institutions of men.

His impromptu speech, delivered gently into the microphone, was an explanation of Vinoba Bhave's Bhoodan movement:

'Vinoba's is a entirely new technique,' he said. 'Land must be redistributed, land must belong to the tiller, landlordism must go. But let us do this by the method of love. Vinoba Bhave started going from village to village on foot and asking those who have land, to give part of it for the benefit of those who do not. Just as simple as that; in fact so simple that it sounds non-sensical, foolish, but it seems to be working. We are all human beings, the landlord is a human being, the capitalist is a human being; there is something in all of us to which this man is appealing and there is good response—hundreds and thousands of acres of land have already been given to him. You know that I have dedicated my life to this new movement.

'It is the beginning of an all-round social and human revolution; human also because it aims at changing man along with society. It is an application on a general scale of Mahatma Gandhi's non-violent technique of revolution.

'No heart or mind has been changed by law; no individual made virtuous by coercion. Gandhiji's technique of conversion was based on faith in the possibility of improving man.

'Bhoodan is thus a great mass movement of conversion and... what Bhoodan says about land is, according to Gandhiji, true of all our possessions, including even knowledge and skill.'

As per a Foreigner's Account: "We had very little idea of the implications behind his speech on that Sunday morning, but we were moved by a sense that we were observing an audience prepared to make profound self-sacrifices for its ideals. We watched with emotion the band of white-clad people who walked away from the meeting to begin a hard trek through Bombay streets appealing for gifts of money, clothing, or food.

Before he parted from us to attend another meeting, Jayaprakash offered to take us to his ashram in the Gaya district of Bihar where we could stay if the conditions were not too severe for us. This instant of mutual trust changed the course of our lives.

In 1958 we had, of course, no conception of Jayaprakash's mighty vision of revolutionising the political, social, and economic structure of India's six hundred thousand villages by persuasion; no appreciation that he had thrown down the gauntlet to the government and all political parties, by insisting that the new interpretation of Gandhi's philosophy was the correct method for uplifting the rural areas. India was yet to hear him describe his 'Revolution Beautiful', his spearhead for radical development that would create in the people a new will to life, a new sense of values, a new hope. But we accepted intuitively both that he was unselfishly devoted to helping the poor and that he would let no harm befall us.

The trip from Bombay to his ashram was over one thousand miles by train, bus and finally jeep. To Jayaprakash, we found, travelling is almost an occupation, and he has perfected the art of leaving a train as immaculately clad as when he boards it. In the fifteen years we have known him, we have heard him speak constantly of how so that he can write and think for several months without interruption. But this time never comes round.

We have always gained an amused enjoyment from trying to phone him from Australia. We give his Patna address as a starting point and then wait until the postal authorities have found out his programme. On occasion they have told us when he would be in Delhi, but by the time the connection has been made he has gone again.

People who wish to speak with him often board his train at a particular station and travel several hours to the next station with him. It is an excellent means of gaining a few private hours of discussion with him.

That night the train chugged slowly up the slopes of the Western Ghats but dawn broke over the flat red earth of the Deccan plateau.

Dust from the plains and soot from the engine filtered into our compartment leaving a thick grey film over all our things. It smeared across our faces and with perspiration marked our legs and arms with fine corrugations. The fan, provided for first-class passengers only, churned the hot air round and gritted the dust and soot in our eyes and between our teeth. For us it was an unusual experience, for Jayaprakash, a constant one.

'We're getting off at Allahabad,' he had told us while he talked to us between stations late in the afternoon. 'We are going to take a meal with the Rajah of Manda. He had just given all his property— fifteen hundred acres of land and everything on it— to one of our Bhoodan workers, and the Rajah has invited us to celebrate.

Dusk brought coolness and hid the dust, and later that night we drew into Allahabad station.

We collected our baggage and climbed down on to the long crowded platform with the assistance of Brahmanand, Jayaprakash's private secretary. Blue-shirted compartment sweepers, with reed hand brooms, dusters and dustpans, jostled the red-shirted porters at our door. Dozens of families with canvas bedding rolls, brass tiffin carriers, baskets, and belongings tied in squares of cloth, crouched or slept on the open platform. Beggars with distorted limbs, grasping their bowls, suddenly whined around our feet. From third-class compartments farther along the train, an angry shouting broke out as spindle-legged peasants struggled to push themselves into the already bursting compartments. They clung tenaciously to the iron railings at the door, continually regaining their foothold as they were pushed clear by others.

We stood in confusion, confronted suddenly with the problems of human misery that sheer numbers of people create. In the patient resignation of the waiting people on the platform, in the angry frustration of the thwarted third-class passengers, and in the desperate humiliation of the beggars, we recognised three of India's major psychological problems—all related to poverty.

A party of men sent by the Rajah rescued us and drew us into the quiet, empty first-class waiting-room, where Jayaprakash talked quietly to friends, and a small plump woman argued vociferously with the porters over their fee. It was his wife Prabhavati Devi handling, as usual, a massive load of baggage and issuing instructions about the new train reservations that had to be made since our journey was broken. Prabhavati, we found, fought a losing battle to stop Jayaprakash from overworking. She eschewed all luxuries, wearing only a white *khadi* (homespun cloth) blouse and sari, without any personal jewellery or cosmetics.

Outside the station, we were squeezed into a car with Jayaprakash and Prabhavati and driven through the evening mist to a large two-storeyed stone building, set back from the road in its own grounds. Its architecture derived from English Victorian. Inside the building it was gloomy. We climbed a wide draughty staircase and entered a large, dark green, cheerless room. From its high ceiling electric punkhas descended. We sat on sofas in the centre of the room with a large empty space between us and the walls.

There were introductions, and we sat silently observing the people who had come to celebrate this event. The Rajah was a quiet, earnest young man with a shawl caught round his shoulders against the cool night air. The Bhoodan worker who had persuaded him, and who had received his gift, was a small, meek, nervous man with a beard. He sat inconspicuously in a corner. Dhirendra Majumdar, the president of the Sarva Seva Sangh, and a government minister, monopolised the conversation with Jayaprakash, while Prabhavati also kept up a quick barrage of comments in Hindi. The others listened respectfully to them. Here was a pattern of deference and paternalism that we were often to observe in the years to come. And while in our youth we were happy to give way to it, fifteen years later we were to come to see this pattern as a fundamental brake on the freedom of the workers in the Sarvodaya movement.

We ate in a large room adjoining the gloomy green one. Between twenty and thirty people seated themselves on mats on the floor in two lines facing each other. When everyone was called to the meal, Jayaprakash apologised for neglecting us and insisted on placing us between Prabhavati and himself. We settled ourselves cross-legged in the manner of everyone else, while servants moved up and down the line placing small quantities of food on the steel platters before us.

We were very tired by this stage, and Jayaprakash grew more and more concerned about our slow progress through the meal.

His concentration upon us became almost embarrassing as he called the servants to give us a little more of this or that.

Try that. That's nice—' That's sweet, try that—' 'No, that's hot with spices. You won't like that—' 'Have a little more tapioca. You'll like that.'

The climax to this concern came when a servant brought a jug of hot milk and liberally filled Jayaprakash's and Prabhavati's glasses.

'Would you like some?' he anxiously asked Wendy.

She assented tentatively on condition there was sufficient milk in the house.

The servant went away and returned with a glass that was only half full. Even as she reached for it, Jayaprakash in a torrent of excited Hindi, ordered the servant to fill her glass by tipping some of his milk into hers. She placed her hand over the top of her glass and laughed with a mixture of embarrassment and appreciation, for nobody could have withstood such a barrage of affectionate concern and remained emotionally detached.

Jayaprakash appreciated good food. And he treated people's problems of taste over food with almost disproportionate concern.

When we lived in his ashram and he returned there from Delhi, he frequently brought us a large basket of Delhi fruits—long, golden bananas curved like a sickle moon; pomegranates, crimson, crisp, and luscious; guavas, sweet, tangy and delicate yellow; plus Delhi cheese and nuts. For, he would comment (dismissing all provincial cities), 'the fruits in Patna are very poor.'

After the meal in Allahabad, we returned to the station at midnight, collected our luggage from the waiting-room where a servant of the Rajah's had been keeping guard over it, and following Prabhavati who was excitedly giving orders and gesticulating to the porters, we were bundled into a four-berth compartment with Jayaprakash and Prabhavati.

At seven the next morning, Patna, the capital city of Bihar state, was misty and cold. Porters with thin cotton blankets draped about their shoulders and their scarves twisted into a ring on their heads so that they could carry our luggage, jogged along the ugly platform. Outside, horse and gig drivers set upon our group, each yelling his superiority over the other. Prabhavati was suddenly in the midst of this yelling throng, part of the shouting, and in a moment had stilled it. She organised our party and luggage into two gigs, and paid the porters from a purse bulging with small change which she always carried for this purpose.

Our gig drivers eased and cursed their way between lumbering bullock carts, bicycle rickshaws, small snub-nosed cars, spindle-legged labourers dragging carts of wood, peasants leading cows with a forlorn calf hugging the hind legs of its mother, and pedestrians who wandered unregardingly along the road.

The roads into Kadam Kuan, the area where Jayaprakash and Prabhavati had their flat, were so narrow that two vehicles could hardly pass without endangering the stalls on either side of the road. We looked down on the tiny trays of cheap cigarettes, the small baskets of bananas, and the metal cauldron where milk boiled on an open mud fireplace beside a pyramid of earthen cups and a charred kettle. The tea vendor squatted beside a stove, occasionally scooping out a fly or the thin scum of dust that collected on the milk.

Jayaprakash and Prabhavati's flat was situated on the second floor of a long concrete building in the grounds of the Mahila

Charkha Samiti (Women's Spinning Centre) Hostel. There was a workshop at the rear of the living quarters, and the ladies spun a quota of cotton every day on the four-spindled cotton machines known as *ambar charkhas.* Prabhavati had raised the money for this centre and seen it planned and built, and in 1958 she and Jayaprakash both believed that the ambar charkha would make the village people self-sufficient in cloth. As well as this, it would provide extra income in those months of the year when farming people have periods of idleness.

The four-spindled machine was an advance on the simple Gandhi charkha; but the emphasis on village self-sufficiency in cloth remained an essentially Gandhian one. It was to take Jayaprakash many years to reinterpret Gandhi's vision of self-sufficient agrarian communities in terms of modern industrial techniques.

Jayaprakash's flat, which was still his permanent address, consisted of three rooms, each of which opened on to a wide, concrete verandah.

He had a large library with books in glass-fronted cupboards along two walls, a cotton carpet on the floor, a low, floor-level desk, and bolsters. His guests, after leaving their shoes at the door, sat on the carpet. Next to the library was a long narrow bathroom with a shower over a red concrete floor, a washbasin, and a toilet at the far end. On the far side of the bathroom was the bedroom with a collection of wardrobes, a chest of drawers, a glass-fronted cabinet containing presents given on various occasions, trunks, and a wire-fronted kitchen cupboard with oddments of honey, cooking spices and dried fruits. Photographs of them both, of friends, and of Mahatma Gandhi, decorated the plain white walls, and barred windows with wooden shutters opened on to an unparapeted apron of concrete running along the outside wall of the rooms.

Prabhavati's kitchen was at that time a tiny room on the flat roof above this apartment. She cooked on a brazier of charcoal. Later, she had a gas stove and the kitchen had been rebuilt; but it was still essentially a mere collection of concrete shelves built up from a concrete floor with a tap in one corner of the room over a concrete scoop.

Our stay was brief, for the next morning we sped out of Patna by bus on the last hundred-mile leg of the journey to Jayaprakash's ashram. Intermittently we glimpsed the Ganges, now reduced to a silver ribbon of water, snaking through a misty bed of platinum sand. In the monsoons it would be a congested swirl of mud red water. The open fields had an orange glow in the morning light. They were bare but for the small spikes of yellow stubble the cattle now gazed over. The winter wheat had been cut and soon the orange gold would give way to the bleak whiteness of the hot summer winds.

Seventy miles later we climbed down from the bus and walked to the Inspection Bungalow on the outskirts of Nawada township. It was a remnant of British administration, a brick building with concrete floors and verandahs, standing in its own garden.

Under Prabhavati's keen scrutiny the skinny Muslim and his boy, who were in charge of the bungalow, prepared fried eggs and tomatoes for us. Prabhavati and Jayaprakash ate from the tiffin carrier of vegetables and chapattis that she had carried for them.

After lunch we sat on the verandah, where Jayaprakash explained to us at length the social philosophy of the Gandhian movement, but he was restless because the ashram jeep had not arrived and he disliked the prospect of being late for his village meetings. We found he became quite irritable if he were kept waiting or if his programme needed to be altered for a latecomer. Whenever we travelled with him, he always added this rider to his invitation: 'And don't be late.'

Eventually the jeep arrived, and Jayaprakash asked the driver shortly why he was so late. He was a cheerful unshaven chap, who replied that the battery was exhausted and he had had trouble arriving at all. Allan noticed too, as he helped dispose the boxes, bedding, cooking utensils, and cases in the back of the jeep, that oil was leaking out of the engine. Prabhavati and Jayaprakash took the front seat next to the driver and we climbed in the back. Jayaprakash looked round at Wendy perched amidst the luggage and got out.

'Please sit on my seat here in the front; he said. 'I will ride in the back because I am used to these roads.'

She thanked him and refused. But he worried about our comfort for the rest of the journey. Very shortly we began to enjoy speeding along, with the warm wind blowing through our hair.

'I should like to take you to see several famous places; Jayaprakash said, speaking with deep affection about his home state, 'such as Nalanda, the site of an ancient university, which drew students from thousands of miles away, and Bodh Gaya, the spot where Lord Buddha received enlightenment, and where I took a vow of life service to the Gandhian movement.'

Before long we turned off the bitumen onto a fair-weather road. It was a heaped-up bank of earth about six feet higher than the paddy fields on either side. Much of this track had been newly surfaced with a layer of large clods, almost as hard as stones, in preparation for the monsoon. The unprepared parts had a layer of dust about four inches deep on top.

This rose in a solid column behind the jeep smothering the bullock cart drivers and the stray pedestrians who were going the other way. As we had a slight following breeze, occasionally great gusts of it surged in between the tailboard and the canvas top, and whenever the jeep stopped, we were overtaken and blanketed by the lung-clogging curtain. We all held shawls or handkerchiefs over our faces. We felt great admiration for Jayaprakash and Prabhavati, who could have been living comfortably in Delhi instead of being jolted along back roads.

We began to come upon small villages where the houses were mud walled and roofed with mud tiles (which were half-cylindrical in shape), and clustered tightly along narrow alleyways. From each village some of the population turned out in a line on either side of the road, and there were barefooted, shrewish women with babes in arms, sun-tanned farmers with a minimum of cloth twisted round their loins, naked children, and starving dogs. Usually these groups had constructed an archway of banana leaves, coloured ribbons, branches, and even small flags, over the road. As the jeep approached, they placed the palms of both hands together in a *namaskar* and bowed with humble devotion. One or two leaders from each village then approached the jeep through its dust, and respectfully and affectionately touched Jayaprakash's and Prabhavati's feet. Some of these village groups had beautiful garlands of flowers which were placed over Jayaprakash's and Prabhavati's shoulders. Others had hanks of homespun cotton to give as a symbol that they were carrying out his Sarvodaya programme and helping themselves. In every village the profound respect this couple were held in moved us deeply.

As soon as we came into sight, shouting started, and as the jeep moved on again each crowd ran after it despite the dust, beating on drums, blowing trumpets, and chanting in wild unison:

'Jayaprakash *Zindabad* (Long Live Jayaprakash)!'

He reacted soberly, even impatiently, to all this enthusiasm. We judged that it embarrassed him.

We approached the first village, at which he was to speak, by a branch track, which was little better than a succession of irrigation channels and banks with patches of flat, stubbly paddy field in between. Since roads were of less importance to the farmers than water, they had not hesitated to cut drains wherever they wanted them. The jeep passed under a decorated archway where dozens of people were waiting, and they ran after us chanting loudly: 'Sant Vinoba ! Jayaprakash ! Gandhiji! Jayaprakash !'

Hens scattered and the crowd increased as we entered the village main street, splattering mud from the ill-smelling drains with our wheels. House walls closed in on us, rough, gleaming bright orange in the sunlight, throwing off heat and patterned with dozens of cowdung cakes, each bearing the imprint of the maker's five fingers. We manoeuvred a corner and were just approaching the rear end of the village when the jeep was bogged down in a drain. Many pairs of hands seized on the vehicle and heaved it forward. There was a deafening blood-stirring din of drums in the narrow alley, and a cheerleader, with a scrap of paper in his hand which he consulted as he came along, dashed past us leading an enthusiastic chorus: 'Jayaprakash !' and 'Zindabad!'

> 'Jayaprakash !' he bellowed, and 'Zindabad !' they replied.
>
> '*Juga-juga-jeeah* (Long Live)!' he cried.
>
> 'Jayaprakash !' replied the chorus.

On and on it went for as long as the cheerleader had different tributes written on his paper, after which it all began again. We had never, in our lives, been caught up in such a surge of mass enthusiasm.

The village was unhygienic, disease was prevalent, and the inhabitants resembled scarecrows; but the courtyard where Jayaprakash was to speak had been swept spotless after it had received a new plastering with cowdung. A mud wall, about seven feet high, enclosed the meeting place; and under a large canopy, a dais had been spread with clean handwoven cloths. Incense had been set burning. The dais backed onto the wall of a house, and at the opposite end of the yard, cows were standing in their mud-walled bails. Refreshments had been set out for Jayaprakash and Prabhavati.

The chanting died as suddenly as it had begun and the men filed, quiet and orderly, through the gateway to take up seats immediately in front of the dais. When this rightly packed audience had installed itself, the women and children were permitted to enter. They surged across the back and up one side, chattering in wild excitement with little respect for the formal dignities of procedure that the men expected them to obey. On the left hand side of the courtyard were two haystacks, and the women, children, babes-in-arms, and toddlers clinging to their mothers' saris, were crammed into the space between these and the house wall. They made such a din that the men bellowed to them to sit down quietly as they had done; but the space was insufficient, and a number of them ended up standing directly behind Jayaprakash.

Finally every available inch was taken up by men in brief loincloths, who stood back against the cow bails, or perched like sparrows along the tops of the walls.

Well-dressed village leaders and ashram workers placed garlands round Jayaprakash's and Prabhavati's shoulders. Then one stood up and read blunderingly from a large sheet on which the village had recorded its collective decision to become self-sufficient in cloth, to refrain from buying mill-cloth or luxuries such as jewellery from outside sources, and to keep what little money it had within itself by buying food and other necessities only from each other. In addition their declaration promised that they would settle their disputes within the village without recourse to the police (who, Jayaprakash said, swindled them) or the courts (which, he said, bankrupted them).

This meeting, and thousands like it over the next decade, was part of Jayaprakash's work for a reconstruction of the whole of Indian society. It was the beginning, as he saw it, of a social revolution based on the persuasion and mass conversion of the agrarian population to a cooperative, self-sufficient, and self-governing way of life. We left the village meetings late in the afternoon, and swung in between the ashram gates after dark.

The ashram was Jayaprakash's own experiment in social living, in the training of reconstruction workers, and the implementation of new industrial and agricultural techniques for the village. We waited with great excitement for the morning to show us what it was like.

For the ensuing six months we occupied ourselves in unpaid educational work for his movement, then returned to Australia. Two years later Jayaprakash invited us to return to the ashram for a period of three years, which we did during 1960-62. He treated us as members of his family rather than as his employees, often allowing us use of his Patna flat or his ashram house, and introducing us to a number of prominent figures in Bihar and Indian national life. We recorded our impressions of him and of the lives of the Sokhodeora village people in our book *A Mouthful of Petals.* His impressions of us he wrote in a foreword to the volume of Wendy's poetry, *Shadow and Flowers.*

In 1967 Wendy returned to Bihar and with Jayaprakash's assistance toured the famine areas. From this painful experience grew our book *Tiger on a Rein* which gives a detailed report of his work in that desperate year In this critical period, we were able to open contacts between his Relief Committee and the Australian aid organisation, Community Aid Abroad.

We were able in 1969 to make the first exploratory contact which led to Jayaprakash and Prabhavati accepting an invitation from the Gandhi Bicentenary Celebrations Committee to visit Australia. Sir James Plimsoll, for the external affairs department, kindly agreed to Jayaprakash's request for an itinerary, which included a private visit to our home; and it was then that this biography began to take definite shape.

We returned to India to carry out the final research in January 1971."

A Terrorist in the Making

Jayaprakash Narayan whose given name means 'victory to the light' was born in the early hours of 11 October 1902 in a thatched shed near the remote Bihar village of Sitabdiara. He was Phul Rani Devi's fourth child, delivered by the village midwife.

His paternal grandfather, Devaki Nandan Lal, was a sub-inspector of police, who served in the Saran district of Bihar state. Jayaprakash's father, Harsu Babu, was sent to the university where he studied Persian, but he gave up his Bachelor of Arts course when he gained employment with the government as an official in the department constructing the Sone Canal through the Shahabad and Gaya districts of Bihar. He was employed in the building of a bridge spanning the canal which is taken for granted by drivers today. But at that time, it was a matter of great pride within the family, and far beyond it, that this was the longest bridge in India.

The inhabitants of Sitabdiara village, Jayaprakash's family included, were tenants of the Maharajah of Dumaraon, one of the premier *zamindars* (non-cultivating legal holders of land paying land tax) of Bihar and United Provinces. Jayaprakash's family did not work the land they rented from the Maharajah but let out the use of their plots to undertenants, permitting them to apportion their contract out to others of even humbler status, some as far down the social scale as the landless labourer.

Because of the deaths of her two first children and fearing his catching cholera from other children, Phul Rani kept Jayaprakash close to her in the house and indulged him. To help fill his solitude, she allowed him to play with the household's animals. When his father bought him a pair of pigeons, he was delighted and spent hours feeding and watching and talking to them. Jayaprakash developed into a very quiet, shy little boy.

In the end, however, his lonely search for playmates among animals almost led to disaster. His father kept a mare which dropped a foal, and Jayaprakash went secretly into its stall to pat the new arrival. The mare, taking fright, lashed out with her hooves. Jayaprakash was found bleeding and carried home. His mother called the village herbalist. His father, despite Jayaprakash's pleas, sold the mare and foal. Thereafter they always discouraged him from trying to learn to ride, as they also discouraged him from trying to learn to swim.

Anything involving risk was avoided. Harsu Babu was fond of hunting, and possessed a double-barrelled shotgun, but never took Jayaprakash hunting with him. The most he ever allowed the boy was the chore of pulling a brush through the barrel to clean it, or helping to make the cartridges by turning the handle of the little machine which sealed them with a paper wad.

As his father moved about regularly on account of the canal construction, he eventually decided to leave Jayaprakash with his step-grandmother. Hasru Babu's mother had died while he was an infant and his father had remarried. Thus Jayaprakash's step-grandmother took over the responsibility for his education from the household tutor, Aditya Mishra, who had displeased Harsu Babu at one time and had avoided being sacked only because of Jayaprakash's fondness for him and his plea that the man would remain unemployed if dismissed. Jayaprakash's sisters, however, were never sent to school and so they travelled with his parents, having little contact with Jayaprakash.

From numerals, multiplication tables, Hindustani alphabet, and the reading of myths and legends at home, Jayaprakash moved on to the village primary school when he was about six. The family paid fees for him right through the upper primary school: there was no government school in his village.

Jayaprakash's family attended the usual religious festivals of the Hindu year but his father never took part in any private ceremonies within the home. His mother, by contrast, was a devotee of Shiva whom she worshipped in a special corner of the courtyard each morning.

In Jayaprakash's recollections, his mother was always kindhearted, his father indulgent but irascible. His father must have been gentle, although he may have fretted at his wife's absorption in the boy. He had unusually liberal attitudes for the times, never raising his hand against his sons and on one occasion only seriously losing his temper with Jayaprakash. Jayaprakash had made a bow and arrows from some branches and, on this occasion, was firing them as high as he could. By design or accident, or a little of both, an arrow soared over the roof of one of his father's subordinate officers and fell into the inner courtyard where it struck the head clerk's daughter-in-law on the cheek near her eye. The head clerk complained to Harsu Babu, whose outraged sense of propriety brought forth the only display of anger which his son remembers.

The family home—still maintained though Jayaprakash visits it only rarely—was built on a high earthen plinth to keep it above the river water when in flood. It consists of a gracious series of rooms built in two squares around two inner courtyards. The lower courtyard and rooms were reserved for the servants. There in a corner, a pomegranate tree grew beside the courtyard wall. The earthen floors of the courtyards and rooms were regularly smeared with cowdung paste and the brick walls periodically whitewashed or tinted heliotrope. The sense of space and peace emanating from the colours was enhanced, in the absence of ceilings, by the high arched roof of tiles laid over neatly cut bundles of reeds. The bricklayers and tilers had built for coolness but to a western eye the rooms have a pleasing resemblance to the nave of a church.

During the day the upper courtyard was the world of Jayaprakash, his mother and step-grandmother, the men sitting together and gossiping on wooden tables on the wide porch outside the front door, overlooking the mango orchard. In the evenings the enormous front door, made of beams almost a foot thick and studded with ornamented brass nails, was securely fastened against thieves, and the courtyard was lit by oil lamps or, in later years, kerosene lanterns. The family ate from broad steel platters, seated along a mat in a corner of the courtyard. On occasion, after the evening meal, Harsu Babu invited groups of travelling musicians to his courtyard. The servants and a few poor neighbours crept in and sat in the shadows behind the family to hear the twang of the sitar, the pathos of a love song, the twinkling rhythm of the tabla.

During Jayaprakash's lifetime, floods damaged or destroyed this family home four times. Each time his grandfather or father rebuilt it.

When he was nine, Jayaprakash made his first break with the village. He was admitted to the seventh class of the collegiate school at Patna. This was arranged for by his parents' eldest son-in-law who was an assistant in the office of the High Court there. Jayaprakash was taken to Patna by his grandparents in a bullock cart. While at Patna he had little contact with his parents during his adolescence. He continued to be retiring and intensely studious, and by 1918 he had reached the final class. He sat for the state public matriculation examination at the close of the academic year and fared so well that he was awarded a district merit scholarship to Patna College. Books took the place of affectionate family life.

However, the political situation prevailing in the nine provinces of British India had a far more profound influence upon him than his school studies, so that by the age of fourteen he had cast himself in the role of an extreme nationalist.

A new group of militant nationalists was arising in Bengal in the face of the unpopular measures the Viceroy, Lord Curzon, had introduced. At the height of the agitation following the partition of Bengal, Bal Gangadhar Tilak, in a Congress annual conference, made a declaration of historic importance. 'Swaraj,' he said, 'is my birthright and I will have it.'

The ground swell of Indian aspirations and protest brought about a British backlash. Law and order was imposed through a series of arrests, including that of Tilak.

But terrorist activities became more conspicuous and they had had an overpowering influence on Jayaprakash by 1916. He was not religious but tinder the influence of the Bengal terrorist fringe he began to read regularly one of the Hindu scriptures, the Bhagavad Gita, taking heroic inspiration from the great battle described in the book and from its overriding religious concept that man is immortal and can never be destroyed. His reading was not conducted to gain for himself religious merit of any kind, but to strengthen himself internally. This belief in immortality had become part of the terrorist intellectual discipline. The members brainwashed themselves: nothing can destroy you; the British can beat you, shoot you, torture you, hang you, but you will still be there. You will be nobly reincarnated.

The timid, overprotected boy had found adventure at last in his imagination. He became Swadeshi in his attitudes, using crude handmade village shoes instead of British manufactured ones, and cleaning them with Indian mustard oil instead of British shoe polish. He dressed in a kurta of hand-spun and handwoven material and an ascetically short dhoti instead of wearing British-owned textile mill products. He took cold baths even in winter to toughen himself against all forms of sensual self-indulgence.

With all the extremism of adolescence a terrorist was in the making.

Prabhavati Devi and Mahatma Gandhi

Some miles from Jayaprakash's village was the home of Braj Kishore Prasad, a lawyer who, after something of a conversion in his middle years, became the president and father figure of the Bihar Provincial Congress Committee. In this village home his wife, Phul Jhari, was delivered of their first daughter Prabhavati. Neither she nor her husband kept a record of the exact date of the confinement, and all she could remember was that it had occurred between June 15 and 21 in the year 1906.

Prabhavati grew up in the close company of her cousins, her two younger sisters and her brother at her father's and her uncle's home. Her sister who was about two years younger fell ill with pneumonia and, after anxious care night and day, died at the age of six.

Phul Jhari connected the death in her mind with the primary school her children had been attending, and her fear of alien British institutions grew. She refused to permit Prabhavati to attend school. Braj Kishore employed a private tutor to come to his house to teach her the mother tongue, Hindustani. Later she learned the ancient root language, Sanskrit. Finally, before her spasmodic education ended, some fleeting attention was given to

English. This education was not of a high standard and it lapsed by the time she had reached her early teens.

Part of the religious belief of her parents was the embracing of vegetarianism and asceticism, so that although the family was well off they lived simply. Phul Jhari kept only two servants and did most of the housework herself. She kept Prabhavati close to her, guarding her and exerting a constant influence. Prabhavati had a much more limited relationship with her busy father. As a consequence her interests developed in a practical rather than an intellectual direction.

Prabhavati claims that she enjoyed all the daily household chores and regularly begged the milkman to let her help when he brought his cow to their door, milking out the quantity that the family wished to buy. He often gave in to her entreaties with the result that on one occasion the cow grew restless at the slow and inexpert handling, kicked the bucket of milk and sent it flying. Prabhavati was brought up very devoutly and taught to spend time in prayer each morning, a practice which she kept up throughout her life.

When she was eight years old and Jayaprakash twelve, Gandhi, who was then forty-six, arrived in Bombay on 9 January 1915, returning home from South Africa. In 1916 on behalf of the indigo sharecroppers of Champaran he was drawn into his first civil disobedience campaign against British rule.

Prabhavati's father, Braj Kishore Prasad, was among the many disciples Gandhi attracted on his return to India. Braj Kishore carried the major load of the ensuing Champaran campaign. Non-violent resistance to the law was entirely new to India and so socially disreputable that Braj Kishore was very hesitant The idea of accommodating ourselves to imprisonment is a novel thing for us.' Braj Kishore told Gandhi, 'We will try to assimilate it'.

Eventually an official commission heard the evidence Braj Kishore and his assistants presented and the wealthiest planters agreed to refund part of the money they had illegally extorted from helpless tenants. Then Braj Kishore returned to Darbhanga, impressed by Gandhi's belief in raising the poorest in society first by persuading the wealthy to a change of heart and by his determination not to be bullied in his own country by foreigners.

Prabhavati's first recollection of Gandhi is of an occasion when he was a guest at their home in Darbhanga and caused a family upset. This was probably sometime during 1919 or 1920. Gandhi, who had four sons but no daughters and was now a celibate, asked Braj Kishore to allow Prabhavati to live with him and his wife Kasturba at his ashram in Ahmedabad as an adopted daughter. Braj Kishore was very keen on her taking up this discipleship, but his wife was alarmed and possessive enough to refuse to let her go. Prabhavati remembered the reactions of her parents but she had not known whether Gandhi's invitation had been serious or simply exaggerated affection.

Once Gandhi had broached the possibility of Prabhavati joining him at Satyagraha Ashram, he continued to repeat his invitation and to influence Braj Kishore. However, as she moved into her early teens Braj Kishore began to look for a husband for her despite Gandhi's appeal as an educator, a spiritual mentor and a freedom fighter. This was something of a problem to him because, owing to Gandhi's influence, there was a social unconventionality in his arrangements: he was trying to arrange a marriage without the customary provision of a large dowry for a son-in-law. If he failed, she could join Gandhi.

Jayaprakash Narayan was suggested to him by a Patna High Court friend, Shambhu Sharan Verma, who although much older than Jayaprakash was his nephew; and he negotiated the match between the respective fathers. Jayaprakash proved to be a very pleasing prospect to Braj Kishore for he was of an extremely quiet, respectful and sober temperament, and had already shown evidence of an intellectual brilliance which boded well for a future career. He had recently received a government scholarship and was enrolled at Patna College, the foremost educational institution of Bihar, in a science course. In 1919 he had successfully completed his first year and was now moving confidently through his second year of studies.

The marriage was solemnised at Darbhanga in October 1920. Jayaprakash was eighteen years of age and Prabhavati fourteen. In accordance with Hindu custom, Jayaprakash took Prabhavati to his family home in Sitabdiara for a month. During this time she worked and stayed with his mother sleeping in her room at nights. After this time Braj Kishore called her home again, but after the normal interval of about a month he decided not to return her to Sitabdiara because Jayaprakash's father, the head of his family, was absent from the house and so unable to see to her proper care. His work as a minor official in the canals department kept him on construction sites in various parts of Bihar State. So Braj Kishore decided to send Prabhavati to live in Gandhi's ashram, which since its commencement had moved from Ahmedabad to a nearby village, Kochrab, and then had moved from Kochrab, because of an outbreak of black plague there, to a site about four miles removed near Sabarmati Central Jail. Here it had begun under canvas, but a number of buildings had since been erected.

While these family matters were being decided, public events, which were to culminate in an immense upheaval, were beginning to bear upon Jayaprakash's life, awakening in him a burning passion for national freedom. Sir Sydney Rowlatt issued his report on 19 July 1918, recommending that Britain continue press censorship and imprisonment by secret tribunals which had aroused the deepest bitterness in India during the course of World War I. The Rowlatt Act became law on 18 March 1919, and it was against this that Gandhi, after careful preparation, launched his first political attack on the Government of India.

Mahatma Gandhi's nationwide hartal paralysed economic life in March and April, but he was ashamed of the unanticipated violence which occurred when police clashed with demonstrators, and he called a halt to the movement. This was not enough for the government of Punjab which deported the two Congress leaders and the Ali brothers who might have continued to control the hartal. In reply an angry mob surged through the streets of Amritsar, lost all reason and murdered the manager and assistant manager of the National Bank and the manager of the Alliance Bank.

Brigadier-General Dyer was called to Amritsar. On 12 and 13 April he issued a proclamation banning meetings, which reached a limited audience. So when a meeting of some 10,000 to 20,000 people took place at Jalianwala Bagh on the afternoon of the 13th, he ordered his troops to fire without warning into the dense crowd which had no way of escape. With 1,650 bullets he scored

379 dead and 1137 wounded. He made no provision whatsoever for caring for the wounded.

The mass murder was applauded by Sir Michael O'Dwyer, British acting-governor of Punjab, but condemned by the Hunter Commission. Dyer capped his atrocity with an uncivilized order that all Indians must crawl on fours when passing the street where Miss Sherwood, the headmistress of an Amritsar girls' school, had been assaulted by the mob that, on 10 April, had killed the bank managers.

India was deeply embittered. Jayaprakash was filled with disgust and impotent indignation. Gandhi and the Nehru family flung themselves into political action. There was a delay in their counterattack until the findings of the Hunter Commission had been released and it was made known that admirers in Britain had collected a purse to provide Dyer with a pension.

At this time there was cooperation between many Muslims and Hindus in the Indian National Congress, and Gandhi became a spokesman for a Muslim organisation. Anger at the peace terms that Britain was forcing upon Turkey—which included deposing the Turkish Sultan who was also the religious head or Caliph of all Muslims—led to a Caliphat (or Khilafat) Movement in India. Its members sanctioned Gandhi's policy of non-cooperation with the British. The non-cooperation would protest against the peace treaty, the Amritsar Massacre and the Rowlatt Act. It was timed to begin on 1 April 1920.

A special session of the Indian National Congress in Calcutta in September supported the Khilafat Non-cooperation Movement, and the annual convention in Nagpur in December—attended by an unprecedented twenty thousand people—gave it unanimous approval.

Prabhavati's father Braj Kishore Prasad, Motilal Nehru and his son Jawaharlal, Vallabh Bhai Patel and other lawyers, left the British courts and never worked in them again. Rabindranath Tagore, Gandhi, and many others handed back their titles. In an inspired fervour thousands of students pulled out of schools, giving up their education and future career for achieving the greater, unselfish goal of national liberty. Millions were electrified by Gandhi's promise that they would have freedom within a year if they refused to cooperate with the British.

Jayaprakash had paid his deposit for his second-year science examinations at Patna College as they were only a few weeks away. He had used his scholarship for the first two years of his four-year course at Patna College. And in December 1920 he sat for his test examination preparatory to the University examination in intermediate science which was due in March 1921. It was then that Gandhi came to Patna. His call for non-cooperation ignited into a flame of enthusiasm Jayaprakash's dream of being part of his nation's revolt. He flung his textbooks into a water tank to emphasise his refusal to attend a British institution any longer.

After all their sacrifices, made in order to afford being able to send him to school, his parents were furious with him and set about enrolling him in Banaras Hindu University. But he refused to attend there either, because this institution was aided by British funds. However to continue his education, he enrolled in Bihar Vidyapeeth, a tertiary institution set up by the Bihar Congress for all non-cooperation students. Such schools were financed by public donations to the Tilak Fund—set up in memory of the Congress leader who had died on 31 July 1920.

Gandhi's promise of freedom within a year was inspiring but unrealistic. On 19 February 1921, the Montagu-Chelmsford reforms were accepted by the House of Commons and became the new Constitution of India. Instead of granting independence, only a small measure of Indian participation in government was assured. Gandhi sent the Viceroy an ultimatum which was rejected, and then launched his campaign. The Congress campaign of non-cooperation shook the government, and its members overreacted with the customary savagery of threatened politicians: thirty thousand demonstrators were jailed; police unmercifully bashed crowds; riots, murders, and widespread violence occurred throughout those parts of India that were outside Gandhi's control; finally a Congress procession in United Provinces was attacked but it retaliated and killed twenty-two policemen on 5 February 1922. In horror, Gandhi stopped the entire campaign, accepted moral responsibility in court, and was sentenced to six years' imprisonment for making inflammatory and seditious statements.

The Indian National Congress was outlawed and the struggle subsided.

Jayaprakash felt completely crushed. Not only were his high hopes for his country dashed, but Bihar Vidyapeeth had no facilities for him to proceed with his studies beyond the second year. It seemed he had sacrificed himself for nothing. It was common for Indian students to go to England for higher studies but although Jayaprakash felt some inclination to study at Oxford or Cambridge, his parents could never have afforded it, and he was in the grip of passionately anti-British emotions.

An opportunity seemed to present itself when his friend Bhola Pant, who had gone to the United States of America for higher studies, invited him warmly in his letters to come there and offered him hospitality. He assured Jayaprakash that students from poor families could work their way through college. Jayaprakash obtained his passport and visa and wrote to Prabhavati requesting her to accompany him. She refused.

Jayaprakash's departure for America was delayed for a year by his mother's affectionate opposition, and by his concern for her health for she was becoming increasingly affected by dropsy. Only after the family had prevailed upon her to relent, did he decide to go. Prabhavati still refused to accompany him and knowing he could not support her, he accepted her decision. He set out on 16 May 1922 from Patna, going by train to Calcutta with three young friends from Bihar Vidyapeeth. While Prabhavati continued to live a traditional, religion-oriented life, he was to be plunged into entirely new experiences.

To begin with, at the age of nineteen, in Calcutta, he saw a tram for the first time. He bought a passage on a steamer going to Kobe. On board he made friends with Mehta, Ghose and Gopal Reddy. Upon their arrival in Japan they took a train together to Yokohama where they were able to buy passages to America on a ship belonging to a Japanese line, which had been acquired by Japan as part of German reparations for World War I. They landed at San Francisco in October and were welcomed at the docks by Bhola Pant and his friends.

Meanwhile, Prabhavati lived in Sabarmati Ashram with Kasturba, as a daughter. As a part of ashram life, Gandhi preached complete abstinence from marital relations. Young and immature, married by ceremony but without marriage's consummation, and in the absence of a husband's influence, Prabhavati was completely overawed and dominated by Gandhi's personality. Like the other disciples, she undertook the vow of celibacy.

American Education

Jayaprakash landed at San Francisco on 8 October 1922. He was astonished and a little fearful at the *size* of the buildings, the roar of the traffic in the streets, the free mingling of the sexes, the endless procession of fair-complexioned people wearing strange clothes and allowing their women's legs to be seen. The flappers caught his attention: to be like men they wore shingled hair, smoked Camel cigarettes and drank alcohol in speakeasies (where liquor flowed despite prohibition).

After a halt of one night he completed the last stage of his journey to the University of California, situated at Berkeley. To his intense disappointment he learned from the Registrar that the term was already well advanced and he should wait for the opening of the coming term to enrol. In his despondency he was glad to find other Indian students on campus with whom to share his troubles. They advised him to look for work to cam his tuition fees.

Jayaprakash's first job was on a ranch, setting out grapes to dry in the sun to be made into raisins in the factory on the ranch. The workers were allowed a half-hour lunch-break in their nine-hour day. This job lasted a month. Then Jayaprakash returned to Berkeley where he lived in a rented room, earning his board by working in restaurants, waiting at tables or washing dishes, and by taking odd jobs on Sundays. With the money he had saved and what he brought from home he managed to eke out two months of waiting and his first term as a science student at the University of California.

During the vacation Jayaprakash picked grapes at a Sacramento Valley vineyard and when this was over he worked in San Jose as a packer in a fruit-and-jam canning factory. This experience of ranch and factory work and odd jobs while he was at college began a revolution in his thinking. He had been accustomed, until this time, to feudal economic relationships in his village and an inflexible caste system characterised by hereditary specialisation of occupation and hierarchical social organisation. He now had to adjust himself to a democratic and capitalistic way of life with its greed for accumulating possessions. The equality of human beings and the dignity of labour became real things to me,' he said decades later. 'I noticed how foreman and workers addressed each other by their first names. There was no feeling of being below or inferior or anything like that.'

He was charmed by the grace of the University buildings and the spacious beauty of its grounds so that he always felt a sense of nostalgia, keeping Berkeley, 'at the top of my list of places I like to revisit.' So he was reluctant to leave and to part with the members of the Hindustani Association, but Bhola Pant kept writing to him, begging him to come to Iowa University where the fees were considerably lower.

In Iowa City, Pant helped him find part-time employment in a terra cotta factory, a foundry, a garage as a mechanic, while he continued his science course; but he worked mostly in restaurants.

During the midterm vacations and the summer break in 1924 Jayaprakash travelled to Chicago where Indian students from all the neighbouring states used to go in search of employment. 'We used to find a bed-kitchen in the slums to live in because it was cheaper there. It would cost about $10 a month. Two or three of us would share a room, and often used to have a double bed in the room that two of us would occupy,' he recalled later.

While he was making a visit to the home of the authors in Australia in 1969, the sight of a Woolworths store brought back memories of a week he had spent working in the Sears Roebuck emporium in Chicago.

During his second year in America he began to loosen his personal ties with his fellow-Indians and to follow American social and political affairs. America was enjoying her greatest boom. Progress seemed inexhaustible with the appearance of radios, loudspeakers, newly designed aeroplanes, record-breaking trains, and soaring sales of the T-model Ford.

Thrift and foresight fell out of fashion. While Jayaprakash scrimped and saved, all about him a whole people seemed to be going hedonistic Underneath the greedy effervescence of consumption, lurked the misery of shanty towns, the desperation of unemployment, the explosives and mob oratory of the 'Wobblies' and pitched battles in streets in which the police were always the victors.

In 1923 Britain's first Labour Prime Minister had arrived in Westminister to the tune of The *Worker's Flag is Deepest Red*. The ideas of the Russian Revolution had spread everywhere. To Jayaprakash, Warren Harding and Calvin Coolidge—who was elected to the presidency in 1924—were totally uninspiring political leaders feathering their own nests at the summit of a reactionary and inhuman state. He began to find himself more interested in sociology than in science and to view his career in a different light. Because of his expectation of national revolution in India he did not consider that a study of science would assist him much in his work as a revolutionary.

When the next term began he enrolled in the social sciences course at Wisconsin University. He wore sports jackets and slacks like the other students and large multicoloured bow-ties. By day and night he pored over the writings of the 'bourgeois' social scientists and the radicals—Marx, Lenin, Trotsky, Plekhanov, and Rosa Luxemberg. He read the three volumes of *Das Kapital* and everything else available in English that Marx had written.

The students he came into contact with belonged to a cosmopolitan club. Still subject to loneliness and insecurities Jayaprakash formed a very close friendship with Avrom Landy, a graduate assistant in the German department of the University, whose ideas exercised a strong influence upon him. From Landy he borrowed pamphlets written by M. N. Roy, the famous Indian member of the Communist International, and the two books *Aftermath of Non-Cooperation* and *India in Transition*. These he read voraciously and began following the fortunes of the Communist International.

He came to regard Marx then, as he still does, as one of the greatest minds of the human race for his pathfinding work in sociology. Jayaprakash does not seem to have felt any conversion to dialectical materialism nor any deliberate turning away from a belief in some immaterial form of ultimate reality. Soviet Communism was the finest instrument to remove the world's inequalities of wealth; Marx's principles yielded the best analysis of Indian society and offered the best techniques for putting an end to its exploitations. His sociological concepts filled his mind and simply crowded out any philosophical speculations. While he claimed to be a Marxist, he nevertheless faced the ignorance of Chicago landladies with an unshaken pride in the fact that he was a Hindu, and never forgot his amusement at one woman who assumed when he told her he was a Hindu, that he therefore came from Honduras.

Out of shared beliefs and a desire for affection and companionship he accompanied the Polish Jew, Avrom Landy, to the meetings of a group of Marxist-Leninists at the Madison home of a Russian Jewish tailor. The group was formed of first generation Americans whose parents had originated from middle or northern Europe, and radicals of many shades of opinion. Not only were Jayaprakash's intellectual interests greatly broadened by the contact with them at the time, but he remained attentively alive to the writings of sociologists throughout the world.

He went regularly with Landy to the study evenings organised by the cell of the communist party which existed among the students in the university. This group not only provided him with intellectual stimulation and keen discussions but also with a sense of belonging; it offered him sympathy for his lack of money; and, as an outpost of an international movement aimed at removing the inequalities of wealth from all human societies, it appealed deeply to his idealism. He was aware that the socialism of the Labour Party in Britain was failing lamentably to end poverty and unemployment, and he sided energetically with the left-wing Labourites in their condemnation of Ramsay Macdonald. He could see quite clearly that capitalism in America, for all its success, was littering the streets with men in rags, hunting desperately for a living.

To him, in the twenties, communism seemed the only way towards a more just economic society, towards the poor being treated as human beings. Europe's new saviours of mankind, Hitler and Mussolini, so popular with British and American conservatives, he completely rejected. Nevertheless, he was never a member of the American Communist Party.

At this time his studies proved so engrossing that Jayaprakash did not write to his family members or friends for a year and they became exceedingly worried about him. He told Prabhavati very little in his infrequent letters. She recalled that the little she knew about his years in America she had discovered almost forty years afterwards when she overheard him giving replies to the questions of an American newspaperman, Welles Hangen.

Jayaprakash was rarely if ever interested in giving news about himself and his daily activities or his emotional reactions to happenings. As a rule he wrote only to expound his views on political issues so that his friends and associates would know his standpoint. And it is still habitual with Jayaprakash to give almost daily consideration to whether he should issue a press statement on some political occurrence, but fail to answer a private or a business letter for months.

However he did write to Prabhavati telling her that he had received an invitation to study in the Soviet Union, making a request to her that she should accompany him. This was, in one sense, his bid to begin their marriage, to start building a deep personal relationship through shared purposes. Prabhavati once again refused to go with him.

There was immediate shock in the family when his appeal for funds reached his father. Prabhavati's father discussed the situation with Dr. Rajendra Prasad who appealed to Jayaprakash's intelligence and his nationalist spirit. He insisted that the important fight against injustice was in Jayaprakash's own country, not in the Soviet Union.

Jayaprakash thought over the objections carefully, but his glowing new ideals weighed more heavily with him. The term at Wisconsin ended and he again looked for work to support himself as before, but now also in the hope of saving his fare to Moscow.

During the summer of 1926 he had much more difficulty finding work in Chicago among the unemployed of the city than he had had in California.

This winter of 1926 he trudged the bitterly cold streets from factory gate to factory gate fortified against Chicago's sleet and searing winds only by two meals of rice a day, with sometimes the addition of canned beans. Scrimping on his food and playing recklessly with his health soon caused a near-disaster. Trouble began with a throat infection. 'An Indian doctor who practised in the Negro quarter removed my tonsils, but he left the infected roots. I was ill for three months and I almost died.'

During his illness he wrote no letters and his silence alarmed his family. They eventually learnt of his illness through his friend Bhola Pant but only shortly before Jayaprakash was forced to cable to father for money to meet his urgent need for the $900 which his hospital treatment had cost him.

His father mortgaged his lands to provide help. By the time Jayaprakash had met his bills he no longer held any hopes of going to the Soviet Union.

Some months later Landy obtained a lecturership at Ohio State University. He suggested that Jayaprakash also go and room with him, which he did at Columbus. On 31 August 1928 he graduated as a Bachelor of Arts. Then, instead of returning home, he applied for and was granted a postgraduate scholarship. He was also distinguished in being one of the few non-Americans chosen at that time at Ohio State University to be a graduate assistant.

The degree of Master of Arts was conferred upon Jayaprakash on 13 August 1929. The subject of his thesis for his degree was 'Societal Variation'. It was declared the best paper of the year. Despite the glow of triumph which his success and the acclamation of his fellows bestowed on him, his ambition had still not been fulfilled, and he planned to continue his studies until he had completed his Ph.D. But this dream did not become a reality, for he felt unable to continue living in America when he received the news that his mother was bedridden. When he learnt that her condition had become precarious, he left Columbus.

References from six of his Ohio University professors found Jayaprakash to be one of the brightest students the University had had, possessed of an unusually high ability, enquiring mind, critical capacity, and brilliant originality. They testified that in his private life he was modest, good humoured, engagingly popular and morally beyond question. His most remarkable trait was his idealism, his high hopes for human welfare and his struggle against materialism.

Professor Dumley's observations were perceptive of traits which were to persist throughout Jayaprakash's life. Dumley wrote that he possessed 'the germs of leadership', was 'aggressive in thought but not in action', and had 'ideals of human welfare.'

Jayaprakash returned to India convinced that the central problem of human society was inequality of wealth, property, rank, culture and opportunity. To him this inequality was strange and disconcerting and painful, and its root cause, the private ownership of the gifts of nature which led to economic exploitation. He had observed in both countries that the overwhelming majority led lives of poverty, hunger, filth, disease and ignorance, while the select few had comfort, luxury, culture, position and power. The passage of time never obscured his consciousness of monetary disparities between individuals and nations, nor did it soften his distaste for the spirit of materialism, so that he was as sensitive to human selfishness in the 1960s as he had been in the 1920s.

In his university studies he had read widely of man's varying proposals and experiments for reforming society through charity, philanthropy and Utopias, of appeals to the more fortunate to be kind to the less fortunate, the denunciation of riches and the exaltation of the virtue of poverty, and programmes for curtailing human wants. All of these he rejected for taking the fact of inequality for granted and for trying to level out inequalities while they continued to grow.

'The socialist solution to the problem of inequality,' he repeatedly told mass meetings of trade unionists in Indian cities, 'is to abolish private ownership of the means of production and to establish over them the ownership of the whole community. Socialism is an inevitable reaction to the capitalist system. Wherever conditions of capitalist exploitation exist, socialism will spread to the four corners of the globe. India is no exception.'

He maintained vigorously that India's industrial backwardness, feudal landholding system, and Hindu traditions did not invalidate the application of socialist principles. The laws by which wealth accumulated were as true in India as anywhere else in the world and this private accumulation could only be stopped by social ownership of the means of production. Indian traditions were not averse to the sharing of life and its privileges. The Hindu ideal of the perfection of the individual could not be compared with the self-seeking individualism of capitalist society. He agreed with Trotsky that individual perfection could only rise to the level of a Plato or a Marx through socialism, because socialism aimed at the utmost common good.

A Man Inspired

Jayaprakash sailed from New York in October 1929, a week before the Wall Street Stock Exchange crash ushered in worldwide economic depression. In Britain he made the acquaintance of a number of Communist Party members while he waited for a berth to Bombay.

He reached Patna on 28 November 1929, where Prabhavati met him at his sister's house and they stayed there a night. Jayaprakash had left Prabhavati to go to America when she was a thin, uncertain girl of fifteen. Now he was confronted with a practical, assured woman of twenty-three, her purpose to serve the cause of Indian liberty as firm as his.

Gandhi, once he had become acquainted with Jayaprakash's political views, had humorously dubbed Prabhavati his 'hostage from the socialist movement'. However, if there was any element of emotional possessiveness underlying his affection there was also an intelligent appraisal of her difficulties. He encouraged her to improve her knowledge of English to be able to speak more readily to Jayaprakash and his friends, and insisted upon her reading socialist literature so that she would be able to understand Jayaprakash's thinking. He influenced her for the sake of comprehension, not for conformity, telling her she must go the way her conscience dictated, and allow Jayaprakash to go the way of his, for there was a fundamental difference between his—Gandhi's—philosophy of non-violence in which she had been reared and in Jayaprakash's newly acquired belief in violent revolution.

As his wife, Prabhavati had fulfilled her duty to Jayaprakash by coming to Patna. However as eldest son, Jayaprakash's first duty was to his entire family, especially his elders, and so he left her the following morning, and in company with an excited party of men friends—including old school ones and new socialist admirers among whom was Ganga Sharan Sinha—he travelled to Sitabdiara. His mother was overjoyed at his return. He was saddened to see her so ill but found relief in the family assurances that she was in no imminent danger.

A large function was held to welcome him home and to celebrate his academic achievements, unprecedented in the family. The house lay open to visitors for five days. Then he enthusiastically yielded to the urgings of family and friends to go to a Bihar Congress conference in Monghyr.

The speeches roused his passion for freedom and for powerful revolutionary action so that when he returned from the conference to Patna he was ready to give all his energies to the Independence Movement. Prabhavati was very keen to return to Gandhi at Wardha and re-enlist Jayaprakash as his follower, and she prevailed upon him to accompany her there by train. Gandhi was then attending a vital meeting of the Working Committee of the Indian National Congress.

Jayaprakash went with mixed feelings. He hoped to discuss with Gandhi what employment or public role might best suit him, having in mind the possibility that through Gandhi's intercessions the vice-chancellor, Madan Mohan Malaviya, might permit him to open a department of sociology at Banaras Hindu University. As a boy he had been fascinated by the story of Gandhi's satyagraha in South Africa, and his 'brief experience of soaring up with the winds of a great idea' had 'left imprints on the inner being ' that time had not removed.

But M. N. Roy's writings had persuaded him that Gandhi 'was against the social revolution and would at a moment of crisis hasten to uphold the [British] system of exploitation and inequality.' Freedom was his 'unchanging goal', 'one of the beacon lights of his life', and the Marxist science of revolution seemed to him to offer a surer and quicker road than civil disobedience. Lenin's success seemed immeasurably more thrilling than Gandhi's failures.

In Wardha he and Prabhavati were allotted a room on the ground floor of the two-storeyed building where Mahatma Gandhi was staying. Next day she attended to Gandhi's needs as he sat upstairs with Congressmen. Towards evening the session ended for the day and the fifteen members straggled downstairs.

In Jayaprakash's recollection Jawaharlal Nehru came down as he was standing in the doorway of his room. Nehru came to him with outstretched hand saying, '*Main Jawaharlal hun* (I am Jawaharlal).' Jayaprakash felt shy in the presence of the president elect of the Congress, but replied, 'Main Jayaprakash hun; and shook hands. They felt an immediate liking for each other.

As Prabhavati recalled Jayaprakash was very quiet and retiring, and both of them felt an acute reticence at meeting Jawaharlal. As Gandhi wished them to meet him, however, they were hoping that the introduction would be arranged for them, when one morning they emerged from their door just as Jawaharlal appeared before his, opposite. He walked across, took Jayaprakash's hand warmly and announced who he was.

Prabhavati stood in the background unable to pluck up courage to join in the conversation, much to the amusement of the jaunty, mercurial Minoo Masani. He whispered confidently to her: 'Well, now you've been shown how to do it Prabha behen, you go straight up and say, I'm Prabhavati Devi.' However she would not, and Jayaprakash went on talking without noticing.

Jawaharlal talked keenly about events which had occurred in India during Jayaprakash's absence. In reply to Jayaprakash's remarks about his being president elect, Jawaharlal explained that about three months previously, on 20 August, the reception committee preparing for the next Congress conference to be held at Lahore on 31 December, had elected Gandhi to succeed Motilal Nehru as president for 1930. Gandhi had declined, however, and proposed him, Jawaharlal.

The British government had rejected the Congress demand for granting full dominion status within the British Commonwealth. Jawaharlal and his father and the other members of the Congress Working Committee had just spent the day considering giving up, once and for all, this moderate demand, and replacing it with a radical call for complete and immediate independence. Gandhi, he added, wished to make one last bid with Lord Irwin before 31 December, and would therefore go to Delhi very shortly.

Despite his pleasure and pride in meeting Jawaharlal, this had not been Jayaprakash's purpose in coming to Wardha. The interview helped to fill in the time he had to wait to be personally introduced to Gandhi. Frail, gap-toothed, sparkling with energy for his sixty years, Gandhi welcomed Jayaprakash enthusiastically and affectionately, treating him as a son-in-law, the husband of his 'adopted' daughter. Although Gandhi assumed he would join the independence struggle, his being accepted as a family member instead of as a political associate provided Jayaprakash with no occasion to dispute his theories of social change with Gandhi He felt very shy and most anxious to pay proper respect to Gandhi—both because of his age and his national fame—and so his conversation consisted mainly of answering questions about himself. After their talks he experienced that sense of wonder which so many thousands of people felt; that Gandhi had an enormous interest in him, had treated him as an equal, and that he mattered individually to Gandhi whatever his personal differences might be.

Around him the atmosphere was ablaze with the glory of self-sacrifice and Jayaprakash, being a highly emotional man, was intensely affected. He felt they were all on the verge of India's great leap forward to liberty. The days were crowded with intensity and suppressed excitement and expectations of victory; day-long, nightlong arrangements; a flow, in and out of his life, of tried warriors and passionate young recruits. Jayaprakash's enthusiasm was roused to 'white heat'.

It was while he was in this state that Gandhi broached with him the extremely private matter of his relationship with Prabhavati. Gandhi told him that Prabhavati was a wonderful woman who had been like a daughter to him, a pure soul with a great capacity for service, and she had responded to his persuasions to become a *brahmachari* (a celibate), and had taken a vow which should be respected by any person with a sense of moral decency. He referred to the Hindu belief that there are four paths to the knowledge of truth, four yogas, by which men could realise their fullest natures— Jnana Yoga, the path of the intellect;

Karma Yoga, the means of work and action; Raj Yoga, the experience of power and rule; and Bhakti Yoga, the way of loving devotion. Though Jayaprakash was a remarkable thinker, the taproot of his life was devotion, and his passion to help the poor and his country sprang from his profound sympathy for their plight. Because of this love he was prepared to work, to strive, to endure self-sacrifice. Surely he also felt such unselfish love for his wife? If he felt he was not devoted enough to Prabhavati to respect her vow, and take a similar vow himself, then of course, Hindu law would allow him to put her aside for another wife, but this was neither his duty nor his way of fulfilment.

Intellectually tough, Jayaprakash was however emotionally inhibited and susceptible to another's ascendency over his affective life. He succumbed to Gandhi's moral pressure.

Jayaprakash, Prabhavati and Jawaharlal left Wardha with Gandhi, travelling together by train to Delhi with a small crowd of followers. They stayed in the house of the Chandiwalla family, while Gandhi called upon Lord Irwin to no avail, before making their rail bookings to Lahore. *En route* there were further opportunities for conversation with Jawaharlal. He told Jayaprakash about his eighteen months in jail, in company with his father, for organising an Allahabad merchants' boycott of British cloth. Jayaprakash questioned him eagerly about his impressions of Europe on his 1926-27 tour and about his reception in the Kremlin. Nehru described his reactions to the Soviet experiment of a new, planned society, showing a sympathy for socialism—albeit of the Fabian kind—whereas Jayaprakash explained to him that since Wisconsin University he had been an 'intellectual adherent of the Communist International'.

They found they had much in common for they were both highly educated, highly original thinkers, saw Indian affairs from an international perspective, and had a passion for the life of politics and for national independence. Each of them was critical of Gandhi's economic theories and his technique of civil disobedience and non-cooperation, feeling that socialism was more likely to lead to a better world.

'Why don't you come and join me at Allahabad if you have nothing fixed? We are in need of a secretary for the Congress Labour Research Department. Would you come?' Jawaharlal asked him.

'I should be very happy to do that, 'Jayaprakash replied.

Thereafter, private concerns were quickly put aside for the drama of the conference at Lahore. Meeting on 31 December 1929 and 1 January 1930, only a month after Jayaprakash's return, the Congress delegates elected Jawaharlal their president and voted to make India independent of the British Commonwealth. The Indian flag, red, white and green—the red later replaced by saffron— was hoisted. The Congress president was declared the president of the newly independent country, and was henceforth to be addressed as 'rashtrapati'. The Indian National Congress was declared India's legal government. If the resolution had any weight, Jawaharlal was now the Viceroy's successor.

Unfortunately euphoria outran practicality, and no real plan of action was drawn up.

A week later, on 9 January, the *New York World* published Gandhi's statement that 'the independence resolution need frighten nobody', which he repeated in his paper *Young India* and in his March letter to Lord Irwin. This brought from India's and Britain's few communists bitter condemnation that he was a lackey of the British imperialists and Indian capitalists, only interested in maintaining his domination over the mass movement while placing upon it the maximum restraints. This was their consistent attitude from 1928 to 1934. Their attack seemed most unjust to Jayaprakash and he was offended at the slur they cast on the freedom movement which had so captivated his emotions.

Inspired beyond any earlier dreams by the display at Lahore of mass support and mass emotion he willingly accompanied Jawaharlal to Allahabad where he and Prabhavati rented a house for a time until the Nehru family moved to their new home, Anand Bhavan, which was destined to be anything but an 'abode of happiness'. Thereupon Jawaharlal set up the All India Congress Committee office in the old home, Swaraj Bhavan (abode of freedom), and invited a number of the Congress clerical and organising staff to live on the premises. To Jayaprakash and Prabhavati he allotted his father's now vacant rooms on the first floor. Affection and intimacy grew between Jayaprakash and Jawaharlal, and between Prabhavati and Nehru's wife, Kamala, and their thirteen-year-old daughter, Indira.

Soon after he joined the team at Swaraj Bhavan, Jayaprakash's mother's condition became critical, and five days later Phul Rani Devi died of a heart attack in Patna. Grief-stricken, Jayaprakash attended her cremation on the burning ghats on the banks of the majestic Ganges.

Jayaprakash pushed aside any sense of loss by working diligently in the Congress office organising the mass contacts of the Congress organisation, corresponding with trade unions, using whatever influence he could bring to bear to coax unions back to the Congress fold, whenever they had fallen under the influence of the old liberals, the communists or men considered opportunists. He made international contacts with the British labour Party and the British Trade Union Congress and carefully read their publications. He engaged in surveys to discover what the problems of industrial labourers were and to what extent the Congress could help in ventilating their demands and, of course, in identifying the Congress and its struggle for independence with the workers.

Jayaprakash did his best to ensure that Congressmen went to factories and spoke at workers' meetings to gain influence with them and to themselves become educated on the problems of India's working people. At that time the personality and beliefs of their leaders largely determined which political party a union supported. Jayaprakash regularly met V. V. Giri (later President of India) who was then the organiser of the Trade Union Congress and N. M. Joshi, the Liberal, whose efforts he admired, though he considered that the Servants of India Society, the (Mrs. Annie) Besantites and the Shiva Rao disciples were all too conservative, too concerned with private charity.

One of his heartfelt concerns was to achieve the introduction of labour laws, for only a minute fraction of the Indian workforce was covered by factories acts, and these acts were ineffectually policed. Nor was there any accepted form of voluntary or compulsory conciliation or arbitration between management and labour.

Though his efforts in 1930 did not achieve immediate results, one of the contributions his group in the Indian National Congress did make towards a more egalitarian society was to succeed in applying the conventions of the International Labour Organisation to India, influencing the enactment of legislation in line with ILO policy.

However, Jayaprakash had to take a break of two months from this work, for his father was in serious debt and he had to find a well-paid job to raise some money. Through his Congress connections he was able to obtain employment in Delhi as private secretary to the millionaire Congress supporter, G. D. Birla. Jawaharlal, however, invited him to return to the All India Congress Committee and with Birla's help managed to enable Jayaprakash to do so. From this time on Jayaprakash and Prabhavati lived very austerely on whatever modest allowance the Congress (and later the Socialist Party) was able to provide from the private donations collected by it. Most of the nation's political leaders and freedom fighters and all its illegal printing presses were supported by gifts. After the 1954 Asian Socialist Conference, Jayaprakash's finances were improved and stabilised through the generosity of a Burmese friend who made him from that time on an allowance of almost Rs 500 per month.

Meanwhile the Indian people's ordeal of fire began. On 26 January 1930 the Congress enthusiastically celebrated Independence Day, resolving at public assemblies: 'It is the inalienable right of the Indian people to have freedom. We hold it a crime against man and God to submit any longer. If we can but withdraw our voluntary help and stop payment of taxes, without doing violence even under provocation, the end of this inhuman rule is assured.' But Lord Irwin did not fold his tents. When he refused to grant the eleven freedoms Congress requested, Gandhi informed him by letter on 2 March that the Congress would embark upon a campaign of non-violent disobedience. By 13 March he had decided to symbolise peaceful resistance to all government power by a personal act violating the sales tax on salt, and informed Irwin of this. Irwin's advisors dissuaded him from making an arrest until Gandhi had broken the law, so permitting one of history's most publicised pilgrimages.

On the eve of Gandhi's action, the campfires of thousands of supporters twinkled beside his Sabarmati Ashram near Ahmedabad. With the dawn of day Gandhi, aged sixty-one, led seventy-eight of his disciples on a walk of two hundred and forty miles to the coast. There was general fear that the walk would kill him. The procession which followed the small band was, however, two miles long. Before the Salt March began no one could have predicted the impact it was to have, and Jawaharlal was disgusted with the insignificance of the issue. He had hoped for a strenuous no-tax campaign, like the Irish and Americans had waged against the British, and also for the desertion of their jobs by all professional people to reduce the British rule to impotence and topple it. Jayaprakash sympathised with his view.

They walked for twenty-four days meeting cheering crowds and winning worldwide publicity. Louis Fischer and other American newspapermen who reported events and publicised Gandhi's moral philosophy were in this period a democratic thorn in Britannia's martial flesh. On reaching the beach at Dandi the processionists walked into the waves, collected water in battered pannikins and ceremonially boiled it in pots to extract the salt, symbolically indicating that God has freely given mankind both salt and liberty.

Having survived, Gandhi on 9 April instructed the Indian people to manufacture contraband salt to picket liquor shops, opium dens, and British cloth shops, to burn foreign clothes, to spin their own cotton yam, to desert government schools, and to resign from government service. Everywhere the Congress branches tried to carry out their programme but, as in the twenties, the indignation and rebelliousness which was released could not be kept under control.

There were widespread strikes and massive demonstrations. The Government of India made arrests indiscriminately without trial. Political and trade union detenties went on hunger strikes in their cells. Then on 23 April, the authorities arrested Khan Abdul Ghaffar Khan, the 'Frontier Gandhi' whose followers had only just joined Gandhi and danced on the banks of Ravi river at the Lahore conference. Armoured cars were sent to shoot down the demonstrations against his arrest in the city of Peshawar. But his 'Red Shirts' attacked and defeated the vehicles and took control of the city. The Second Battalion of the 18th Royal Garhwali Rifles was sent but instead of doing the slaughtering expected of them they refused to fire. So from 25 April to 4 May the city was controlled by Indians. Lord Irwin, having issued an ordinance preventing anyone publishing information on what the Government of India was doing, recaptured the city. Memory of this event had power to enrage and inspire Jayaprakash for the rest of his life.

In Allahabad, Prabhavati joined the Nehru family in publicly obtaining salt water and extracting the salt, and in picketing shops which sold British cloth or liquor. There were also hours of work in Anand Bhavan for the wounded or dying were brought there and their bullet wounds had to be tended to secretly at night by doctors coming surreptitiously under cover of dark.

Simultaneously the worldwide economic depression was affecting India. Britain was buying less raw materials, so agricultural prices were depressed for the already pitifully poor villagers, reducing them to a diet on which, reported the Bengal director of public health, 'even rats could not live'. Industrial workers were sacked by the hundreds. They had lived in the growing cities, thirty to a room, and now they had to move to kennels made of cardboard and palm fronds. If the peasants of the United Provinces were to pay the land taxes the British administration was demanding they would die of starvation. Jawaharlal assisted in rousing them from their submission into a no-tax campaign and was arrested for it on 4 May while boarding a train at Allahabad Junction.

Eventually Irwin took the gamble of proceeding against Gandhi. He was arrested at 1.00 a.m. in his camp at Karachi on 5 May and jailed without trail for eight months. The official government communique for that day clearly showed that it was not his non-violence which was feared but the 'outbreak of violence'.

There was such an explosion of outraged indignation at Gandhi's arrest that the British introduced Emergency Powers legislation under which the Government of India assumed absolute power. The Indian National Congress was outlawed and its bank funds confiscated. Jayaprakash's office was ransacked, its records seized and burned, and its door locked. The furniture and property of the Nehru family and of the other arrested Congress members was confiscated.

More strikes occurred and trade unionists seized control of the industrial town of Sholapur, near Bombay. Mrs Sarojini Naidu led a non-violent attack on the Dharasan Saltworks where troops clubbed down the demonstrators and committed obscenities on their private parts, unfortunately observed by another troublesome American newspaperman whose description disgusted world opinion.

Jayaprakash became an individual atom of a giant movement in which millions of people felt a bond of unity against an oppressor; he was a man in hiding whom the police net had missed, struggling for the masses, influenced by their poverty and passion, swaying them by his intensity. He had been sent to Bombay to organise textile workers and went underground, not being known well enough to the authorities to have been watched. He kept Congress members in contact with one another's activities and revived their spirits. He printed illegal literature and distributed it to supporters. He kept record of British atrocities, of those in jail and of help given to their families. He organised both boycotts and no-tax campaigns.

Prabhavati was arrested in a women's demonstration and imprisoned in Allahabad Jail together with Kamala Nehru (of whom she was now deeply fond), Mrs Sarojini Naidu, Jawaharlal's mother and his two sisters, Sister Nan (Swarup Pandit) and Sister Betti (Mrs. Krishna Hutheesingh). She was temperamentally incompatible with Jawaharlal's sisters and there was considerable friction between them in prison. They had lived very wealthy, sophisticated lives, their father Motilal even being sent bottles of whisky and soda by his friends while he was in prison. The effect on Jayaprakash of Prabhavati's detention was to make him drive himself even harder in the struggle to topple the British.

In Patna his brother Rajeshwar Prasad, one of the most active workers of the Patna Youth League, was jailed for six months. Prabhavati's father, Braj Kishore Prasad, was also rounded up.

Gandhi, the Nehrus, Prabhavati and the leading Congressmen were released on 26 January 1930, the anniversary of India's first 'Independence Day'. Irwin held talks with Gandhi from 19 February onwards and they issued the terms of their Pact on 4 March. The Viceroy wanted the civil disobedience stopped or 'suspended'; Gandhi compromised with 'discontinued'. An amnesty was accorded to all persons arrested for non-violent offences, and administrative concessions to make salt in certain areas were granted. Some of the repressive ordinances were withdrawn: the ban on peaceful picketing, under which Prabhavati had been imprisoned, was ended; over a hundred thousand detainees were freed; the Indian National Congress was legalised; confiscated, forfeited or attached properties were restored except in special circumstances. Gandhi withdrew the no-tax campaign in the United Provinces when the government agreed to halve rents in recognition of the desperation of the peasants. He agreed that the Congress would accept representation at the second session of the Round Table Conference.

Jayaprakash and Jawaharlal and many of their friends accepted the withdrawal of the movement with great reluctance and were both angry and disillusioned with Gandhi. Their indignation was increased further when he failed to save Bhagat Singh and his two young terrorist friends—who had thrown a bomb into the Delhi Legislative Council chamber—from being hanged in jail on 23 March. Nevertheless, the Karachi Congress conference on 31 March, despite Subhas Chandra Bose's black-flag demonstration against Gandhi's sellout, endorsed the ending of the Satyagraha and agreed to Gandhi's going to London for the September Round Table Conference. The weeks of negotiations had persuaded the country to wait submissively for the settlement which was coming.

The honourless opposite, however, was being planned. Irwin's attempt at peaceful and dignified settlement was swiftly closed. He was replaced by an anti-negotiator, Lord Willingdon, the hard-line governor of Bombay, who promptly and publicly declared Gandhi a humbug, and promulgated new ordinances reintroducing imprisonment without trial, confiscation of property, and an Emergency Press Act silencing news of his rule. In addition, he began the tripolarisation of Indian political settlements by intriguing with Sir Fazli Hasan and his group—who were financed by the Aga Khan—against Hindu-Muslim dialogue, and by refusing to allow Gandhi to be accompanied to London by Muslim supporters of the Indian National Congress.

Jayaprakash went on with his trades union work for the Congress, becoming increasingly convinced that the miserable poverty of working people could never be removed while British imperialism drained his country dry. He continued in this work until Gandhi's empty-handed return to Bombay on 28 December 1931. Then he and Prabhavati accompanied Jawaharlal and T. A. L. Sherwani on the train from Allahabad to Bombay to meet Gandhi, intending to take part in the impending conference of the Congress which would hear Gandhi's account of his London negotiations. The travellers were, however, offending against Willingdon's new ordinances which confined them to their homes and prevented them from such movement. So on the way Nehru and Sherwani were arrested Jayaprakash and Prabhavati, being in a separate compartment, were missed by the police. They did not reveal themselves and were able to reach Bombay unimpeded; they delivered the conference papers to Mrs Sarojini Naidu, who was then acting president of the Congress, and joined the crowds who welcomed Gandhi on Ballard Pier.

On 1 January 1932, Gandhi and the Congress Working Committee formally reviewed the disobedience movement of the previous year. Jayaprakash had written a history of the events for this meeting from the reports his office had received of the numbers of demonstrators jailed and atrocities witnessed. Three days later they had further experience of British contempt for civil liberties. While they trusted. British honour would devise a new Constitution for India, an attack upon the Congress was secretly prepared by the revengeful authorities. On 4 January, Gandhi was arrested and the mass arrest of fifteen thousand Congressmen followed. In February another eighteen thousand demonstrators were jailed.

Escaping the net once again Jayaprakash set up an illegal, underground office of the Congress in Bombay, the position of acting general secretary of the All India Congress Committee conferred on him by default. He was assisted by Lalji Mehrotra in keeping contact with other men in hiding all over India who were seething with the same disgust and indignation, and fellow conspirators who were running off Congress opinions on any shabby printing press or worn-out cyclostyling machine and passing them surreptitiously to readers. They felt that Indian freedom now rested upon their shoulders and that they must resist every repressive law in whatever manner they could, must speak and write the truth when the government ruled in secrecy.

During this time, Jayaprakash was planning a secret meeting of the Congress Working Committee which he managed to stage successfully in Banaras in July 1932.

Shortly after this secret meeting, the India league of England dispatched a delegation of members of the British Parliament to study the repression being carried out by Lord Willingdon and to look into Congress charges of police brutalities.

Jayaprakash was apprised of the visit and came from United Provinces back to Bombay to meet the delegation. The police observed him there in company with British members of Parliament, reported him and a warrant was issued for his arrest. The action was not swift enough to silence him however, for by this time he had travelled with the delegation members to Puna where he wanted to introduce them to Peter Alvares and to Guru Swami, the secretary general of the Railwaymen's Federation.

Then Jayaprakash conducted the delegation to Madras to meet certain South Indians who could supply damaging evidence. On police lips, his name pursued him through railway stations and along telegraph wires. While he stood on Madras railway station seeing off one of the groups of the delegation on its way to Karnatak he was under police observation. But his shadowers waited until the train had drawn out so that the British parliamentarians were unable to observe the arrest. Then as Jayaprakash was stepping into the car, in which a merchant Congress supporter had had them driven to the station, the police confronted him, 'Are you Jayaprakash Narayan?'

'Why do you want to know?'

'Because you are under arrest!'

The two men took him away by police car. His chauffeur reported what had happened, the news was passed along the Congress grapevine, and eventually Rajagopalachari instituted a civil petition in the Madras High Court to test the validity of his arrest, for he had been apprehended in Madras on a warrant issued in Bombay. The High Court however held his arrest to have been in order. He was then transferred secretly to the Arthur Road Jail in Bombay, and from there, in January 1933, he was taken by train to Nasik Road station from where a police car took him to Nasik Central Prison. Meanwhile Prabhavati, not knowing his whereabouts, returned to Gandhi's ashram.

The Man who Founded Indian Socialism

The men who were detained together in the cells and exercise yard of Nasik Jail were a remarkably talented company: Morarji Desai, Ashok Mehta, Ram Manohar Lohia, Minoo Masani, J. C. Kumarappa, Yusef Meherally, M. L. Dantwala, N.G. Goray, Achyut Patwardhan. But the closest and most enduring friendships developed between Jayaprakash and Masani, Patwardhan, Lohia, Meherally and Mehta.

Nasik Road Central Prison consisted of an L-shaped block of rooms, thirty-two in one row and twenty-two in the other, surrounded by high walls. During the day the prisoners were allowed to sit, walk about, talk or read in the open yard, but they were locked into their rooms at sunset. There were a few A class prisoners who were better fed than the others. There were also C class criminals. Jayaprakash, Mehta and Meherally were B class prisoners, receiving a ration of rice each day with whatever vegetables were in season, at the fixed rate of nine annas per day.

As the months went by, Jayaprakash began to suffer from his limited prison food and its unhygienic preparation. He had a prolonged attack of dysentery followed by colitis. Then he experienced sharp pain in the sciatic nerve when he stood to shave in the mornings, leaning forward to see himself in his mirror which he set against the bars where the sunlight came in. An army doctor, Colonel Bhandari, diagnosed a slipped disc and prescribed a series of leg-folding exercises from a lying position, similar to yogic asanas.

Jayaprakash, Mehta, Masani, Patwardhan and Lohia saw capitalism as crumbling, and morally and socially discredited by its greed and inhumanity. It was a time of crisis demanding a desperate remedy and the educated became either fascist or socialist. They discussed the times endlessly, trying to evaluate social developments such as the introduction of the world's first Five Year Plan in the Soviet Union.

They agreed in their discussions that all history was a process of class struggle and that proletarian revolutions were inevitable. The bourgeoisie owned the means of production and used it to earn profits for themselves from the proletariat who had to live from wages and were related to their employers only by a cash nexus—always being forced to produce more than they received. The abolition of private ownership, they believed, would destroy this hegemony, and a consciously prearranged and planned society would bring about a classless state in which human relationships would be harmonious and cooperative, and the coercive state would wither away.

India was related to this unstable and socially unjust system in the manner which Lenin had clearly described. As capitalist enterprises in Britain, France and Germany increased in size they became monopolistic until, within national states, competition between individual entrepreneurs virtually ceased. Control of society passed from individual manufacturers to a financial oligarchy of bankers and financiers. The European greed for higher profits found its gratification in using cheap labour and raw material from underdeveloped Asian and African societies. The high returns from capital investment in these poor areas and the increasing production from these investments created pressures for larger markets. International affairs then became a competitive scramble between capitalist countries for peasant populations and feudal tropical territories to exploit. War was the inevitable outcome of this imperialism.

Since Jayaprakash had influenced his group of close friends to consider themselves Marxist-Leninists, they questioned him and one another very closely on what their relationship should be to the Communist Party of India. They agreed that Gandhi was confused about social and human motivations when he asserted that there was no need for the state to strip the wealthy of their privileges because he would gain their support for his social revolution by persuading them to look upon themselves as trustees of their wealth for the benefit of society. They were impatient with Gandhi's policy of compromise with the Viceroy which the Congress had adopted since his Salt March. None of the older men in the Congress seemed to have a modem approach. But there was no question about their loyalty to it, because it was the only mass organisation struggling for national freedom.

Jayaprakash considered that Marxism was the only acceptable theory of socialism. He had as little hope for Gandhi's trusteeship as he had for the constitutional tactics of the British Labour Party or the capitalist planning of President Roosevelt's New Deal. Only in the USSR, he believed, was socialism being built up successfully, and if the Russians could achieve collectivisation of agriculture with 'an ignorant, intolerant, narrowly-selfish peasantry' so, too, could India. The only qualifications he made to the wholesale copying of the Russian experiment in state ownership of the means of production, distribution and exchange, were that India should be slow instead of hasty; should use encouragement and promotion instead of coercion; and might need fewer labour-saving devices because of her shortage of land.

Therefore joining the Communist Party of India seemed both logical and advantageous. However there was scarcely a communist party in 1934. Its membership had not yet climbed above twenty, and the most capable of them were in jail and undergoing a trial in Meerut for sedition.

The internationally notorious Meerut trial dragged on from 1929 until January 1933, when the prisoners were found guilty of conspiracy to overthrow the state. Believing that the accused were sincere nationalists, Motilal Nehru acted as president of an appeal committee, and Jawaharlal and Jayaprakash—after his release from Nasik— keenly assisted in the appeal, indignant and certain that an injustice had been done. Their opinion was eventually vindicated. An international agitation and court appeal, which followed the savage sentence of transportation to the Andaman Islands, was successful in drastically reducing the penalties.

Had these few communists been supporting the national independence movement at the time of his return from America, and the subsequent non-cooperation movement, Jayaprakash's 'dream of creating a great India' and his indignation over the Meerut Conspiracy Case might have urged him out of the Indian National Congress into the Communist Party of India. He and the other Marxist-Leninists were going to 'wipe off poverty, injustice, filth, indolence, ignorance from the face of this great country'. They would abolish maharajas and landlords and ensure that no peasant was landless. Their technique was class struggle and the revolutionary upsurge of the toiling masses.

However, the strategies of the tiny Communist Party of India followed the policies of the Communist International, rather than deriving from a passion for national freedom. Though the Communist Party did support the Congress independence struggle between 1934 and 1948, it did not in the years 1928-34 nor 1948-50.

While Jayaprakash was hunted, caught and jailed, the communists attacked the 'bourgeois nationalism' of the Congress. Gandhi, they wrote, was a lackey of Indian capitalists and not a sincere freedom fighter. So they refused to join his struggle. This disgusted Jayaprakash. He called it a 'folly' and 'shameful' behaviour. It angered him that none of them had been 'anywhere on the battle lines' in the struggle he had just waged from underground.

So began his feelings of increasing alienation from the policy of Stalin's Communist International, and also from the political climate of the Soviet Union which, until 1928, had been to him 'the paragon and exemplar of all communist virtues'. He argued with his friends that the Comintern was dividing the labour and socialist movements throughout the world; that the communists were being isolated from the nationalist movements in all colonial countries; that their policy was contradictory not only to Lenin but also to general Marxist theory.

As a result of such discussions, ranging over months, the seven friends decided to attempt creating a new political party in India, a party devoted to both independence and socialism, to both freeing and uplifting the peasants and workers of the country. They agreed that their party members should retain membership of the Indian National Congress but nevertheless function as a ginger group, operating at all times as 'true Marxist-Leninists'.

In April 1934 Jayaprakash's and Masani's terms of imprisonment were up. Ashok Mehta, Mohan Dantwala, Dr. Ram Manohar Lohia and Achyut Patwardhan bade them farewell, full of excited hope for what they might achieve now that they could participate again in India's political events. Afterwards they sat down in despair at the thought of the months they still had to serve in their cells.

Jayaprakash emerged from Nasik determined 'to break the chains of slavery', to guarantee every Indian citizen equal rights, to abolish all distinctions of birth and privilege, and to do away with all titles emanating either from inherited social status or the state. In Jayaprakash's Utopia, every person would receive according to his needs and would work according to his ability. And in addition to providing material equality and a sound economic standard of living, the state would promote the moral and intellectual development of the individual.

Moreover his mind was full of the important question of when the Congress, gingered up by the Socialists, would launch the final offensive against the enemy. Had the Congress Working Committee any clear conception of the battle? What should Congress members do to prepare themselves for it? How should they strike? Should they wait until the British chose for them a time which would naturally be more favourable to the British Empire than to Indian freedom? However, his impatience went unrewarded: Gandhi called off the satyagraha in August 1934.

For the next five years these queries turned over and over in his mind. 'I suppose the technique of satyagraha,' he wrote in angry contempt to Jawaharlal in November 1938, 'does not permit one to prepare plans of offensive in advance. The only plan one may conceive of is that we must spin more and do other soul-stirring things like that. But will you be satisfied with it?'

Jayaprakash returned to Patna to visit his father and to seek the help of his father-in-law, his classmates from school-days, and other young radical Biharis to establish the first socialist party in India's history. Masani returned to proselytise in Bombay.

From his father-in-law Jayaprakash was able to learn of Prabhavati's whereabouts and he wrote asking her to join him in Patna. Then he plunged into organising a convention which met in Patna on 17 May 1934 to inaugurate the Bihar Congress Socialist Party and make arrangements for an all India conference. He was elected general secretary. (Through his speeches, his articles for newspapers and his booklet *Why Socialism?* he quickly became the group's most articulate spokesman and its leading anti-Gandhian.) The meeting laid down as party policy, the capture of the state through elections, centralised state planning, the collectivisation of agriculture and the dictatorship of the proletariat—the peasants and lower castes and outcasts of India. On Jayaprakash's initiative the Patna meeting decided to call an all India convention of socialists to coincide with the Congress Annual Conference in 1934.

Membership of the Congress Socialist Party was exclusive. It was limited to a few thousand only, and based upon Leninist principles. Cadre membership, not mass membership, was the basis of the party Constitution. The national executive drew up the policy and submitted it at the annual conference when it was generally rubber-stamped, the members then being responsible for carrying out the decisions. A clause allowed for collective affiliation of trade unions. No one could be a member of the Congress Socialist Party if he was not a member of the Indian National Congress.

Jayaprakash plunged into the practical details of creating a political party: finding a suitable office and meeting the rent for it; paying the office staff and the officials; collecting donations; arranging annual conferences for the state organisations and keeping a watch on who would be elected to office; settling arguments on whether elections had been valid; and contacting branches and encouraging them. He had to accept or refuse invitations to address party meetings and to consider state requests that the party hold its annual all India conference in their capital city. He determined whether the donations he had collected had been used for correct purposes, kept lists of members who were active or promotable, wrote a weekly newsletter, decided whether or not to disband some of the provincial unit committees, and took part in the ubiquitous party process of suspending or expelling members.

As general secretary, Jayaprakash gave advice on how branches should be reorganised after some of the members defected to the M. N. Roy political group, helped in preparing the party badge, arranged meetings, boycotts, picketings, helped in famine relief in Kutch in 1939, and took part in various enquires into injustices done by the wealthy to the village poor or into the justice of the arrest of party members.

Jayaprakash rushed from one end of India to the other, exhorting people to join his party, explaining over and over to small party groups or large meetings of trade unionists that the objectives of the All India Congress Socialist Party were to eliminate exploitation, the profit motive and poverty. To achieve these objectives, the party pledged itself to a social plan consisting of fifteen practical measures.

The state should be secular, recognising the equality of religions, debts owed by peasants and workers to landlords or moneylenders, and recognise the right of all to work or maintenance. The state should socialise all key industries, banks, insurance and public utilities (measures partly introduced by Nehru and Mrs Indira Gandhi years later) and establish a monopoly of foreign trade. The privileges of Princes, landlords and other exploiters should be eliminated without compensation. Land should be redistributed to peasants who should be encouraged to form production, distribution and credit cooperatives and to farm their lands cooperatively or collectively.

Meanwhile his mass movement work on behalf of the Congress went on actively. As a patriot who had suffered imprisonment, as a founder of a new party, as an attacker of the status quo, Jayaprakash became a prominent national figure during the latter months of 1934. Men heard of him, came to his meetings to form their own opinions, fell prey to his charm, passion and charismatic appeal, and joined him.

The British authorities and the collaborating Indian members of the state legislatures began to consider him a serious threat and kept a constant surveillance on him.

By 1934 the turmoil of the past four years of discussion, demonstrations, emergency legislation, jailings, police firings and clubbings of women protestors, resulted in a partially-successful demand for greater freedom for India. The British Parliament began to introduce the first provisions of its new Government of India Act. The sufferings reaped meagre reward. A Federation of Indian Provinces and the Princely States (which were British Protectorates) was to be implemented. Elected Indians would control the state legislatures.

The Comintern shifted its stand on national independence movements and the Communist Party of India made a sudden volte-face from its earlier calumny of Gandhi and the Congress, and sought to penetrate it by advocating the formation of a National Front. The Congress conservatives were unimpressed but not the Congress Socialists.

Jayaprakash had already presented resolutions calling on Congressmen to boycott state legislatures, as a number of them had done since the resolution of the 1929 Lahore Conference. He attacked, as communalist and anti-national, the group within the Congress which had decided to revive the Nationalist Party and return to their parliamentary seats without the sanction of a full session of the Congress. On 1 October 1934 the Congress Socialists carried this policy further. No Congress Socialist was to participate in the elections which Britain proposed to conduct, or to be an office-bearer of any Congress organisation. The All India Socialists Conference on 21 October at Worli in Bombay endorsed this policy, affirming India's goal of complete independence from Britain and the establishment of a state wherein power was transferred to the masses. No truck was held with the Princes, for their private and public scandals and their extravagance were inexcusable. This conference also declared its opposition to participation by India in any European war in which the British imperialists might become involved and followed this up with an Anti-War Day in Bombay on 11 November. While the British were celebrating the Armistice Day ending World War I, Jayaprakash, as general secretary, and other speakers appealed to the Congress to avoid being drawn into any European war.

Because of his fear that Congressmen intended to betray Indian freedom, Jayaprakash proposed at this conference that the Socialists form a United Front with the Communist Party of India, which had been declared illegal in July 1934 and had, in consequence, grown from twenty to a hundred and fifty members.

The 1935 Government of India Act introduced fully responsible Cabinet government in the eleven provinces of British India, giving more than fifteen hundred Indians an opportunity to be elected members of Parliament. To the disgust of the socialists, one-man, one-vote democracy was ignored. The total enfranchised population was thirty-four million—only one-tenth of India's population— who were permitted to vote because of their property ownership or their educational standard. In the central government, powers were divided—revenue, defence and foreign affairs portfolios being reserved for appointees. As Indians had no control over the budget, and government, the police were still under the Viceroy's charge, and the viceroy and governors of the provinces had the right to veto all legislation. Nehru and Jayaprakash condemned the proposals as introducing a 'Slave Constitution' at the annual Congress conference.

Gandhi recommended that Congressmen accept office in the new provincial Parliaments. Jayaprakash was quick to point out that he had fallen from his high pedestal of non-violence, soul-force, and non-cooperation with the evil of imperialism. Gandhi replied with chopped logic that this would not be a venture into the field of power politics but an opportunity to serve the people. Jayaprakash's supporters were in a minority and the Congress decided on taking part in the new constitutional arrangements.

Jayaprakash's difference of opinion with him served to strengthen Gandhi's affection for the 'young firebrand' but within the Congress, Jayaprakash's opinions and his closeness to Gandhi and Nehru won him such opponents as Vallabh Bhai Patel. The relationship of the Congress Socialists to the Indian National Congress in this pre-war period was ambivalent. Nehru's affection for Jayaprakash was not completely open and unqualified. He kept one eye on his own aims for the Congress and his status among its members. Jayaprakash did not consistently oppose Gandhi but often deferred to his opinions or wishes. A. P. Sinha and Pyarelal Nayar supplied recollections of conversation: 'I will organise peasants' unions and build up the workers' movement but I will not join in propagating khadi,' Jayaprakash told Gandhi. 'It will not win us freedom and villages cannot be self-sufficient.'

'Very well Jayaprakash,' Gandhi replied. 'Your work is very valuable but there is much in what I say also.'

'And non-violence is not my creed. I cannot accept it as a technique of social reconstruction.'

'If you accept it as a weapon that is enough for me, Jayaprakash.'

'We will not get power by satyagraha. There must be a revolutionary upsurge of the toiling masses. Every group and party and individual in the world that seeks to enforce its schemes over the nation, seeks to capture the State. When the State is in your hands you can legislate, you can use the whole magnificent apparatus of propaganda and education that modem science has made available; you can enforce your will. And if there is resistance, you can use the coercive arm of the State—the police and the army—to crush it.'

'Will you win power through the will of the electorate or by a *coup d'etat*?'

'After the achievement of independence a *coup d'etat* may not be necessary.'

The State is a soulless machine. And without popular support how can it possess coercive powers? That is the meaning of my satyagraha. You cannot change men's hearts by legislation, Jayaprakash. Conversion must precede legislation. We have today the power to enforce rules of sanitation but we can do nothing with it because the public is not ready.'

'We persuade individuals to become members of the Congress Socialist Party but no party in the world today can build up socialism unless it has the machinery of the State in its hands. In possession of the State it can create a socialist heaven on earth. Why should the overwhelming many of our country suffer poverty, hunger, filth, disease and ignorance while the select few have comfort, luxury, culture, position and power? The socialist endeavours to tackle this problem of inequality at the source so as to check the very growth of inequalities. Your solution of trusteeship takes the fact of inequalities for granted and just levels them up a little. Why can't we force the wealthy and the potbellied capitalists to give up their treasure? You admit that their vast possessions are gained through exploitations.'

'My revolution is bigger than the Russian one, Jayaprakash. I not only win the capitalist's money by persuasion but he also lends me his business talent, his experience, his know-how, his specialisation. Under my non-violence we can ask for and expect to induce our opponent even to immolate himself for the sake of a higher principle.'

Jayaprakash worked energetically to present socialist resolutions to the All India Congress Committee and to have them adopted there. He always looked to Nehru for support because they had agreed on most issues in the past. Nehru had told him repeatedly that he was a socialist, and he had supported Nehru in persuading the Karachi Congress Conference of 1931 to commit itself to the aim that, 'The State shall own or control key industries and services, mineral resources, waterways, shipping and other means of public transport.'

He therefore brought forward resolutions both to the Bihar Provincial Congress and to the All India Congress Committee for the socialisation of the entire economic life of India: 'the elimination of Princes, landlords, capitalists, moneylenders, and all other parasites and exploiting interests', the redistribution of land so that no one might possess more than was necessary to maintain an average family at an average standard of living, the collectivisation of agriculture (which temporarily appealed to Nehru), and the liquidation of rural indebtedness.

Another of his defeated resolutions called on the Congress to alter its Independence Day Pledge so as to shun Gandhi's spinning and weaving and Hindu-oriented removal of untouchability programmes, and to admit that the surest method of achieving complete independence was through the organisation of the peasants and workers on the basis of their economic class interests. 'We do not believe,' he asserted, 'that charkha and khadi will resuscitate the seven hundred thousand villages of India, nor remove the grinding poverty of the masses. We do not believe that regular spinning or the use of khadi or products of village handicrafts will in any way make the Congress members better fitted for continuing the struggle for freedom in an intenser form as contemplated by the Working Committee.'

When he was elected Congress President in 1936, Nehru secured Jayaprakash's nomination to the fifteen-member Congress Working Committee. But the idea of collaborating with the British, after all the suffering he knew they had inflicted on the Indian people, stuck in Jayaprakash's throat.

The Socialists reversed earlier policy and agreed to Jayaprakash's accepting the position, but he tendered his resignation as the general secretary to the national executive of the Socialist Party at Lucknow. This however was not received.

Nehru nevertheless did not respond to socialist overtures for a National Front and another anti-British campaign. Though he held meetings with them, and though Jayaprakash trustingly sought his support for his party, Nehru never joined or openly appeared to support them. Jayaprakash resigned from the Congress Working Committee as soon as it became apparent to him that Congress would contest the elections.

During 1937 Nehru threw himself into a twelve-to-eighteen-hours day of electioneering against the Muslim League and the liberal Party. The Congress won an absolute majority in five of the eleven provinces and was able to form governments in eight. At first these Congress governments resigned because the provincial governors would not give up their veto but a 'gentleman's agreement' was reached by mid-year and for the following two and a half years, until the commencement of World War II in 1939, these provinces enjoyed a large measure of self-government.

Once Nehru had raised his guard in 1938 against Jayaprakash in the interests of his own career he did not lower it. Jayaprakash had a naive trust in Nehru. In his letters of this time to Nehru he expressed his thoughts with complete frankness assuming an identity of ideas with him, and evidently without conceiving that Nehru might not be so disinterested as to never feel personally under fire.

He told Nehru that now that the Congress had acquired power it was being converted 'from a democratic organisation of the millions of the downtrodden people into a handmaid of Indian vested interests', that 'a vulgarisation of Gandhism made this transition easy and gave the new Congress the requisite demagogic armour', that the new Congress assemblies had shown in their dealings with the All India Trades Union Congress that they wished to bind the workers' organisation hand and foot and deliver them to the employers. 'We are faced today,' he wrote, 'with the real danger, of Indian industry being made a synonym for Indian nationalism.' Jayaprakash assumed that Nehru would respond to his appeal to give fresh impetus to the people's urge for social freedom.

Instead of manoeuvring to win parliamentary seats, the Socialists shunned the elections. Jayaprakash as general secretary—his heart filled with joy and his hopes rising high because of the communist policy change towards nationalist struggle—recommended, at the January 1936 Socialist Conference at Meerut, the admission of Communist Party members to their party on individual applications being submitted to the national executive. This was to be done in secret as the Communist Party was banned. Jayaprakash wrote (in *Towards Struggle)* that in a rush of hope as to what might be achieved by this Anti-Imperialist People's United Front, the national executive unanimously adopted his resolution. The Communist Party was slow to respond to his advances, being unwilling to drop its suspicion and bitter hostility towards the Socialists, until P. C. Joshi became their general secretary. He had a personal liking for Jayaprakash and arranged that communists apply for membership. If enthusiasm is to be measured by the size of headlines in the socialist magazines of the period then the Anti-Imperialist Front was expected to topple the British overnight. For the anti-imperialist people's front: Long live soviet Hindustan, proclaimed a Communist Party central committee pamphlet dated 20 July 1936. Urged another: Transform the elections Into Mighty anti-imperialist Demonstrations (5 December 1936).

So while Nehru assumed office in the Delhi Legislative Council, Jayaprakash handed over branches of his party, particularly in the south, to communists, agreed to have socialists and communists work together in the trade unions, and urged his group to get communists elected to the All India Congress Committee.

Jayaprakash was not deceived by the flattery he received from the Stalinists—epithets like 'the Indian Lenin' and 'India's Revolutionary No. 1' were used to describe him—but as he was to do repeatedly in later years, he allowed his enthusiasm and idealism for a great cause to blind him to the pettiness and selfish power-lusts of individual men. For months he was either elated or completely sanguine about the hopes of his United Front, arranging two places for members of the Communist Party of India on the national executive of the Congress Socialist Party (and hence within the Indian National Congress).

As part of the United Front activities, Jayaprakash organised a demonstration in Patna in April against forming of ministries by the Congressmen elected in Bihar state (by now the veto problem had been seemingly solved and the princely states had declined to join the Indian Federation). He was arrested and not released until 26 June. Within days of his release his father died. His keen sense of loss was relieved by the many expressions of shared grief and comfort he received from friends throughout India, and the national executive postponed its meeting until he had performed the funeral rites and recovered from his loss.

Receiving some money from his father's insurance policy he pooled his resources with Ganga Sharon Sinha and rented a house in Kadam Kuan, the cheapest area in Patna. Prabhavati lived with them but Ganga Sharan Sinha's wife and daughter remained in his village. Their occupancy of the house was interrupted by residence in jails but continued until 1954.

For Prabhavati the years from 1934 until the end of World War II were a time of loneliness, worry and estrangement, not consciously admitted. She lived for the most part in Gandhi's ashram enjoying his and Kasturba's parental affection and serving them, while Jayaprakash was away travelling for up to four months at a time. Jayaprakash did not attempt to influence her against brahmacharya nor did he in words ever show a retreat from his vow to lovingly respect her wishes. If he ever reproached her it was only with the intensity of his self-sacrifice for the proletarian revolution. He returned to her, Gandhi's 'hostage from socialism', clad only, she said, 'in a dirty dhoti, looking like a fakir', and frightening her with his emaciation. He never admitted to himself that a resentment arising from his subconscious added heat to the disputes he had with Gandhi over matters of—on the face of it—moral and political philosophy. He had never been ready to admit that emotional factors had any relation to his public career.

Whatever anticipations of close affection and tenderness Prabhavati had allowed herself remained unfulfilled, and she remembered all her life how Gandhi on one occasion had attempted to console her by remarking: 'Jayaprakash isn't married to you. He's married to socialism.'

Even had Gandhi not interfered in their emotional life the odds against marital happiness were tragically high for them. Their marriage had been arranged for them at an immature age and thereafter directed by their parents and the social mores of Hinduism. Then there had been eight years of separation and Jayaprakash had returned highly educated in western thought while she had lacked formal education. Jayaprakash had supported himself by labouring while she had been dependent on Gandhi. She was a disciple of Gandhi, he of Marx. She had experienced only her own society and he was not able to completely share with her his experiences of the American pattern of life. His agnosticism confronted her traditional Hinduism. So they had to live out the years as best they could in a decade of national turmoil.

When Jayaprakash mildly wrote years later that he had pursued freedom as a goal in his life he concealed the intensity of that pursuit, which had consisted of eighteen hours of political work daily year after year, nor did he choose to remark that his high position in public life had been accompanied by a lack of family life, parental responsibilities, and private happiness.

These years were to be called by Prabhavati the 'bad part' of their lives, worse for her than her imprisonments in jail. In recollecting those years she was so moved as to tell us in 1969, with tears in her eyes, that Gandhi would be happy, today, if he could be alive to see how she and Jayaprakash had come together in later years.

Although Jayaprakash especially liked chicken and ate meat, fish and eggs, he agreed for Prabhavati's sake to become a vegetarian. Since Sinha wished to continue eating eggs he employed an attendant who cooked for him on a separate *chula* (mud stove). Jayaprakash's food was simple but varied as Prabhavati keenly collected recipes wherever she travelled in India. Jayaprakash was very hospitable and constantly invited acquaintances: 'You also come.' Until the guests left Prabhavati was jolly, courteous, but later unleashed her annoyance. These times, or the occasions on which Jayaprakash was unpunctual for meals, were the only troubles in their household of which Ganga Sharan was aware.

Jayaprakash for his part used to be irritable with Prabhavati for taking such a large quantity of luggage on their journeys. 'Let us travel light', he constantly remarked. 'What are you taking here, Prabha?' — 'I was taking the stove.' — 'Well, leave it behind.'—'How can I give you tea?'—'We'll do without tea.' Then an hour or two later would come the change of heart. 'A cup of tea would be nice. I think we should have brought the stove, Prabha.' Or else he made her leave her food and tiffin carrier behind and then remarked: 'We ought to have brought something more with us. You meet people in the train and you have to give them something to eat.'

Although something of a perfectionist in clothes, food, his demands for cleanliness and beauty in his environment, and in his dreams for reforming society on a grand scale, he was not always practical in helping his wife to manage his own household budget. One day a pedlar came to the house hawking 'kabuli shoes'. Let us have it,' he said, out of generous sympathy for the pedlar's humility and poverty.

'I never use those sandals,' Ganga Sharan said. 'I want covered shoes in winter.'

'But let us have them. They are more comfortable than our old shoes, Ganga Babu,' Jayaprakash insisted and bought a pair for each of them. Then four or five days later he demanded irascibly, 'Why do we keep so many pairs of shoes?', and that evening he gave five pairs away. With an 'I think we should give it to him', he gave away coats, sweaters, clothes of new design which he had temporarily taken a fancy for.

He was repeatedly in difficulties with his train fares and gave his wristwatch to ticket collectors or bearers, usually managing to get it back by borrowing from friends who met him on the platform at his destination. He became quite casual about this, although sometimes he had to cover up by pretending he had mislaid it in the house. Once for a holiday he agreed to go to Rajgir hot springs about sixty miles from Patna, and arranged to meet Prabhavati and Ganga Sharan on the station platform. They had to leave without him and wait half a day for him to appear. The Patna ticket office clerk had refused to take his watch as surety for a ticket. A vendor selling a tray of books on the platform gave him a rupee for a ticket to a junction where he thought he might catch up. From there he caught his connection without a ticket and was caught out by a collector who knew him. Finally he stepped from his carriage saying to the anxious Prabhavati and Sinha, 'First you release me before you receive me. Would you pay this gentleman my fare?'

The most excruciatingly embarrassing incident for Sinha arising from this 'never bothering for money' occurred in late February 1938, when the two men were bound for the Lahore Socialist Conference. Jayaprakash went away on party work having asked Sinha to 'manage their fares'. Sinha loathed soliciting donations but at last obtained the necessary money. The day before they were to go to Lahore, far to the north of Delhi, Jayaprakash asked for his half of the money and Ganga Sharan unsuspectingly gave it to him.

Next morning when Jayaprakash was in the bathroom Prabhavati came to Sinha and asked him surreptitiously: 'Did you give some money to J. P. yesterday? Was it your fares? Well, now he has none. He gave it all to a poor friend. I'm warning you beforehand. But don't let him know I told you.' She gave him the food she had prepared for the journey.

The two took a horse-drawn gig to the station. When they reached there Sinha attempted to pay the driver. Jayaprakash, secretly trying to keep the remaining money for their fares, hurriedly said: 'No, no, Prabha will pay him when he goes back there. We have an account with him. Ganga Babu, you go and buy the train tickets while I look for a seat.' He deliberately gave the impression that he was keeping his half of the money for their expenses on the way. The ticket office clerk gave Ganga Sharan one rupee in change.

They boarded the train. At one stage of the journey, P. C. Joshi, the general secretary of the Communist Party, got into their compartment and talked with them for hours about a host of political matters including demonstrations against forming any Indian Federation which included the maharajas unshorn of their feudal wealth and power. At about 3.00 p.m. when the train stopped at a station, Jayaprakash demanded, 'Can't you get us a cup of tea, Ganga Babu?'

Ganga Sharan called a hawker because he could not afford the pot of tea served with china cups and saucers from railway restaurants by the train attendants. This tea is not good, Ganga Babu,' Jayaprakash fastidiously complained. Ganga Babu defended himself by saying he had only four annas left and Jayaprakash dropped the subject.

Joshi returned to his travelling companions in his own compartment and after they had finished Prabhavati's food in the evening Jayaprakash began tentatively: 'Ganga Babu, suppose I tell you that I haven't got a *pice*. What will you do?'

Sinha pretended that he thought Jayaprakash was jesting. 'We still have twenty-nine hours to go and I have four annas. But if you tell me that, I'll get out at the next station and go back or I'll commit suicide!'

Then Jayaprakash finally confessed contritely: 'So-and-so came to me in great need and I gave my money to him.'

> 'You shouldn't have given him the money. He's a rogue.'
>
> 'I'm sorry. I didn't know.'

Thereupon, his conscience cleared, Jayaprakash turned in and went to sleep peacefully while Sinha lay awake worrying about how they were going to eat. In the morning while Jayaprakash awoke refreshed, Sinha was jaded from a restless night.

> 'What about breakfast, Ganga Babu?' he asked cheerfully as they pulled in at a major station.
>
> 'Well, I'll try to see what fruits I can buy.'
>
> 'No, no, let's have a good breakfast.'

He called the bearer. The previous evening a professor had joined them in the compartment and to Sinha's horror he invited this man also to breakfast as his guest.

'Bring me scrambled eggs. What kind will you take, Ganga Babu? No, don't be angry. Eat with me. Fried? And bring eggs for the professor, too.'

He plunged Sinha into the sharpest anxiety, knowing he might be able to stall off paying the bill for an hour or so, but there must come a time when the bearer would arrive back for the used plates to return them to the platform restaurant and would demand payment. Ganga could almost see himself back in the jail for debt when Dr. Ram Manohar Lohia and Mrs. Purnima Bannerjee appeared on the platform. Jayaprakash called them and after the usual greetings ordered breakfast for them also. Then he winked at Ganga. 'I think our worries are over now, Ganga Babu?'

> 'What worries?' Purnima demanded. 'Why are they over?'
>
> 'I can't tell you unless Ganga Babu permits me!'

At the Lahore Socialist Conference, Jayaprakash proposed for elections to the national executive for the following year a slate of candidates, a third of whom were communists. Namboodripad responded with his own list which gave the communists a majority. By a narrow margin only Jayaprakash's slate won. The threat of a takeover or split was narrowly averted but after this only a limited measure of unity remained on a personal level between Jayaprakash and Joshi. Next year his close friends Masani, Ashok Mehta, Achyut Patwardhan and Dr. Ram Manohar resigned from the national executive.

Jayaprakash declared to the Congress Socialist Party in December 1939 that 'the Communist Party of India stood as the sworn enemy of the Congress Socialist Party and of every other progressive organisation with which it had worked before.' He addressed a mimeographed 'War Circular No. 2' to all party units and members declaring that during the past weeks the Communists had left nothing undone to destroy unity with them. He regretted this as the policies of the Socialists and the Communists were really identical—to move the Congress to more action, to seize the chance of revolt now that they felt the old world collapsing.

At the Ramgarh Congress Conference in March 1940 the Communists published a new statement of policy entitled 'Proletarian Path', advocating a general strike as well as no-rent and no-tax actions culminating in armed revolutionary uprising to make use of the war crisis. Their changed policy parallelled Jayaprakash's calls to factory workers for which he was undergoing trial just at that time. Nevertheless at Ramgarh, the national executive of the Congress Socialist Party resolved to expel all members of the Communist Party of India from its ranks.

Resisting Imperialist War

In April 1939 Britain began to send Indian troops to Aden. The British Parliament passed legislation giving complete emergency power to the Viceroy and repudiating the Congress demand for immediate self-government. The Congress Working Committee resolved: The Committee... cannot possibly give any support to Great Britain for it would amount [to] an endorsement of the imperialistic policy which the Congress has always sought to end.'

Jayaprakash and his Congress Socialist sector committed themselves strongly to the anti-war faction. 'For our part,' Jayaprakash said, 'we do not wish to embarrass or create difficulties for the United Nations. But we cannot help it if our war of liberation comes in the way. If it does, it is not our fault, but theirs... After we are free we shall march shoulder to shoulder with them in an assault on all kinds of oppression and brutality—Nazi, imperialist, capitalist.'

Jayaprakash exhorted his public audiences of trades unionists and city crowds to take advantage of the war to stop British exploitation of Indian working people and overthrow the British rule. 'Stop paying your rent and revenue taxes,' he shouted. 'Establish your own government. Set up your own police and courts and boycott the British administration. Establish your right to rule yourselves by organising a general strike of all railwaymen, postal workers, defence workers and any other government employees.'

In Jamshedpur on 18 February 1940, on G. Town Maidan he repeated these ardent appeals to the Tata Iron and Steel Company workers, adding the direct appeal: 'Stop all cooperation with the conduct of the war against Germany. Overthrow the British administration. Tata's is the biggest steel works in Asia. You should stop it supplying steel for the prosecution of the war. I call upon you all to strike.'

Present in his audience by prearrangement was a police magistrate accompanied by the reporter of the Criminal

Investigations Department, who recorded the Hindi speech in shorthand. On the basis of their evidence Jayaprakash was arrested.

At Sevagram Ashram, on hearing of the arrest from Prabhavati, Gandhi wrote a statement of his reactions (dated 12 March 1940) which he forwarded to the Viceroy and published in his newspaper *Harijan* of 16 March:

> The arrest of Shri J. P. is unfortunate. He is no ordinary worker. He is an authority on Socialism. It may be said that what he does not know of western socialism nobody else in India does. He is a fine fighter. He has forsaken all for the sake of the deliverance of his country. His industry is tireless. His capacity for suffering is not to be excelled. I do not know what speech has brought him within the law. But if... the highly artificial sections of the Defence of India Act are to be utilised for catching inconvenient persons, then any person whom the authorities want can be easily brought within the law.... It is open to the Government to precipitate a crisis if they wish to.... During the first civil disobedience the Government had forced the issue by arresting the Ali brothers. Is this arrest a prearranged plan, or is it a blunder committed by an overzealous officer? If it is the latter, it should be set right.

The court assembled at Singhbhum on 15 March. Jayaprakash made himself liable to conviction by pleading guilty. He declined to cross-examine the witnesses but submitted a written statement stating that his actions did not constitute guilt because he was devoted to the victory of freedom and democracy for all of humanity and the charges framed against him of trying to impede the efficient prosecution of the war was only the fulfilment of a patriotic duty.

He expressed the hope that his incarceration would draw the attention of Indian political and labour leaders to the political backwardness of the labourers in Jamshedpur and at least give some momentum to the demand for payment of war bonuses by the profiteering capitalists. He insisted that his country found both Britain and Germany driven by the same selfish ends of conquest and domination, exploitation and oppression. Britain was fighting not to destroy Nazism, which it had fostered, but to curb a rival whose might could no longer be permitted to grow unchallenged, to maintain its world dominance, its imperial power and glory.

'I have no desire to help Germany or to see Germany victorious. I desire the victory neither of imperialism or Nazism.... In the present circumstances, however, India has no alternative but to fight and end British imperialism. Only in that manner can it contribute to the peace and prosperity of the world.

'A slave has no obligation to defend his slavery. His only obligation is to destroy his bondage.'

He gently thanked the deputy commissioner, S. W. Russell, for his courtesy and consideration. Also, he forwarded a copy of his statement of Gandhi who commented on 26 March 1940 on the injustice of punishing a patriot for openly saying what tens of thousands thought and thousands said, and commended Jayaprakash for his humanitarianism and lack of malice.

On 27 March Jayaprakash was sentenced to nine months rigorous imprisonment in Jamshedpur Jail. He had to follow events in the newspapers and pass many of his hours reading. He became even more deeply disenchanted with international communism as he considered how Stalin had beaten his nation into industrialisation, agricultural collectivisation, compulsory education, and had increasingly suppressed opposition culminating in the hideous public purge of the 1936 Moscow State Trials. Renowned communist political leaders whose writings he had 'eagerly devoured' and who were to him 'revolutionary heroes, who had made, as Lenin's closest lieutenants, the greatest revolution in history', had now been imprisoned and executed. Being a political prisoner himself he was passionately condemnatory.

He pursued the painful process of rethinking the Marxist-Leninist basis of his party which had been extinguished in South India because of the United Front. He realised that the nightmarish experience had taught them a great lesson in politics: that there could not be any unity with a communist party affiliated to the Kremlin or the Comintern.

He came to the conclusion that Soviet communism would not lead mankind to social revolution or to socialism, because the destruction of capitalism in Russia had not given people freedom, social justice or equality. It had merely given them a new class of bureaucratic rulers, overcentralisation of political and economic authority; in a word, total statism. Though still believing that violence was a necessary 'midwife of revolution', he resolved that 'in a society where it was possible for the people by democratic means to bring about social change it would be counter-revolutionary to resort to violence' and that 'socialism could not exist, nor be created, in the absence of democratic freedom.' The theory of the dictatorship of the proletariat he rejected as meaning in effect the dictatorship of a bureaucratic oligarchy.

His disillusionment with the Soviet Union and his indignation at the way Indian communists had duped him was so profound that it affected his political attitudes for the remainder of his life. He determined that the policy of his party must become democratic; it must emphasise the need for democracy for the poor, the need for social and economic decentralisation, and it must insist that the means of introducing social change and socialism to India were *morally consistent with the projected ends.* Freedom had become a passion for him and he was determined he would not see it compromised 'for bread, for power, for security, for prosperity, for the glory of the state or for anything else.'

He was released towards the end of December 1940. During his imprisonment France had surrendered on 22 June and the evacuation of British troops from Dunkirk had followed. The Congress members and Gandhi's constructive workers had begun individual satyagraha by reciting in public: 'It is wrong to help the British war effort with men or money. The only worthy effort is to resist all war with non-violent resistance.' They had, of course, been detained without trial. Jayaprakash had written unavailing letters to Gandhi urging him that the situation was ripe for a revolutionary attack on British power. Nehru had been arrested and sentenced to four years' rigorous imprisonment for his speeches. Protest meetings at British repression had landed fourteen thousand in jail.

Jayaprakash undertook a tour of India in hope of a socialist revolt. He set up secret organisations in Bihar, United Provinces and Gujarat as well as in Calcutta and Bombay. On 1 January 1941 he was, however, detained without trial in Bombay. The detention was carried out on behalf of the United Provinces government in Lucknow with the full knowledge of Sir Reginald Maxwell in New Delhi.

Jayaprakash was taken to the Arthur Road Prison in Bombay where two days later the prison doctor treated him for his sciatica. Lucknow agreed to meet all expenses and requested that he be transferred to its concentration camp at Deoli after his medical treatment. For the ensuing two months there was a flurry of telegrams and letters about him between the chief secretaries of the three governments. The Government of India directed Bombay to transfer him to the remote Rajput desert camp of tents and barbed wire, then telegrammed a month later that this transfer was rather drastic unless he showed signs of giving trouble. However he already had been transferred the day before and after two days of travelling under armed escort he arrived at Deoli Detention Camp on 23 April 1941.

He quickly found that the rules, conditions and amenities at Deoli were abominable, because the Government of India considered all prisoners there terrorists or communists and it was entitled to treat such people without humanity. His indignation was roused by the system of punishments and solitary confinement and the lack of trained medical attention. A climax was reached after S. Kumar, the 'medical officer', assaulted a ward boy in the 'hospital' and alleged that a patient, B. M. Rai, was merely feigning lunacy at the instigation of his fellow security prisoners. After being kept in solitary confinement for one week on a reduced diet, Rai had gone insane and he received the attention of the civil surgeon from the town of Ajmer only after he became uncontrollably violent.

On behalf of themselves and twenty other prisoners, Jayaprakash and a new friend, Mohanlal Gautam, applied to the camp superintendent, R. F. Craster, an Englishman, that the 'medical officer' be removed immediately, that the civil surgeon from Ajmer attend the camp twice a week, that the 'hospital' cases be transferred to a real hospital at Ajmer for adequate treatment, that those in solitary confinement be released immediately. Their demands were rejected; they issued a hunger strike notice which was scorned; they began their refusal to eat on 30 May (one source says 22 May). They took no food until 3 June when better medical care was promised and Jayaprakash and Gautam had written to their Socialist friends who publicised their grievances.

N. M. Joshi, a Liberal member of the Central Legislative Assembly, a supporter of Britain, having read the government communiques and press notices, was so appalled that he made it the concern of his conscience over the ensuing year to press Sir Reginald Maxwell and the Assembly into improving or disbanding Deoli Camp. He obtained permission to visit the camp for two days from 20 July and published his recommendations. Gandhi publicly called them 'over-moderate'. He commented that prisoners were fed bad and insufficient food and there was no warrant for keeping them in a place so far away from their homes and families.

Prabhavati went to visit Jayaprakash at Deoli Camp. After her visit Jayaprakash conceived the plan of sending a letter to his Socialist friends and hence requested permission for her to visit him a second time. He also wrote to her. Knowing that his letters were read by the prison authorities Jayaprakash got into the habit of cutting his letters in half and posting the two sections to her separately.

She was contacted by the police and returned fifteen days after her first visit. However the superintendent was highly suspicious of the purpose of a second visit and had warders closely watch their meeting as they sat together in an office room.

While they talked Jayaprakash surreptitiously drew out the letter from its place of concealment between his foot and sandal and slipped in into the upper fold of her sari. His action startled her and in their lack of understanding and deftness the paper rustled. The warder heard it and snatched the letter from Prabhavati. Jayaprakash was hustled back to his cell and she was taken almost immediately into the office of the superintendent, an Englishman.

The letter was lying on his desk; although she had not read it she recognised her husband's handwriting. The superintendent questioned her severely. Her inadequate knowledge of English put her at a disadvantage but she replied that she had not known of Jayaprakash's intention and she considered his act had been morally wrong. Avoidance of any such act had evidently been part of her undertaking when she had been allowed to make the visit. Nevertheless he refused to credit her words and denied her any future visits. He returned a deaf ear to her pleadings, for her promises not to carry messages were not credible to him.

In great distress she then went to the home of the assistant superintendent, an Irishman who spoke a little Hindustani and with whom she felt a greater rapport. He listened sympathetically to her account of what had happened and assured her that he would try to reverse the ruling. That night she stayed at the government dak bungalow and returned to the home of the assistant superintendent the next morning.

He asked for a little more time and she stayed another night. The following morning as she was seated in the sunshine on the verandah of the dak bungalow spinning cotton thread on her charkha which she always carried with her, four policemen armed with rifles converged on her and questioned her.

'What would you do if J. P. passed you another letter?' they demanded. 'Would you pass it on to the superintendent of the jail?'

She was surprised at their approach, but replied: 'No. I would not give it to you. I would tear it up. You could watch me.'

> 'You would deliver it, you mean.'
>
> 'No, I would not. That would be wrong. I would tear it up.'

She was told Jayaprakash would be punished by having his privilege to write and receive letters cancelled and neither she nor anyone else would be permitted to visit him.

Conditions at the camp continued to be as egregious as before and indignation mounted for two months against the forgetting of promises for improvement, until 1 October when the security prisoners of Camp I sent Craster a final memorandum repeating their earlier demands for adequate medical treatment, and adding new demands for abolition of different classifications of prisoners, grants and allowances to the families of the detenus (who had never been proven guilty of any crimes), the granting of personal allowances, an increase in their inadequate diet allowance, repatriation to a jail in their own province, release on parole in the event of serious illness in their families, association with three men who were 'isolated prisoners' and the abolition of solitary confinement. The Socialists and the Communists, including S. A. Dange and Muzaffar Ahmad, threatened they would launch a hunger strike if their demands were not met and a small socialist group threatened to fast unto death.

Sir Reginald Maxwell rejected their demands. He then arranged that the Government of India, in an attempt to avoid dishonour or having to improve Deoli, release a communique to the press on 16-17 October and a summary of the letters Jayaprakash had passed to Prabhavati, using them as grounds for an accusation of sedition against him which would destroy his credibility as a man honestly requesting human decencies.

In the letters, or the 'Deoli Thesis', entitled 'Support People's War', Jayaprakash had recommended plans to consolidate the Congress Socialist Party by winning over important members of the Revolutionary Socialist Party and the Hindustani Republican Socialist Association (designated by the government as terrorist organisations) and isolating the Communists who were now on Britain's side since Hitler's June 1941 invasion of the Soviet Union. He described Gandhi's individual satyagraha as a fraud and called upon Socialists to use violence to overthrow the British.

Until the humiliations and sufferings of Deoli's sadism, Jayaprakash had been, like many communists, an intellectual believer in revolution without actually having the slightest ability to hurt anyone or damage anything. It was a curious psychological contradiction in contrast to the simple, mindless brutality of the politically conservative trained soldier or the police towards the Indian satyagrahis in the 1930s. Furthermore, he had been until now ambivalent in his attitude because of Gandhi's strong influence. Now he recommended attacks on British installations and communications. On the very edge of accepting Gandhi's belief in moral means in political life, he was thrown back into the hands of the terrorists, who had beckoned him when he was an adolescent, because Britain had again used the methods of the barbarian.

In Madras, The *Hindu* refused to print the government release on the grounds that there was no proof of the authenticity of the letters nor the circumstances under which they had been written. On the other hand 77 M; *Statesman* was offensive to the point of making Jayaprakash write to his solicitor friend, P. P. Varma, who filed a suit on his behalf for defamation against the editor. As general secretary of the Congress Socialist Party, Purushottam Trikamdas issued a statement from Bombay that the publication of the communique was perhaps intended to create a misunderstanding, if not a scare, among the public regarding the party's activities.

A suggestion was raised that the documents seized from Jayaprakash had been carefully edited to misrepresent him, and the home secretary, R. Tottenham, quickly issued a press note that not only snippets thought convenient to the government but entire letters had been published. Jayaprakash was steadily becoming a national hero.

Gandhi then joined the public controversy by issuing a statement from Wardha in *Harijan*. Prabhavati, deeply angered by the imputations cast upon her, had sought his advice and yielded to his persuasion not to take any action as her statements would be suspect because of her involvement. Gandhi refuted the charges of deception heaped upon her and strongly criticised the government for its cruelty, demanding in the name of humanity that the demands of the Deoli prisoners be granted. He was however stung by the taunt that his policy of non-embarrassment, which had not awakened a mass upheaval that would interfere with the government apparatus, was a farce. He appealed to Jayaprakash 'for the sake of his noble wife to reconsider his philosophy and, if his reason can approve, to repudiate the method (of violence] as a lapse of sound reason and of loyalty [he] owes to the Congress.' In addition he did his best to persuade some of the newspapers to drop their demands for tightening restrictions on the Deoli prisoners.

Gandhi's criticism of British hypocrisy, in "From Sevagram", was read then, and for many years to come, by hundreds of Indian patriots as giving his own assent to the use of force although this had not been his conscious intention:

> Frankly, all nationalist forces, no matter by what name they are described, are at war with the Government. And according to the accepted canons of war, the method adopted by Jayaprakash Narayan is perfectly legitimate. Jayaprakash has had his training in America for seven long years and is a student of the methods adopted by western nations in their fight for freedom. To practise deception, to resort to secret methods, and even to plot and murder are all honourable and turn perpetrators into national heroes. Are not Clive and Warren Hastings British heroes?

On 22 October Jayaprakash and over two hundred prisoners began their hunger strike. Three days later Sir Reginald Maxwell rejected their demands. N. M. Joshi wrote to Sir Reginald that he intended to move for adjournment of the Legislative Assembly to discuss the grave discontent of the Deoli detenus. This motion was rejected without a division by the repressive legislators.

As the hunger strike continued public agitation increased. On 1 November, the Bihar Provincial Congress Socialist Party under Trikamdas's presidentship passed a resolution of 'deep concern' and two days later a public protest meeting was held in Calcutta. On 6 November, Sir Reginald, pressed by Joshi for information, issued a smooth assurance: 'The Government took every possible step to persuade the security prisoners not to embark on a hunger strike and informed them that their demands were being carefully considered and that any attempt to force the issue on their part would, etc.' Jayaprakash, after ten days of hunger strike, wrote to Gandhi requesting him to send Rajendra Prasad or Pant to make an on-the-spot enquiry into camp conditions. Pressure mounted throughout India.

On the sixteenth day one of the prisoners, J. Chatterjee, was so ill that he was released and given treatment in hospital, and Jayaprakash was so weak that he was forced to eat some food. Joshi arrived and appealed to the camp committees of the three camps to call off the strike unconditionally. The men told him they had prevented Craster's intention to forcibly feed them by threatening combined resistance and he assured them that efforts were being made for their repatriation to their own states. The communists decided to give up their hunger strike, but, not trusting government promises, Jayaprakash continued his, although he was very weak and had caught influenza. For his intransigence he was punished by being put into solitary confinement.

Either because the dissidents had been crushed or because Jayaprakash had refused to capitulate, Sir Reginald resumed his interrupted consultations with the provincial governments about repatriation. Gandhi's anxious request to the government was granted: his secretary (for twenty-four years) Mahadev Desai was granted permission to interview Jayaprakash. In the meantime Gandhi wrote to Jayaprakash begging him to give up his strike even if the Government of India accepted only his demand for repatriation. Jayaprakash adamantly refused in a telegram which explained his feelings and reasons. Mahadev Desai finally persuaded him to give in, after he had been almost completely without food for thirty-one days. The Government of India announced its decision to repatriate security prisoners in Deoli Camp just over a fortnight later, on 9 December.

When Jayaprakash, now a great national hero, recovered his strength sufficiently he was transferred in early 1942 to Hazaribagh Prison, situated in the jungle-clad mountain region in the southern part of Bihar state. There to greet him was Ganga Sharan Sinha, also detained without trial.

Again the time crept by in dreary physical routine and intense intellectual stimulation while beyond his cell walls, mass murderers stalked the earth. On 7 December 1941 Japan attacked Pearl Harbour, Manila, Hong Kong and Malaya. By May 1942 Burma had been captured, Japan controlled the Bay of Bengal, and a union with the forces of Rommel in Libya seemed possible. India was gravely threatened. The British had shown themselves incapable of successfully defending their Empire, but would not arm Indians. British refugees from Singapore, Penang and Burma were cared for and transported as well as possible, but the hundreds of thousands of Indian refugees were deserted by the British civil and military authorities. As the famished survivors reached India and related their horrible stories of racial discrimination, a great wave of resentment swept the country. Gandhi drafted a resolution calling on Britain to grant India independence. Failure to comply would be met by another campaign of non-violence. The resolution was then submitted to a meeting of the All India Congress Committee of over two hundred members which met in Bombay on 7 August 1942. Although Jayaprakash was still in Hazaribagh Prison, Prabhavati was one of the members present. Gandhi spoke with fire and bitterness: This is open rebellion. Here is a mantra "Do or Die". We shall either free India or die in the attempt.' An American press correspondent coined the phrase, 'Quit India' movement, a term which caught on throughout the world.

In the ensuing months, hundreds of thousands of his admirers and followers believed he had summoned every man to revolt in whatever way he chose, 'making no distinction between violent and non-violent acts'.

Some time after midnight on 8 August 1942, Gandhi and the other delegates to the All India Congress Committee went home, to be awakened before sunrise by the police. Gandhi, Mrs Naidu, Mira Behen, Mahadev Desai and Pyarelal Nayar were imprisoned in the Aga Khan Palace at Yeravda.

As captain of the Bihar Women's Congress Brigade, Prabhavati also attended the meeting, but escaped the police round-up by catching a train leaving Bombay. After a change of trains at night at Mughal Sarai she had the feeling that she was being observed and followed and might be assaulted. She returned without incident however to her Married Women's Spinning Centre in the Kadam Kuan area of Patna. But by this time the Bihar government and police had received instructions about her, and she was arrested shortly after her arrival. She was imprisoned without trial in Darbhanga Jail.

As soon as it became known that Gandhi had been arrested on 9 August 1942, nationwide protests began. Protest meetings were met with police beatings and shootings and arrests. Jayaprakash's socialists engaged in an outburst of sabotage, much against Gandhi's wishes. In an atmosphere of external threat men took to extremes. Telegraph wires were cut, railway lines pulled out, railway stations, post offices and aerodrome installations were burned. In the first three weeks 1,088 persons were arrested. In Delhi alone on 11 and 12 August, the police fired forty-seven times. In United Provinces 76 were killed and 114 injured; in the Central Provinces 64 were reported dead and 102 wounded.

By the end of August police-state methods, used by a nation fighting fascism for democracy, had crushed the Indian 'rebellion'— 1,028 Indians had been killed, 3,215 seriously injured and at least 10,000 had been jailed. The Congress funds were seized and it was outlawed for the next three years.

A Price Upon His Head

Jayaprakash contributed to India's independence movement one personal quality which was invaluable to the Congress. Throughout his life, he had an immoderate, larger-than-human aspect to his thinking; once he took up an idea he pursued it with relentless passion. Of this unbending intellectual characteristic he was to write later, when he had time for introspection in jail:

> Perhaps I take things too seriously: I still remember how Jawaharlalji had taunted me at Tripuri when I had expressed my indignation that in the very midst of a crisis some friends had to talk about seeing the Marble Rocks. That was foolish of me, of course. How can life be made so narrow and restricted? Perhaps my fundamentally socialist way of looking at things makes me so completely possessed with political issues of the moment. ("Inside Lahore Fort," 67)

This trait combined with his lucidity and uncanny perceptiveness about politics drew people to him.

Jail did nothing to dampen his passion for freedom or his untiring energy in liberty's pursuit, or to weaken his resolution with feelings of depression or failure. He met every doubt expressed to him with absolute confidence in his answers. The 1935 Constitution, he told them positively, had been 'a wretched fraud', and all Nehru's 'futile parliamentarianism' had achieved was a greater slavery than before. India had been pitchforked into war and not one vestige of autonomy was now left to the provincial legislatures. The Act was dead and there was no going back to it. It would be the height of political imbecility to expect Congress to resuscitate that fraud.

He sternly attacked the faith and hope Congressmen placed in Nehru's being able to influence world opinion and arrange a compromise with the British which would culminate in freedom. Nehru and other Congress leaders had been released from jail immediately prior to the Japanese attack on Pearl Harbour. But in Jayaprakash's opinion India could not live at peace again with those who had perpetrated unspeakable indignities and bestial cruelties upon her.

He wrote of Jawaharlal:

> Pandit Nehru released from the jail might make statements which American correspondents might lap up with avidity but there would be no strength behind those statements, despite the beauty and grace of their expression. Nehru imprisoned, is a greater problem for the Roosevelts and Churchills than Nehru proliferating nobly worded statements and casting his spell over the envoys of great nations. (Ibid.)

Against Nehru's attempts to reach a reconciliation with the British he pitted his own will to fight, and like many of history's great politicians much of his status sprang from his assurance that his calls to the little people to sacrifice themselves and their families would be answered.

Sir Stafford Cripps had been the devil's advocate, he said. The British offer of no power during the war and a fraudulent offer of it at its end had been rightly rejected by the Congress. Rajagopalachari and his Congress friends who had supported Britain in the war were saboteurs of the freedom movement. Towards the Muslim League he was unbending in his contemptuous condemnation of its failure to even once participate in the freedom struggle, of its being in league with Britain, and of its hope to gain Pakistan without effort. Mr. Jinnah, he declared, was a deliberate traitor to his country, a conceited historical fool for all his Fuhrerian attitudes.

He was exhilarated to read the newspaper reports of Gandhi's 'Do-or-Die' mantra because he hoped that now the country would rise in spontaneous revolt, move out of the way the weaklings and cowards and traitors who had dared to raise their voices against struggle, and march on to liberty. But he expected nothing from satyagraha. As he saw it, Gandhi had called for total refusal to cooperate with British rule since Jayaprakash had been a schoolboy. It was no surprise to him therefore to hear of the 9 August arrests in Bombay, although he considered them a cowardly trampling upon freedom by imperialist jackboots.

Reading of the uprisings, ten of the detenus began plotting a jail break and they rehearsed it several times. The planner seems to have been Jayaprakash's cellmate, Dr. Mukherjee. They were relying upon the agility of Jogendra Shukla. One of the prisoners whom Jayaprakash unsuccessfully tried to persuade to join the group was his tall, angular Patna friend, A. P. Sinha.

Sinha was five years his junior and had joined the Congress at the age of ten. In Hazaribagh Jail he had been a keen reader of Jayaprakash's summary and notes on Marx's *Das Kapital.*

'I cannot accept your method, J. P.,' he replied in answer to his encouragement to escape. 'My passion to be free possesses me but I believe in non-violence.'

'But that controversy is meaningless. Every fighter for freedom is free to choose his own method.'

'Not Congressmen.'

'Yes, Congressmen. If there is violence in India the British government itself is responsible for it. Ninety-nine per cent of the murders committed in India are the acts of the British fascists and hooligans and not more than one per cent are of an infuriated and sorely tried people. You know what the home secretary to the Government of India, Sir Richard Tottenham, has said. He boasted to American correspondents that he had bought enough sandalwood to bum the remains of Gandhi.'

'I am a devout Hindu, J. P. I cannot take life.'

'I will not take the life of any person. But without harming persons I can burn installations and disrupt communications. Is it violence to destroy the property of the British thugs and cut-throats who let loose a hell over the heads of our people?'

'J. P., to use violence will compromise Gandhi's position.'

'No, Gandhi's adherence to non-violence is so complete, his position in respect to it so clear, that not a hundred thousand

Churchills or Colonel Amerys will be able to compromise him with all their imperialist lies. Whatever we do we can't prevent British statesmen whether Tory or Labour from telling lies. Lies are one of the central pillars of the British Empire.'

'But, J. P., to us Gandhians the secrecy that you will have to indulge in to do acts of sabotage cannot be a foundation on which to build a mass movement. You are forever in the dark. The millions of people can only be persuaded to rise up if you use the open frankness of non-violence.'

'Have the British been open? Were they frank when Gandhi returned from the Round Table Conference? Were we open when we kept alive the illegal Congress organisations in the thirties? What has just happened on 9 August after Gandhiji's arrest? The Congressmen who had escaped the police hastily met in Bombay to by the foundations of the illegal organisations that are functioning now. If they don't hide out to prepare the detailed programme of the national struggle, how can there be any struggle? Are the people to bow their heads whenever the British arrest the leaders? Are they being disloyal to the Congress to struggle?'

Without a chance they could avail of to escape as August wore on, the reports which reached them, were both inspiring and depressing. The Congress had gone underground. There was a mass upsurge. There were police firings.

Sinha finally pleaded, 'Let me help to cover your getaway. You have got the passion that can make people's spirits soar up. You can inspire them to self-sacrifices, to accept sufferings. You are a great national leader.'

Mukherjee and Shukla conspired urgently to get him out, believing that 'his courage would cast a spell on all who came near him', his oratory would move crowds to action, and that his acts of bravery and his sufferings in Deoli were essential to a new mass movement arising out of the persistence and fortitude of small groups of people throughout India. There could never perhaps be a tight organisation to hold the movement together, but it depended on constant inspiration, a constant upsurge of passion that men of Jayaprakash's compelling personality and youthful fire could inspire.

Feeling it was too risky to approach any of their jailors for help and unwilling to take the time necessary to make contact with comrades outside they kept their plans within the closed circle of ten men. They chose that comer of the jail courtyard which was darkest at night and timed the march of the guard on duty who passed by this spot every eight minutes. As for scaling the twenty-foot wall, A. P. Sinha recollects that, 'Jogendra Shukla was like a monkey. He could go up and down the wall with ease. He used to show us every day. He did it for practice.' How often or whether Shukla actually tried the ascent in their rehearsals could not be verified but after thirty years his strength and dynamism had left this impression upon his friends.

On the night of 8 November 1942 their planning was finally and breathlessly put into effect. Diwali was being celebrated throughout the country. The Hindu warders had been allowed to go off-duty to celebrate it, and throughout the jail there was a relaxed, festive atmosphere, with some of the prisoners and Muslim warders enjoying a special feast. Countless tiny wicks burned in earthenware saucers containing oil. In the cells of the plotters six beds were arranged so that the tiny lights shining through the mosquito nets seemed to reveal the contours of sleeping men; for in the end it had been deckled that only six could make the attempt. Four men had to make the sacrifice of staying behind to regale the guards with funny stories, to lull their suspicions with gifts of cigarettes, and to deceive those prisoners whom they suspected would give them away to the warders. The warder on duty was deliberately engaged in conversation.

At 10.00 p.m., Jogendra Shukla, Ramanandan Misra, Suraj Narain Singh, Shaligram Singh, Gulab Chand Gupta and Jayaprakash stealthily moved into the courtyard on bare feet. They hurriedly set a table against the wall and Shukla knelt upon it. They tied a knotted rope of dhotis around Suraj Narain Singh's waist. Either Singh or Gupta stood upon Shukla's back, and Suraj Narain Singh climbed upon his shoulders, swayed unsteadily and managed to grasp the top of the wall and draw himself up. Next, while his friends inside clung to the knotted dhotis he let himself down the other side of the wall, his bare toes finding a foothold in the cloth. As soon as he reached the ground he drew the line tight to allow his friends to ascend from their side. In six minutes the six men were free. At the approach of the sentry their friend inside had no time to throw them the bundle of shoes, warm clothing and money that they had prepared.

The six untied the dhotis, draped them about their shoulders, and fled into the darkness. They reached the cover of the prickly scrub of the Hazaribagh-Monghyr hill tract and they kept on running until about an hour before daybreak.

After six hours of flight the escapees felt exhausted and famished and their feet were scratched and bruised. They stopped and kindled a small fire in a thicket and slept fitfully. Awaking, they massaged their feet and tied strips of dhoti around them as protection against the stone-strewn undergrowth. Next they searched their pockets for money, finding to their horror nothing at first and then Misra discovered a one-hundred-rupee note folded small. This was little better than before because in this jungle area the few people of the remote villages earned less than one rupees a day and would be most suspicious of them even if they were able to find change.

They moved on again urgently, subdued in spirits, and kept up the best pace they could until they reached a rare hot spring that bubbled into a clear, rocky pool shaded by a broad-leafed mango tree. There, as they bathed their swollen, bleeding feet, a more leisurely search turned up a four-anna piece, and taking this Shukla went to a nearby village where he bought crushed rice and salt. They ate it raw.

For the remainder of the day they moved onwards as rapidly as their clumsily bound feet allowed over twisted roots, prickles and outcrops of grey black granite. They were awkward and painfully slow getting through gullies which were thick with thorny bushes or bamboo clumps. They guessed that by now the pursuit must have begun.

For each man in Hazaribagh Jail the cells were equipped with two earthenware pots glazed with coal tar which the *bhangi* (scavenger) removed twice daily at 6.00 a.m and 6.00 p.m. To delay the discovery of the escape Mukherjee managed to pass water and stools in both his own and Jayaprakash's pots so that the arrival of the cleaner passed off without the alarm being sounded. Unfortunately, however, later in the morning an order of the central government concerning Jayaprakash reached the Punjabi superintendent of the jail, Colonel Nath, who sent warders to bring him into his office. Jayaprakash not being found the alarm was sounded. Nath searched frantically but unsuccessfully and was promptly suspended from his position by the governor of Bihar state. Nath contacted K. S. V. Raman, the district commissioner, who posted police and soldiers in the jungle as fast as he could transport them.

Meanwhile, by the evening Jayaprakash was in such pain in his back and legs that he could no longer walk. He thought it was sciatica although in later years doctors suggested to him that he had suffered some spinal injury that might have been set right in its early stages by surgery. Again the six lit a small fire and clustered together for warmth in the cold winter night. Around them hovered the black shapes of craggy ranges two thousand feet high and inhabited by Bengal tigers and dangerous black bears. Awake they constantly glanced around them, fearful of resting too long in case of being surprised, listening always for sounds of pursuit behind the bamboo clumps, in the valleys, in the thickets they had to pass.

In the morning they carried Jayaprakash, two at a time. Here and there they came across villagers grazing cattle in the scrubby jungle and they were able to find a bullock cart owner. They tried to hire his cart to carry Jayaprakash but the driver demanded an advance payment of three rupees. Sooner than offer the currency they had, they proposed he take Jayaprakash's watch but he refused. Thereafter, whenever they approached a village Jayaprakash had to walk to avoid attracting unwanted attention, and when they were hidden again in the scrub, was carried. Though they were to travel hundreds of miles on foot, eating trashy food from isolated villages, these three days were their leanest, when all they had was four annas worth of crushed rice and salt.

On the third night they crossed from Hazaribagh into Gaya district and slept under some low bushes at the foot of a sloping black rock face, which today is pointed out to visitors as 'J. P.'s rock.' From here Jayaprakash limped into the village of Sokhodeora to the mud-walled home of friends of a local Congressman whom he knew to be in jail. Here he was eagerly received, given food, money, clothing, and sandals and shoes.

Then the group moved along the verge of the range within the jungle but only a short distance from the villages of the plain so that they could get drinking water from a deserted well or buy food from an unfrequented shop. At no time did they feel they could relax their vigilance, for the villagers they met were naturally curious about the strangers in their normally quiet world. It was a natural religious duty to enquire into the caste or sub-caste of a stranger at one of their wells in case of pollution.

Jayaprakash's sympathy for the lowest caste and outcasts was greatly deepened during this flight as the latter were too humble to try to interfere with the escapees and too simple and honest to suspect them of being hunted men. He later returned in 1957 to construct an ashram devoted to village development near Sokhodeora.

One night after dark they bought food from a tiny village shop by lantern light and asked to be allowed to sleep the night on the earthen floor. They usually avoided staying in villages where they might easily be betrayed and caught, but it was raining and bitterly cold and they needed shelter. The shopkeeper was so terrified of their being dacoits that he agreed to let them stay, while for their part they were so apprehensive of being denounced to the police that they slept badly and retreated to the jungle well before dawn.

Soon after this they hid for three days in the offices of Ramanandan Misra's father-in-law, a well-to-do landlord in Gaya district through which they were moving.

Now within reach of the roads and the train line at Nawada the six men separated. Jayaprakash and Ramanandan Misra hid under a heap of jute bags on a bullock cart, provided for them by Misra's father-in-law. The others walked and then caught the train. In Gaya township Jayaprakash's bullock cart driver was interrogated while his passengers lay still, listening apprehensively and guarding against an inadvertent sneeze. The town was on the alert both because British troops were stationed there and because of the search for the escapees. A reward of five thousand rupees had been offered by the authorities for Jayaprakash's capture, dead or alive. This reward was subsequently raised to ten thousand, and the other five men had five thousand rupees each on their heads. From Gaya where he was hidden and helped by a prominent landlord, Bani Bihari Prasad Bhup, Jayaprakash planned to travel to Banaras. A third-class rail ticket was bought for him and he reached the station in a horse-drawn carriage. His week's growth of beard helped to alter the contours of his face, but he also pretended to be ill and kept a cloth to his mouth to improve his disguise. He got into the hopelessly crowded third-class compartment, his hopes of getting away rising higher as the time of departure approached.

Despite his worries he reached Banaras without being discovered. Under cover of the evening light he walked cautiously from the railway station to Banaras Hindu University where he was perfectly confident of being able to stay with friends. He knocked at the door of a Chemistry professor who had, or made it appear that he had, difficulty in recognising Jayaprakash, half-bearded and in the rags of a village farmer. He stammered ashamedly that he could not hide Jayaprakash in his house because he had guests staying with him who might become suspicious. Jayaprakash did not believe his excuses but turned away in disgust and loneliness after the fruitless whispered conversation.

Another Banaras University teacher hid him that night. Jayaprakash did not speak of this incident until more than ten years later and even then he would not reveal names.

While he sheltered here, near the red towers and lawns of the university and amidst the comings and goings of young students, he wrote to Achyut Patwardhan and other fellow Congress Socialist Party members at the parry's underground headquarters in Bombay. They sent him money, addresses in New Delhi, and suggested he could have a tremendous effect upon the independence struggle if he did propaganda work from hiding, as he had done during the thirties.

Risking another train journey he reached Delhi undetected where other friends housed him and the Sethia family, who were jute merchants, gave him money for the illegal printing of his anti-British appeals. In early December under the title The *Freedom Struggle Front,* he issued a review of events and a call to expand the organisation of a secret wing of the Congress, pledged to avoid killing but devoted to disrupting British rule by setting up their' own self-governing village authorities. In a general sense he continued to maintain that violence was the handmaiden of revolution.

His own district and adjoining areas of Bihar had overthrown the British institutions and set up their own *panchayats* (local councils) in August 1942. In Balia district in the United Provinces, in Midnapur in Bengal, in Satara in Bombay, the British administration had been put out of action and nationalists had organised education and welfare work, settled disputes in their own councils, punished 'offenders' and 'traitors', raised taxes and levied fines, ordered arrests of local officials and civil servants, and disarmed the police. For their loyalty to Jayaprakash the Bihar villagers had borne the brunt of the British repression in India. The RAF machine-gunned their villages from the air and police on foot burned and looted homes.

The face of India was still plastered with old and new slogans in paint, in chalk, in betel juice; the millions of oppressed calling on the British to quit, and Jayaprakash worked night and day to fan these flames of resistance into open revolution and to reorganise enough Congress workers to direct his revolt. Jayaprakash called on students to lead the struggle:

> We have to publish and distribute our literature, maintain our contacts and communications; we have to raise and to train a militia and bands of technical workers for sabotage... and we have to continue our present clashes and skirmishes with the enemy. (Tendulkar, Jayaprakash Narayan, 74)

In January 1943 he issued a new programme of action to be launched from the 26th, 'Independence Day'. Again the tone was that of a party general secretary, lacking the fire of Gandhi's call to 'Do or Die'. At the end of February he issued the first of his three famous letters to all fighters for freedom, arguing that the open rebellion envisaged by their incomparable leader Mahatma Gandhi had failed because there was no efficient organisation and after the first phase of the rising was over there had been no further programme put before the people. Most importantly he argued that the views of the Working Committee and the All India Congress Committee about non-violence were different from those of Gandhi, and Congressmen were acting loyally in forming guerilla bands. 'I have no hesitation in admitting that non-violence of the brave, if practised on a sufficiently large scale, would make violence unnecessary, but where such non-violence is absent, I should not allow cowardice, clothed in shastric subtleties, to block the development of this revolution and lead to its failure.' He insisted that skirmishes, frontier clashes, patrolling must go on while they all prepared for 'the last phase of the revolution'. The letter was covertly handed about in the barracks of the United States Army in India, appealing to the men not to cooperate with 'the British who are waging a fascist war against us'. Whoever among you may become a prisoner of war will consider it his duty to escape from the enemy's prison as soon as he has an opportunity.' He requested them not to believe the British statements about him but to consider him an escaped prisoner of war. The government communiques about him regarded him as a dangerous criminal.

With the other Congress leaders behind prison walls, Jayaprakash was now India's greatest public figure, her foremost hero, acknowledged to be the leader of the Independence Movement even by the government in its propaganda pamphlet *Congress Responsibilities for Disturbances.* The pamphlet attempted to undermine the Congress by playing Congressmen off one against the other and to persuade the world that all the violence of 1942 had been the fault of discreditable Congressmen.

Gandhi published a long counter-attack against the government's 'filthy charges'.

If the Government were sincere they would have welcomed the offer of help made by the Congress. Congressmen who had been fighting for India's liberty for over half a century would have flocked to the Allied banner as one man for the defence of India's freedom newly won. But the Government did not wish to treat India as an equal partner and ally. They put out of action those who made this demand. Some of them are even being hounded as if they were dangerous criminals. I have in mind Shri Jayaprakash Narayan and others like him... I have taken Shri Jayaprakash Narayan purposely as my illustration because, as he very rightly says, he differs from me on several fundamentals. But my differences, great as they are, do not blind me to his indomitable courage and his sacrifice of all that a man holds dear for the love of his country. I have read his manifesto which is given as an appendix to the indictment. Though I cannot subscribe to some of the views expressed therein, it breathes nothing but burning patriotism and his impatience of foreign domination. It is a virtue of which any country would be proud. (Ibid., 74-5)

On 1 November 1943 Jayaprakash issued his second letter to all freedom fighters admitting that another uprising of the people had not materialised but calling on them to revive the struggle. Although the leaders were in jail they must keep on fighting. Most of the sixteen-page pamphlet dealt with whether the Congress had originated the present struggle and why it was such a folly that some Congressmen in their depression were seeking their way back to constitutionalism. To those 'who had lost all hope of victory', who 'yearn for the freedom of parliamentary play-acting,' he declared: 'it is inconceivable to me how Congressmen can ever offer the palm to men who have murdered and pillaged and burnt and raped and tortured tender boys in the stillness of prison cells.' People had been butchered for five years, but Allied plans for the post-War world pictured the same old world of slavery, of privilege, class and national tyranny, and capitalist rivalry which had caused the two businessmen for being unwilling to donate funds to the Congress with which a rising on a larger scale could be organised and directed.

In 1943 inefficient and corrupt British rule in Bengal contributed to and failed to alleviate a famine in which, accounts vary, one and a half to three and a half million people starved to death and four and a half million suffered grievously. Jayaprakash called upon Congress guerilla fighters to forcibly seize grain from government depots and distribute it in rural areas. He hoped that the arousal of the starving to direct action could 'convert the country into a seething cauldron in which the Empire can soon be boiled to death'. His guiding star, he wrote, was 'Do or Die'.

But he was not of a nature nor in the mood to conceal himself indefinitely in Delhi and content himself with issuing manifestos. Accompanied by Suraj Narain Singh, he moved northwards towards India's mountain frontiers, avoiding the army units about Delhi as they travelled. They did propaganda work in Bihar sleeping on river banks, behind bushes, under trees, always aware that they were being followed. Always when someone gave them refuge in their house, the police raided the home within a week or fortnight of their leaving it, commonly arresting the householder.

Hoping for a reward equivalent to thirty years of wages, potential informers kept an eye open for him while the police and army combed India. Many released Congressmen or known Congress supporters were investigated or harassed. A great national hero, legends of Jayaprakash grew as police activity spread from one end of India to the other. He led attacks on post offices and railways and cut telegraph lines, taught youths to make and use bombs and published detailed books on guerilla war tactics. It was only natural that the British pictured a killer where there was simply an impassioned social thinker and freedom fighter.

Interrogations at Lahore Fort

From Bihar, under police pressure, Suraj Narain Singh and Jayaprakash travelled by rail, then by elephant and boat into the deodar-forested mountains of Nepal. There they made contact with other revolutionary and terrorist groups and became members of Azad Dasta, a guerilla army of liberation. Daily other freedom fighters from Bihar trickled in to join the fight

The army was trained by three officers who had deserted the British army, one of whom was in charge of the group that Jayaprakash joined. 'But our weapons were all old and in bad condition,' recounted Jayaprakash later. The Government of India soon brought pressure to bear upon the Rana of Nepal and his regime to assist in the hunting and capture of Jayaprakash after he set up a clandestine radio station and made broadcasts into India. The Nepalese police combed mountains and jungles, finally capturing him at gunpoint.

The police party, holding him prisoner, began its return to the frontier to hand him over to British India. As they travelled,

Jayaprakash managed to get word to a boy, an Azad Dasta volunteer not known to the Napalese police, who ran with the news of the capture back to the guerilla camp. They made their counter-attack four nights later after shadowing the Nepalese party.

Evening had fallen. Jayaprakash and five other prisoners with him were being held for the night on the verandah of the district commissioner's house. They had given up all hope of rescue after the four hard days of marching and had gone to bed feeling rather dispirited.

According to Jayaprakash's account of the night's happenings, fourteen of the policemen were sleeping, having stacked their rifles in an upright triangle, and only two had been left on guard. The guerillas silently set fire to some haystacks in the courtyard, whereupon the two sentries aroused some of the others and sent them to investigate what was happening. The guerillas shot the two armed sentries, killing one and wounding the other, and bringing Jayaprakash within the shadow of the gallows.

Jayaprakash leaped from his bed and leading his five friends hastily sprinted for the stacked rifles. A shot hit a bell hanging in the house setting off an uncanny ringing. Grabbing the rifles the prisoners tried to find ammunition for themselves but this had been carefully locked away and they were too flustered to spend time breaking into the house. Then they took to the jungles.

Ram Manohar Lohia was the last to run and narrowly escaped being hit by bullets as the Nepalese police began to regain charge of the fray. Lohia objected feelingly that no one seemed to care about his safety, to which Jayaprakash remembers retorting shortly, 'It's every man for himself.'

They raced through the night, crossing into India before dawn and making their way back through Bihar which was familiar to Jayaprakash. Shunning the trains as now being altogether too risky, they went across country on foot until they were stopped by the Ganges. They went up and down the banks until they found a village punter.

'Would you take us across the Ganga?' Jayaprakash asked.

He was shifty, uneasy, reluctant. 'Okay,' he agreed after some argument. 'But I can't go just now. Not until my mother has pounded some *chiuda* (flattened rice) for me to eat on the way.'

'We'll buy you food,' Jayaprakash promised urgently. 'Let's start now.'

'No,' he was obstinate, 'I cannot go until my food is prepared.'

Suddenly there was no hope of keeping their presence a secret. Other villagers came up and crowded around the group, listening intently to their argument.

They think we are dacoits,' Jayaprakash whispered to Lohia.

'I think we had better get out of here. We'll have to take the risk and crawl across the railway bridge.'

They walked away from the village unhurriedly so as not to arouse any further suspicions, but they had not gone far when eight sturdy men, armed with lathis, came running in pursuit of them. Now they were faced with the bitter irony of possibly being harmed by uncomprehending fellow Indians.

Suraj Narain Singh, who had helped himself to the revolver of the Nepalese guard who had been killed, now turned, panting, upon their pursuers. He stopped suddenly. He shouted nervously: 'Look, we are fighting for the freedom of our country and yours. Is this the way for you to act towards patriots? Well, if you don't turn back and leave us alone, I'll shoot as many of you as I can.'

The villagers retreated hastily.

Days later Jayaprakash returned to Delhi, having shaved his beard at a friend's house, having adopted European clothes and a Punjabi name, 'Mehta', and having gone by bullock cart to Bhagalpur and by train to Calcutta.

In the midst of a widespread manhunt he continued his underground activities until, in a perhaps inevitable reaction against a year of tension, he began to be careless.

Having had a servant, or one of his friends, buy him a rail ticket from the station, he boarded the sleeper train in Delhi on 16 September, intending to travel to Rawalpindi and thence to Peshawar in the Punjab to join Khan Abdul Ghaffar Khan. His attempt was to arouse the Pathan tribesmen of the Peshawar-Khyber Pass area against British rule. This ambitious plan was never to be effected.

Jayaprakash was mildly surprised, he recalls, to find the pseudonym that he had currently been using, written onto the reservation slip which was inserted in the slot on the outside of his compartment door. With his name was that of a Major Khan and family, people who never came to share the four-berth coupe with him. With trains so crowded this surprised him, but he quickly put aside his suspicions.

When the train halted late in the evening he got out to stretch his legs and walked along the platform with his hat pulled down to hide the upper part of his face.

There was a man on the platform whose eyes seemed to burn into me. I should have broken the trip then, but I dismissed the strange feeling and got back on the train,' he recalled.

He spent the night sleeping on the upper bunk, which was Major Khan's, awoke in the morning, rolled up and fastened his bed roll and opened his door to ask for a cup of tea as the train stopped at Lahore station. There were two Indians and an Englishman just outside his door looking at the reservation slip. He called a waiter for his tea, shut his door and completed dressing himself. Some moments later there was a knock on his door. A waiter would have announced that he had brought tea, so assuming someone was searching for an unoccupied seat, he called out: 'Come in. I'm alone. There are seats free here.'

The Englishman came in. To Jayaprakash's astonishment he demanded: 'May I see your ticket please?' Unknown to Jayaprakash he was faced with Lahore's senior superintendent of police.

'Are you a railway official?' Jayaprakash asked.

'No, but I'd like to see your ticket. Are you Jayaprakash Narayan?'

'Certainly not. I don't know what you're talking about. My name is Mehraj Mehta.'

'I don't believe that.'

'I assure you.. '

'All right. We'll search your things and soon find something.'

Seeing Jayaprakash's bedding roll on the top bunk and his clothing on the bottom one, the superintendent was suddenly suspicious that he might have caught more than one rebel.

'Where is the other man?'

'What other man?'

The man who slept on the top berth. That isn't your berth. The bottom bunk is reserved for you.'

'I'm alone as I told you. And my name is Mehraj Mehta.'

Their voices began to rise, until after the most violent shouting of accusations and protestations the superintendent declared: 'Look here! This is not Nepal! You'll have no one making your rescue here. This is the Punjab! I have orders to shoot, so make no mistake. If there's the slightest suspicious move on your part I'll fire. Have you finished dressing?'

The two Sikh plainclothes policemen who had accompanied him came into the compartment and helped handcuff the struggling prisoner. The train was allowed to leave Lahore to avoid crowds to whom Jayaprakash might appeal to help. Outside the city he was taken off the train and bundled into a police car, with an armed Sikh on either side of him. The legend about him had grown so great that the superintendent himself was obviously afraid of him, for he kept warning him not to try to escape. The car was driven to the enormous Fort in Lahore. As they drove inside the walls the superintendent added: 'Don't try to escape. We have sixteen hundred armed police stationed here. This is not Nepal. You won't get away with any escape here. So don't try anything.'

He was taken into a cell fifteen feet by twelve feet The handcuffs were removed, the door locked, and he was kept here in solitary confinement for a month, during which time he neither left the cell nor had any papers or books to read. The guards had orders not to speak to him and they pushed his food in through an opening under a thick iron bar. His captors held him in great awe. Subsequently he was brought out from the cell and teams of three or four police inspectors began an interrogation about his underground activities.

On the first morning at 8.00 a.m., officers of the Punjab, Bihar and Bengal CIDs were present.

'You will have to answer certain questions that will be put to you,' he was informed, 'and you will have to make a statement regarding your recent activities.'

'I am prepared to answer any question that does not relate to my recent "underground" activities. As for a statement I have no more to say than that I am an enemy of the British Empire in India (not of Britain or the British Commonwealth). I am working for my country's independence and I will continue to do so until the object is achieved or my death intervenes."

'You will not be let off until we have obtained from you the information we want.'

'Let us see.'

For the first few days the interrogations lasted sixteen hours a day and he escaped from the questioning only to sleep and use the toilet. Some interrogators told him they had captured the other underground leaders—Ram Manohar Lohia, Achyut Patwardhan, Mrs. Aruna Asaf Ali—and pretended to read from their written confessions which sounded genuine. Others were abusive and bullying. They handcuffed him to a backless chair, slapped him across the face to keep him awake, and threatened to drag him to a basement dungeon and flog him with canes of neem, drawing his attention to men's screams issuing from other parts of the fort. Others flattered him that he was the most important man in India after Gandhi and Nehru.

'They kept changing my questioners,' he told the authors in 1962. 'As soon as I started to fall asleep they would shake me awake. They even changed the style of interrogation: a couple of fellows tried to appeal to my "better nature" by begging me to give the information and so save them from losing their jobs. Then they wanted me to promise not to try to escape, like I did from Hazaribagh Jail, and when I refused to promise they put chains on my ankles. They even expected me to take my daily exercise bound like this. Of course I refused and they had to carry me from my cell. They took them off eventually.'

During the second month of daily questioning the interrogations lengthened, lasting almost continuously day and night. From the fortieth to fiftieth day he was allowed no sleep. One team told him at 9.00 p.m., 'That's all for today. You can go back to your cell for a sleep.' A few minutes later the next team had him pulled from his bunk. 'I ate practically nothing and my head buzzed like a beehive.'

Stories of his torture leaked out and circulated throughout India. To determine the truth of these remains a difficulty because Jayaprakash normally does not refer to these experiences in public speeches or private reminiscences. His brother informed the authors that Jayaprakash was held naked on blocks of ice for two days. One Bombay attorney tried to obtain a writ of habeas corpus for him and was promptly arrested and removed to Lahore Fort. Public indignation flared in street demonstrations and to save its own name the Punjab government feigned caring for human decency by holding an enquiry. A Lahore court severely censured the three police officers who had been responsible for arresting the attorney, a sound gesture since the aim of intimidating the legal profession had been secured temporarily. But the interrogation of Jayaprakash was stopped, without securing his confession.

'I think they would have had to put me through much more to make me talk. In any case there really wasn't much to tell. People imagine this underground business is very sinister and important. The fact is, you spend most of your time just trying to save your skin.'

For a week he was locked in a foul little cell in a dungeon and he went through the quarrel about the chains on his ankles. Six weeks after his torment stopped the home secretary to the Punjab government, A. A. MacDonald, visited him.

'Your interrogation is over,' he stated. 'The Punjab CID has given you up as hopeless.' Jayaprakash requested permission to make a written complaint to the Punjab government. 'Have you any complaints? The question of rights hardly arises.'

Jayaprakash smiled at the man's attempt to whitewash a corrupt government. 'Yes, I do have a few.'

'What are they?' he asked.

Jayaprakash was not so simple as to allow this man to be the reporter of his opinions. 'I shall put my complaints in writing if you will agree to allow me paper and pen.'

'I will think over the matter,' he prevaricated.

A month later he returned and announced: 'You have permission to write to the government whenever you want.'

It took a fortnight to provide writing materials for him and it took Jayaprakash several hours to compose his fifteen hundred word letter to the home secretary. In this he stated his belief that there could be no moral or legal sanction for torturing prisoners simply for refusing to give information. A prisoner was a most helpless creature and the right to petition should never be denied to him, as it had been in his case. Suppression of political opponents was the essence of fascism. He granted that those who believed in violence as a political method must be prepared to be forcibly suppressed by law but even prisoners of war had rights which civilized society scrupulously respected. His bitterness was not directed against his questioners but against the council of ministers of the Punjab government who had sanctioned the policy of interrogations, and he asked that any prisoner under questioning be allowed to petition the government at any time and to see the superintendent and an accredited non-official visitor every week or fortnight.

While Jayaprakash read alone in his cell, Gandhi was released from custody on 8 May 1944, and his actions and statements of the ensuing four months made a profound and disagreeable impression on Jayaprakash. It was given to the press that Gandhi had been released because of illness but Jayaprakash claimed it was political face-saving. Jayaprakash did not want a settlement with Britain during the war for he believed this would do no good to the cause of Indian freedom. It would have been better, his health lasting, had Gandhi remained in prison until the end of the war when his bargaining position would have been stronger.

Jayaprakash's solitary confinement ended after eleven months with the liberation of Paris on 25 October 1944. He wrote with impotent rage:

> It was a great day for Europe, but Europe is far away and beyond my world—sealed off, walled off, barred and bolted Sometimes as the sun goes down and darkness falls over man's deeds, I hear both the howls of the captives, and the thudding of the Ogre's blows.

When I hear these howls.... I find myself turning into a brute—a raging, tearing, brutal vengeance wells up within my being. I fight hard to keep my humanity. ("Inside Lahore Fort," 67)

On that evening he heard the lock outside his cell being opened. He got up thinking it was some routine matter, trying to keep himself from attacking the guard. He found himself unexpectedly confronted by Dr. Ram Manohar Lohia, 'his eyes twinkling as ever through his glasses'. It was a great moment for him which would live in his memory, greater than the liberation of Paris, for he felt no longer a solitary captive of British brutality but a 'human being transported to a human world.'

His treatment at Lahore Fort came close to destroying Jayaprakash's nervous balance: for months after his interrogation he could get little sleep at night, having become attuned to anticipating being awakened and bullied and struck. He requested reading and writing material and finally, some time after allowing him to write his letter of protest to the Punjab government, the jail inspector permitted him to have a school child's cheap exercise book and a pencil, and access to a surprisingly wide range of books. Without these his long period of solitary confinement might well have ended in bitter tragedy.

Five months later, having been sixteen months in Lahore Fort, Jayaprakash was transferred in handcuffs to Agra Central Jail. When the prospects of the Shimla Conference of 1945, however, brought the release of the leading Congressmen, Jayaprakash and his Congress Socialist Party comrades were not released.

Jayaprakash found it humiliating that released Congressmen should submit to restrictions on their movements and activities and believed that they should defy the British and go back to prison. The restraints would never be publicised if no one disobeyed them or refused to collaborate. His resentment spilled over into sarcastic comments such as: 'God's will be done... the coloured men... must not be free,' or his question: 'Will Paris, risen from the dust, allow Syria, Lebanon and Algiers and the millions to rise from the dust?'

Soon after his release on 8 May 1944 Gandhi publicly dissociated himself from the uprising of August 1942 because it had been tainted with violence. He also influenced the underground Congressmen to surrender to the authorities. Believing that the struggle of 1942 could not be disowned Jayaprakash experienced great bitterness.

His love and respect for Gandhi were clouded with bewilderment, sadness, disillusionment. Gandhi appeared to reject the 'poor fools' who lost their lives, their homes, their property for using violence against British rule, while simultaneously condoning violence by endeavouring to have a National Government formed for India which would immediately shoulder a gun and march forth to murder and mutilate the brutal Japanese and the bestial German. 'No one likes to be disowned by his family or excommunicated by his community,' Jayaprakash wrote. 'Gandhi and the Congress had failed in their duty to forewarn the people of how to act under the boot of the British and should now, frankly, unashamedly, identify themselves with the people in their travail and suffering.'

Gandhi in one move had focused and magnified Jayaprakash's disillusionment with the Congress.

Reflecting over the previous fourteen years Jayaprakash concluded that the Congress had never worked according to plan. It had begun its civil disobedience movements haphazardly and without preparation. If Gandhi saw the Viceroy, all Indian hopes were centred on that meeting and when his talks bore no fruit they were rendered impotent through rage and despair. When Congress ministries were formed, freedom was expected to issue from them, and so, when the ministers were bundled back into jail again, all were unprepared. In matters of policy the leadership had merely drifted. Congressmen devoted themselves to party elections and provincial legislature elections, the jackals snatching what the tiger left behind.

Jayaprakash believed that if the Congress gave five years to educative and constructive work among the masses it would bring Britain to her knees and deflate Mr. Jinnah's balloon. So he dreamed of a political master plan, a blueprint for revolution. After the war the Congress should carefully work towards an all India mass civil disobedience campaign within five years and not allow itself to be diverted by negotiations with the Viceroy over a Constitution.

Jayaprakash's underground Socialists sought Gandhi out to gain his further leadership for their revolt against foreign rule. Gandhi's advice was that their secrecy was a sin and a symptom of violence which would not free the dumb millions. Non-violence functioned in the open, he claimed, and awakened the masses. Underground activity should be taboo. Beyond this he would not issue any direction to them.

He told them he had admiration for their courage and heroism, and the highest admiration for the courage, patriotism and spirit of self-sacrifice that their leader, Jayaprakash, displayed, but if he had to award a medal for true heroism it would not go to Jayaprakash but to Prabhavati Devi who had acted as a Satyagrahi, so being a teacher to her husband of the art and practice of non-violent non-cooperation.

The publication of Gandhi's views on sabotage and secrecy not only angered Jayaprakash but evoked protest from a section of the Congress that believed that the British could not be dislodged without sabotage. However, as a result of a series of discussions with Gandhi, most of the Congressmen who were working underground deserted, either surrendering themselves to the authorities or courting arrest by offering open civil disobedience. To Jayaprakash they had become cowardly collaborators.

In September talks were arranged between Gandhi and Jinnah. Jayaprakash believed that Jinnah would not be prepared to talk seriously because he wanted 'vivisection' of the country. He himself proposed full provincial autonomy for Muslim states with residuary powers and minimum agreed powers for the Central government of Gandhi's undivided India. He hoped against hope for agreement between the two leaders because he believed that disagreement would provide Britain with another opportunity to 'throw dust into the world's eyes' by advertising (and exploiting) Indian disunity.

The talks lasted three weeks and after their adjournment the correspondence was published. All Jayaprakash's sympathies lay with Gandhi, not a little because Jinnah had not been to jail. He accused him of a 'pettifogging lower-court manner', of a quarrelsome, self-seeking spirit, of wanting to destroy Indian nationalism. His 'little' Pakistan state would be no better than a British Protectorate.

'I do not believe that without division of the country we cannot be free. Division will solve none of our present problems and will create others more serious than those existing today,' he wrote.

World War II came to an end leaving Britain victorious but exhausted and India in a disastrous situation of inflated prices, shortages of goods, and belated efforts to repair the damage of the Bengal Famine. The British Labour Party campaigned during the 1945 elections for Indian self-government. On winning the vote, it called the Viceroy, Lord Wavell, to London for discussions and appointed Nehru the vice-president of the Viceroy's Executive Council, in effect a *de facto* Prime Minister of India, but did not grant political amnesty to Jayaprakash or Lohia despite the hopes of the Congress Socialists.

Repeatedly in the legislative assembly in Delhi, questions were raised about the continuing detention of Jayaprakash. Early in 1946 the home member visited and questioned the prisoners about their belief in violence. In his maiden speech Masani insisted that Jayaprakash who was a symbol of all that was finest in the nation and a patriot known to all, was in truth a mild, gentle, kindly person 'who would not hurt a fly if he could help it'. He said that on the basis of more than ten years of the closest acquaintance and friendship he could guarantee that Jayaprakash was not guilty of violent methods and was not dangerous. It was said the CID had been surprised by his mildness. He did not believe in revolution but in a democratic humanitarian socialism to lift the masses out of their poverty and degradation. It was a complete anomaly for a socialist government in Britain to continue to detain the very man who would try to lead India towards the objectives of socialism.

Prabhavati passed her time in jail in less intellectual pursuits than Jayaprakash. She was quartered in a long ward like a barrack with about thirty other women detenus. Their food allowance per day was one rupee and four annas, but what was presented to them at meal times was so little to their taste that they requested and gained permission from the superintendent of the jail to have the ingredients bought in the market and delivered to them so they could do their own cooking. The prisoners at the jail were divided into A, B and C categories, the latter being the worst criminals and receiving only ten annas of rations per day. The political prisoners, learning this, also cooked for them and shared their higher rations with them.

The jail roof was low and made of galvanised iron sheeting. When Prabhavati first went there, and in the succeeding summer of 1943, the ward was unbearably hot. The women prisoners asked permission of the warders and of the superintendent to take their string cots out into the walled grounds. Permission was granted for all the women with the exception of Prabhavati. In her case the police feared that Jayaprakash, who had escaped from Hazaribagh Jail and was being hunted, might break into the Darbhanga Prison to rescue her. Consequently four of her companions in a futile effort to influence the warders by their solidarity refused to sleep outdoors if Prabhavati were not allowed to do so.

In the Aga Khan Palace, Kasturba, who was aged seventy-four, was ailing in health until by December 1943 she had fallen seriously ill with bronchitis. Gandhi requested Viceroy Linlithgow by letter to allow Prabhavati Devi to come to the palace to act as nurse.

Prabhavati from taken from Darbhanga Jail guarded by eight policemen armed with rifles, all of whom were bigger than she was and probably worrying about Jayaprakash being at large. When the party reached the state border and the train stopped at a station the guards supplied by the United Provinces came into the compartment unarmed. The huge Sikh in charge of Prabhavati roared at the incoming sergeant-in-charge: 'Where are your rifles? Go and get them!' Upon their return the sergeant ventured a question, 'Where is the prisoner?' 'I'm the prisoner; Prabhavati replied, and was gratified by their astonishment.

Prabhavati and Gandhi spent many devoted hours by Kasturba's side until her death.

Against Gandhi's protests at the 'cruelty' of removing Prabhavati from him, she was returned to Darbhanga Jail under escort, and not released from there until early 1946. She then returned to Gandhi, living as a member of his household at Bhangi Colony in Delhi. After his trial in 1944 Jayaprakash had been transferred to the Red Fort in Delhi, and here Prabhavati visited him on five occasions.

On 2 April 1946 Gandhi suggested that since British and Indian representatives were discussing the necessity for independence, political prisoners, such as Jayaprakash and Lohia, who had been charged with the use of violence should be freed. As a result of his representations Jayaprakash and Lohia were released on 12 April.

Jayaprakash was met at the Delhi railway station by Prabhavati and a crowd of excited, applauding Socialists. Newspaper reporters followed him everywhere. He was besieged with invitations to attend luncheons and dinners, to accept gifts, to address meetings at all hours of the day and night. Most appealing of these was the request to address a mass meeting on the Gandhi Maidan in Patna, and there to receive a purse collected for him.

With the grey buildings of St. Xavier's School and a towering seventeenth-century granary behind him, and with Prabhavati beside him, he looked triumphantly from the platform in the maidan across a sea of tens of thousands of faces turned towards him, cheering him in a thunderous, jubilant roar.

He was exhilarated, inspired.

The Congress leadership is not for fighting;' he told them. 'According to them the era of struggle ended in 1942. Now it wants a compromise with British imperialism. But as in 1942, once again revolutionary forces will compel the Congress to launch a struggle. The Congress Socialist Party cannot start the fight, the Congress alone can. But once the Congress starts it, the Congress Socialist Party can transform it into a revolution in spite of Congress attempts to keep it under restrictions. We have to do it If Congress avoids the fight then the Congress Socialist Party will leave it and form the Indian Socialist Party.

'But we will not join forces with the Communists. They only stand for their own party and Russia whose fifth column they constitute in India. Indian communists are in the last analysis anti-labour and anti-Indian. We must face them and we must oust them from the working-class movement carefully preserving the solidarity of the workers.

The Congress Socialist Party does not extend its hospitality to the British Cabinet Mission as the Congress does. The leaders of the Congress—Gandhiji, Jawaharlalji, Sardar Patel—believe that independence can now be negotiated. But to me, to Ashok Mehta and Dr. Ram Manohar Lohia, and to all our colleagues it is axiomatic that a capitalist, imperialist power will not peacefully surrender its exploited colonies which are the source of its wealth. We must prepare for the revolution that is inevitable.

'For the past one hundred fifty years the British have been dictators, they have enslaved our people. They have been guilty of sanctimonious insolence and racial arrogance, of astronomical looting and exploitation, of the most pitiless forms of violence—which ground down millions of poor people and sucked their lifeblood—of bullets, of looting, of rape and arson. Their imperialist lies to cover their robberies were the greatest lies ever uttered in history. These were that Britain held India down only for our own good, to educate us in the arts of self-government until we are properly able to look after ourselves, and secondly that Britain is really prepared to free India immediately Indians are united among themselves. The real issue is whether Britain is prepared to liquidate her Empire, and the Cripps Mission has refused to do this. You know that Churchill once announced he had not assumed the office of the King's First Minister to preside over the liquidation of the Empire. You know that Churchill has gratuitously insulted Mahatma Gandhi, calling him a half-naked fakir, and Jawaharlalji, calling him an incompetent man of straw. And it is mistaken to fancy that the present British Labour government will care any more for our freedom than the Tories have.

The British are not to be trusted. They are far greater liars than Goebbels and the Nazis. While on one hand they are negotiating with Nehru, on the other they are equipping the police and the army with new weapons. They are training the soldiers in certain army bases to practise shooting on the Gandhi cap as a target. In our own state, Bihar, they are recruiting the *adivasis* (tribals), encouraging them to give a pledge to shoot Congressmen when so ordered.

The British just don't mean anything when they say they are ready to leave India. They have created in this country a strong fifth column for themselves—the Muslim League of Mr. Jinnah and the Princes. The British game at present is to turn our fight for freedom into a domestic fight between the communities. The

British are using the Muslim League as their tool in their game of divide and rule. The British do not intend to give India freedom. India will have to wrest it by force. I entirely agree that freedom is round the comer but let me emphasise that before we achieve freedom an all-out struggle is necessary. A revolution has become necessary.'

The crowd flung back his passion in wave after wave of shouted approbation.

Sarvodaya

On April 19, 1954, Jayaprakash Narayan announced in Gaya that he was dedicating his life (Jeevandan) to Vinoba Bhave's *Sarvodaya* movement and its Bhoodan campaign, which promoted distributing land to Harijans (untouchables). He gave up his land, set up an ashram in Hazaribagh, and worked towards uplifting the village.

In 1957, Narayan formally broke with the Praja Socialist Party in order to pursue *lokniti* [Polity of the people], as opposed to *rajniti* [Polity of the state]. By this time, Narayan had become convinced that *lokniti* should be non-partisan in order to build a consensus-based, classless, participatory democracy which he termed *Sarvodaya*. Narayan became an important figure in the India-wide network of Gandhian Sarvodaya workers.

In 1964, Narayan was vilified across the political spectrum for arguing in an article in the Hindustan Times that India had a responsibility to keep its promise to allow self-determination to the state of Jammu and Kashmir. He hit back at critics in a second article, dismissing the Indian version of the "domino theory" which held that the rest of India's states would disintegrate if Kashmir were allowed its promised freedom. In his graceful if old-fashioned style, Narayan ridiculed the premise that "the states of India are held together by force and not by the sentiment of a common nationality. It is an assumption that makes a mockery of the Indian Nation and a tyrant of the Indian State".

Bihar Movement and Total Revolution

Narayan returned to prominence in State politics in the late 1960s. In 1974, he led the student's movement in the state of Bihar which gradually developed into a popular people's movement known as the Bihar movement. It was during this movement that J. P. gave a call for peaceful Total Revolution Together with V. M. Tarkunde, he founded the Citizens for Democracy in 1974 and the People's Union for Civil Liberties in 1976, both NGOs, to uphold and defend civil liberties.

Emergency

When Indira Gandhi was found guilty of violating electoral laws by the Allahabad High Court, Narayan called for Indira to resign, and advocated a programme of social transformation which he termed *Sampoorna kraanti* [Total Revolution]. Instead she proclaimed a national Emergency on the midnight of June 25, 1975, immediately after Narayan had called for the PM's resignation and had asked the military and the police to disregard unconstitutional and immoral orders; J. P., opposition leaders, and dissenting members of her own party (the 'Young Turks') were arrested on that day.

Jayaprakash Narayan attracted a gathering of 100,000 people at the Ramlila Grounds and thunderously recited *Rashtrakavi* Ramdhari Singh 'Dinkar's wonderfully evocative poetry: *Singhasan Khaali Karo Ke Janata Aaati Hai.*

Narayan was kept as *detenu* at Chandigarh even after he had asked for a month's parole for mobilising relief in areas of Bihar gravely affected by flood. His health suddenly deteriorated on October 24, and he was released on November 12; diagnosis at Jaslok Hospital, Bombay, revealed kidney failure; he would be on dialysis for the rest of his life.

After Indira revoked the emergency on January 18, 1977 and announced elections, it was under J. P.'s guidance that the Janata Party (a vehicle for the broad spectrum of the anti-Indira Gandhi opposition) was formed. The Janata Party was voted into power, and became the first non-Congress party to form a government at the Centre. On the call of Narayan many youngesters joined the J. P. movement.

3

J. P. Movement

The Sarvodaya Way

After Joining the Sarvodaya movement, J. P. completely changed his own attitude towards his own life. No doubt he was a moralist since he attained adolescence and by the passage of time his growth in the field of morality was gigantic. Though he was attracted towards the material aspect of Sarvodaya, yet he was more drawn towards the moral aspect of it. He held that no human society could flourish unless human beings display their individual conduct and behaviour in a rational way which means individuals should be armed with human values of love, truth, compassion, tolerance and brotherhood and many other virtues.

Human society stands on the purity of individuals. Those materialists who argue that circumstances will bring about changes in the character of individuals, are utterly wrong. Changes cannot be brought about in human character by any sort of artificial imposition. Circumstances can force individuals to accept certain values, but it cannot create the desire to accept values voluntarily. J. P. was committed to this basic ethics that betterment and welfare human society cannot be built up by bad human beings, which means selfish, cruel, unsympathetic, violent and greedy. The combination of these human vices cannot help a human being to play a role of a good and accomplished citizen. A good human society cannot proceed with these individuals. The Sarvodaya harps on building such a society of good individuals who will voluntarily abide by the moral principles of society and eliminate, all social vices existing in the society. In this regard J. P. made an impassionate appeal to the people to be conscious of human values and act according to it. He said:

> When we go to God fulfilling our life, we have to carry our good deeds with us, not our wealth or lands. There is no value of the Land in the court of God. He takes into consideration the persons who are pious and donors or who are irreligious and greedy. But those do not understand this, we do not want to impose anything on them. We accept the bondage of heart and mind not of law. If some one does some pious deed under pressure, then it is never considered as genuine.
>
> *(from Bhoodan Yagna)*

Pious deeds come to happen spontaneously. It comes to exist with the changing the lifestyle and thinking process of the individual. To treat all individuals as equal is also considered as a pious deed. Equality is one of the spiritual aspects of life. With the attitude of equality, one can proceed towards a healthy society where all are treated well. To quote Vinobaji in this regard:

> To a wise man, equality is the test of well-being and riches. If it is absent, even the wealth they think would be misfortune. Equality, even it meant poverty was desirable in the eyes.

The Sarvodaya way demands rethinking and reassessing about the democratic norms and techniques which is urgently necessary to induct the spirit of Sarvodaya into democracy. Through the ideas of Sarvodaya, we have to fight with all types of social evils. We have never examined the suitability of Western type of democracy in our country. The democratic apparatus and the pattern of Western democracy which we have from the West is not helping our countrymen to practice democratic philosophy in their life. We should not continue with the democratic rituals of the West. We had our ancient political system of decentralisation of power. The power that is generated from the collective will of the people. True democracy cannot flourish by strengthening the powers of the government. Democracy cannot function smoothly with large-scale planning and centralised economy. The voice of the people counts in democracy.

It cannot be ignored. And the voice of the people can be heard if they are united in hearts and deeds. The country has already gained experience as an independent nation and about its functions. In independent India realities have been changed. And we have to adjust our minds according to those realities. In this context, we have to take the advancement of technology into consideration. Technology has played a greater role in changing the realities of the time. With establishment of equality and welfare, technology can be used properly by serving the entire humanity.

So, a sane society is a precondition of the technological achievement. Sarvodaya thinks of building a sane society where no individual will be left behind in getting a fair deal. Sarvodaya is a way that wants to set right the social, economical, racial and cultural shortcomings by changing the thinking process of the Individuals. The problems of starvation, unemployment, insecurity, inequality and ignorance have rocked our country. The problems are gigantic in nature but can be solved through change of attitude with great ease. The change depends upon the realisation of individuals. But all individuals must realise the problems and think about their solution collectively. So, ultimately we have to come to the change of the attitude of the individuals.

J. P. did not treat Sarvodaya in the reformist way. He treated this as a way of realisation through non-violent revolution. In Sarvodaya, each individual must idealise himself before he embarks upon to idealise the society. Sarvodaya stands for selfless service and self idealisation of individuals. It is through self realisation only man can purify his mind, body and heart. But the major ingredient of self purification is heart. Whatever the heart dictate, mind and body will follow. Once the heart is accustomed to the ideas of self-purification, selfless service will follow. It is only through our change or purification of heart, we can embark upon doing selfless deeds. We cannot do selfless deeds unless our hearts are pure. We need not have to make any special effort for this. The selfless deed shall be rendered spontaneously. Our conscience shall allow our service to be confined to self. Because service towards humanity has been always a way of life. Sarvodaya harps on that way of life. Any transformation could not be brought about in a day.

It could be only worked out through practice. An individual cannot sit idle and declare that his heart has become pure. The purity of heart have to be manifested through our deeds and through our influence over our surroundings. So, transformation is a continued process. It is a dynamic process associated with the march of time. Values are modified with the progress of lime. Such transformation helps to open a vision of new ideology. And that ideology is the ideology of Sarvodaya towards which J. P. dedicated himself. This new ideology gave him the conviction that "All lands and property belong to God". This will help the people to accommodate the new ideology and transform themselves according to that ideology. J. P. knew that the Sarvodaya way is the way to bring the individuals together in heart and soul. It is a way of feeling together, living together, enjoying together and suffering together.

Another important thing of the Sarvodaya way is the means adopted for transformation. The character of the ideal is assessed according the means adopted for its attainment. Purification of means has been an important component of Sarvodaya movement. The same ethics had been adopted by Gandhiji in Indian liberation movement. Those means that have been adopted in the process of revolution make it a continuous process.

The means have a great influence on the goal. The means adopted in the revolution continence to influence the goal even alter the revolution is completed. It also influence the personal and social life of the men who participated in the revolution. After joining Sarvodaya J. P. was very much concerned with the means adopted in the non-violent revolution. We may attain good goal by hook or crook through evil means, but till the means are purified, the goal again rebounds to the evil state and affects the fruits of revolution. The act of purifying the goal after attaining through evil means, is forbidden in non-violent revolution. In Sarvodaya one cannot conceive the process of adopting evil means. As the Sarvodaya harps on purification and transformation of the conduct, character and the attitude of the individuals, there is no question of harbouring any sort of evil in any process of transformation.

All types of evil deeds and evil thoughts should be kept out of the life of the individuals so that he could be an accomplished man to be fit into the society of 'Welfare of all'. It is a basic truth discovered by Gandhiji that no individual can purify himself through evil thoughts, what to speak of deeds. The preparation for a non-violent revolution greatly depend upon the non-violent character and compassionate attitude of the individual. In Sarvodaya, all social changes have to be brought about through the process of persuasion. It is a difficult process no doubt, as it demands the adoption of non-violence in out own character. But once the process is established, it cannot be uprooted through any evil design. If the process is successfully practised by the individuals, then it can be successfully adopted in transforming the society. What is truth in the life of individual, the same is the truth in the character of the society. If the individual adopts the evil as his means, then he will go for a evil society where violence, greed, hatred and intolerance would dominate.

It is through the above means that the individuals can establish a welfare society. It means, we have to treat our neighbours as the members of our family. This feeling would be extended to the whole society. Each individual must feel within himself the sorrows and woes of other members of the society. He must participate with it and make sincere efforts for its eradication. This is easy to practice on the part of Good-loving men. God is not' an object nor He reside in invisible heaven. He lies in every heart in shape of good thoughts and good deeds. God is a way of life. It is a combination of values. Devotion to God means devotion to virtues adopted in one's life. True devotion to God cannot be displayed without kindness, compassion and love. These are the qualities manifested by God through men. So, Sarvodaya ask for that devotion of love and kindness to be expanded to all individuals. Sarvodaya way is the way of God. It appeals to the individuals to open their hearts and be conscious about their surroundings. It wants to do everything through love and kindness. It wants to distribute, peace, and happiness to all individuals of the society through our own character. It wants to fill each human heart with love and sympathy. Sarvodaya will be established, only when we ourselves will act upon these Godly values and appeal to our neighbours to act upon it. Sarvodaya aspires to create a lively bond of sympathy among the individuals and achieve the goal of a Society of Kindness. That would be the new social order for which J. P. was striving at. This social order will bring happiness, peace and security to all the individuals of the society. The Sarvodaya spells out a great future for human beings both of the present and future generations who will no doubt pave the way of happiness and peace throughout the world.

> To a wise man equality is the test of well-being and riches. If it is absent, even the wealth they think would be misfortune. Equality, even if it meant poverty was desirable in their eyes.

Equality is one of the primary objectives of Sarvodaya. It depends upon two important factors. Those are selfless service and self-realisation. A man has to realise within himself that all men are equal to him. No one is high and no one is low. For that realisation man has to purify his mind, body and heart. When a man is accustomed to harbour the ideas of self-realisation, he would be compelled to tread on the track of selfless service. He cannot choose another path: Selfless service is a path in itself and one can move effortlessly over it Once you are on the path you can render selfless service spontaneously to the society, you cannot confine your service to self, even if you desire to do so. Services to humanity are never designed nor premeditated. It is dependable on the ideas of dedication that grows within us. That is known as transformation of self. The evolution or transformation is a continued process of human life. And Sarvodaya has been making efforts to transform the ideas of the individuals. With the march of time new human values enter the arena of Sarvodaya. New interpretations of ideas are also enriching human values. Science has helped a lot in discovering these new interpretations of human values. With that the social order is bound to change. Sarvodaya wants to direct this change for a society of human welfare. Let the entire human society be benefited with this change of values. Some of the primitive values based on ignorance have to be given up and new values have to be replaced. It is through transformation of ideas that helps the mind to open the gate of the new ideology.

That new ideology of Sarvodaya towards which J.P. was attracted is based upon voluntary surrender of individual rights on land and property. The philosophy of equality is based on this concept of collective ownership or social ownership. J. P. endorsed the views of Vinobaji that "All lands and property belong to God." Sarvodaya pursue the people to accommodate this new thought by transforming themselves. J. P. knew that Sarvodaya way was a way of 'living together, feeling together, enjoying together and suffering together.' The spirit of brotherhood long discovered through earlier violent revolutions have to be bathed in the spirit of non-violence. It means the value of brotherhood would be there, but in a relation of different form. Values are old, but the path of achievement is new. The process of proceeding over the path is new too. The consistency and efficiency of Sarvodaya lie in transforming the path and the process. It has completely changed the process from violence to non-violence and persuasion. The spirit of brotherhood has to be inducted in the hearts of individuals by rendering selfless services to others. J. P. hoped that the practice of dedication and selfless service would help to install the spirit of brotherhood among the individuals.

The Sarvodaya way is not a new way. It is as old as mountains and oceans. Vinobaji has brought about some modifications in it to make it applicable for building up a sane society where sufferings of the individuals will be put to end and people shall be lodged in a welfare society where they could be able to display the spirit of true brotherhood. The spirit of brotherhood can be retained only through mutual sacrifice. Vinobaji has shaped all his programmes according to the ideal of Sarvodaya. J. P. warned us regarding the lot of misconception created by certain intellectuals. They continue to harp on primitive values and stick to superstitions that the inequality exists in the society made by God and by ancient and wise forefathers. No doubt our forefathers were wise, but the wisdom of the people at present has been enhanced by scientific attitude. That is the contribution of science. Sarvodaya's goal of welfare of all cannot be set aside because of science. Science cannot function in a humanitarian way unless there is equality of status among the 'individuals. Humanity means embracing all individuals and exhibiting concern towards the well being of every one. The intellectuals may modify their misconception those have been created by science.

Sarvodaya has been moving towards the goal of "Welfare of All". The objective of "Welfare of all" cannot be achieved unless the welfare of each individual is achieved. And we have to achieve this through the peaceful method. Experiments in violent methods have been tasted earlier by the revolutionaries, but it did not succeed in giving justice to one and all. Violence once inducted cannot be removed after attaining the social objective. With the march of time and with the advancement of technology, violent methods became outdated. In the present age, violence has reached the point of saturation. Science and technology has been dominated by war mongering politicians, greedy capitalists and power mongering politicians.

In the mean time violence has acquired unlimited power has posed grave danger to the human race. The improper use of science conducted under the guidance of insane people has endangered the entire creation. At the other end science has made the world smaller and easily approachable from all corners of the globe. Under the evil guidance, the destructive weapons of the science can reach any part of the world and create calamities. J. P. believed that it is only through Sarvodaya. These threats of weapons of mass destruction including Atomic weapons can be wiped out But each individual living in this world must be made conscious about the implication of this threat of global annihilation. Those individuals who want to eradicate violence from the world must practice non-violence and harbour the spirit of non-violence in their hearts. They must act and behave non-violently with their neighbours and with their adversaries. The global violence that we see today is nothing but the manifestation of the spirit of violence that resides in our hearts. The violence that we cherish in our hearts always attempts to find an outlet whenever it discovers any weakness in us. When individual violence interrupts, it ends ultimately in global violence. Sarvodaya therefore, appeals to each individual to remove the spirit of violence from every heart. We must know that the spirit of violence, greed and intolerance must be removed from our hearts, otherwise it will be displayed in Atomic warfare. It is only through individual efforts, the whole human race can be saved from total extinction. Sarvodaya helps us to explore the avenues through which we can remove the spirit of violence from us. These efforts have been continuing since the days of Gandhiji and Vinobaji and J. P. have inherited it They added new dimensions to this effort to eliminate violence from human heart.

The present world order has compelled all individuals to set right their goal of life. We must ask some pertinent questions to ourselves. What is the goal of our life? What is the object of our living? What is our relation with the society? In what way we can contribute to the welfare of all? These are the questions which each of us, specially the intellectuals should ask themselves. The common answer that comes to our mind in this age is that, each of us must aspire for increasing our happiness, develop those instruments by which we can acquire happiness and improve our standard of living. But Sarvodaya does not approve this as the answer to the above questions.

It does not uphold the satisfaction of material wants as ideal. It thinks differently. Sarvodaya confirms that if we keep these individual efforts in satisfying our material wants; welfare of the 'individuals could not be attained by infusing the spirit of self interest. When each individual would be looking after his own self interest without expressing concern for other individuals of the society; then the state of Welfare for All can not be attained. The prospect of material enjoyment will not satisfy the needs of the total human being. Each of us should know that human life is not confined to only 'eating, drinking, and enjoying'. A composite human life is not complete simply by enhancing the objects of senses, objects of luxury and building objects of comforts. The object of human life is something different which we have to learn with the practice of human values. There are thousand and one instances in the affluent countries like America where people remain dissatisfied with comfortable and luxuriant living. They need something more to keep their mind healthy. Mental health is one of the important aspects of a healthy life. The affluent countries go on increasing their necessities and produce objects of comforts and luxuries in order to cope with their unlimited wants. They go on satisfying their wants one after another and surrender to the process of continuous satisfaction that affects the spirit of selflessness which is an important ingredient of the Welfare society. That creates a vacuum in human heart. That vacuum can be filled up not through affluence but through renunciation, which is otherwise called as the spirit of sacrifice or spirit of dedication.

J. P. held that every man should aspire to obtain a developed soul. In order to identify soul, man should not surrender to heaps of material prosperity. It is only through minimising and controlling wants, man can be able to understand ethical part of this life. The self of man which is supreme in character, cannot commensurate with limitless desire for material prosperity. Though it is the duty of man to preserve and serve the body in the best way as he could, but to treat body as supreme is inconsistent with the growth of life. Human being should not treat bodily pleasure as the highest pleasure. If a human being treats his body as the supreme object and indulged in satisfying bodily pleasures, then he would be doing harm to his own self and he becomes a cause for the degradation of society. Human personality cannot evolve simply through the satisfaction of desires. This philosophy of life is linked with the philosophy of Sarvodaya.

He elucidates another aspect of Sarvodaya by stating that we should not acquire more than our needs. The attitude to acquire more and collect more is the cause of degradation of the human character and the human society at large. This attitude prevents us to fulfil the fundamental norm of a human being. When we acquire something, then we must think the process through which we have acquired. We must think, how much we have to retain for ourselves and how much we have to part with for the society. Because, no wealth can be produced single handedly. It needs the cooperation of one and all to produce wealth. So, naturally, society has its share in our wealth that we acquire. It is our duty to part with a portion of our wealth for well being of all individuals of the society. As human beings, we have to satisfy the hunger of the society. Both Mahatma Gandhi and Vinobaji had shown us the way by which we can associate ourselves and sympathise with the hunger of the society. The main principle of Sarvodaya movement is that each of us must share our delight and miseries of others. J. P. holds that this principle is already active in our personal life. What is needed is to expand this attitude to the social dimension. No true human being can love to enjoy at the suffering of others. It is antagonistic to human conduct. It is the technological advancement that is shaking the conduct of human beings by placing before them various objects of pleasure and luxuries. Where technology operates under the guidance of evil people, it becomes a monster and robs all values from human beings. Technology has failed to develop instrument to measure the difference between the primitive man and the civilized man of today. The primitive man held a baton in his hand to kill another man, where as the civilized man is holding Atom Bomb to kill innocents. These killings are against our heritage.

The scriptures teach us that all lives are of equal value and all living beings must tread on the earth fearlessly. So fearlessness is known to be the essence of human civilization. No human being should be afraid of any other. Fearlessness would help human beings to enjoy their rights and liberties in the society. Sarvodaya conceives of a welfare society where no human being would interfere with the fundamental rights of another. If any technological violence happens then the community of fearless human beings would boldly encounter it and save the society from catastrophe. Fearlessness plays great role in uniting individuals and preparing themselves to dedicate for the social change. The strategy of non-violence that Sarvodaya holds acts as an instrument of bravery and unity. J. P. had demonstrated this bravery during his satyagraha against Emergency in India. He had also demonstrated that the power of non-violence is far superior to the power of violence. Even a man being non-violent in heart and soul can boldly face the technological warfare which the mad men may initiate. Non-violence and bravery go hand in hand. The value of non-violence is to be evolved in the society to induce fearlessness into every individual.

Elimination of fear from individual heart is a primary ideal of Sarvodaya. Unless one is fearless completely, he cannot be an instrument of achieving moral ends through moral means. And again he can be only fearless if he has the conviction of solving all internal and external conflicts and tension through non-violence. That was why Mahatma Gandhi emphasised on elimination of fear from personal and group life. According to him fear is born out of falsehood. A man conceals truth when he predicts that sticking to truth would bring for him dire consequences. To quote Acharya J.B. Kripalani in this regard:

> "...As a matter of fact truth cannot prosper where there is fear. People indulge in untruth because of fear of adverse consequences of sticking to truth. Every recantation or repudiation of truth, as one feels it or conceived of it, is due to fear and painful consequences. It may even be said that the history of the progress of mankind is the history of man's martyrdom of man in the pursuit of truth. Fearlessness is intimately connected with non-violence. A man relying upon violence may be brave but he cannot be fearless. He is afraid of injury and death. He tries to avoid them by all the violent means at his command. Brave as such a one is, he become fearless as soon as he refuses to seek protection of arms and cast them aside. Soldiers in the army are brave but they have fear lurking in their hearts. " (Vigil. August 28,1958)

Practice of individual non-violence and fearlessness among themselves will help nations to fight out the dangerous armament race. Through the collective efforts of fearless individuals, the nations can shed fear of entering into armament race. We can take example of fearlessness from Mahatma Gandhi's personal life. His behaviour was the same in his community life also. He went to Champaran in Bihar in 1917 to organise indigo farmers against the illegal taxes imposed upon them by the British. It was then almost unknown in India except for his South Africa "adventures" which was not known to most of the Indians. As soon as he entered Champaran at the invitation of aggrieved fanners being exploited by the European planters, he was served with a notice to quit the area, as he was an outsider and he had no business there. Within a second he took the decision and defied the order of the British Government and offered himself for arrest. This fearlessness of Mahatma Gandhi infused courage into the hearts of poor peasants and they non-violently organised themselves for protest and were ready to face the oppression of the government. It was Mahatma Gandhi's fearless defiance of an arbitrary authority that charged the people of Champaran.

We all must remember that it was owing to the fearless resistance of masses taught by Mahatma Gandhi, the people of India could fight with the tyranny of the British rule. Even those who advocate violent methods in struggle, admit that it is the moral quality of devotion to a cause, patriotism, unity, discipline are more important than the aspect of violence. Violence is a secondary' quality of the revolution. I he moral and discipline factors count more than that To achieve the Sarvodaya order, we have to practice complete fearlessness on the basis of non-violence, till the nation gives up the belief in armed resistance. Vinobaji succeeded in driving away the fear from the hearts of the volunteers of Bhoodan movement. His Shanti Sena did commendable work of fearlessness amidst communal frenzy in many parts of our country. This is a part of the programme of Sarvodaya that J. P. led in the country.

Sarvodaya has laid down its first principle of applying values in our own life. Human lives should be so saturated with values that vices dare not enter into the minds of the individuals. It is only through constant application of values in human life, man can create an atmosphere in the society congenial for human welfare. There are so many programmes of Sarvodaya like Bhoodan-Gramdan, Sampattidan, Buddhidan, Sramdan, Sarvodaya Patra, and Jeevandan that helps man to apply values of love, kindness, sympathy, tolerance and brotherhood, etc. placed by Vinobaji for social revolution. Such programmes would help Indian people to participate themselves in a non-violent revolution that would apparently initiate a social change where human values will dominate in shaping the society. These programmes of Sarvodaya will initiate explosion of love those are lying dormant in human heart. That will make the man conscious of his benevolent role he has to play in the society which is very important to build up human relations. The survival of human beings depend upon his benevolent spirit which he has to expand in the society. But this benevolent spirit must be given a shape through human action. Manual labour is one of the primary component to Sarvodaya. Manual labour is the action that could generate the spirit of equality among the individuals of the society. It could be able to remove the stigma of inequality of status prevalent almost in all countries of the world. In the capitalist countries, as well as in many communist countries (barring China), social status is calculated on the basis of intellectual labour. The bureaucrats and the like, who do not practice manual labour, enjoy greater prestige than the persons doing 'Bread labour'. The true Socialist Society and the Sarvodaya society strive to eliminate the indignity of the manual labour by giving equal status to labourers. The wages received by 'mental labourer' should be at par with the wages of a manual labourer.

In this connection, example set down by Chinese Republic may be taken into account. Though there had been imposition of 'Socialist ideology' in Chinese Republic, the leaders of China including its Chairman Mao Tse Tung and Prime Minister strived hard to create an atmosphere of 'Love for Labour' by doing manual labour with the labourers. The reason behind this concept is that all able-bodied men should not hide them serves from manual labour, as it is a part of developed human heritage. Some young voluntary workers arrived at the Ming Tombs Reservoir to take up the construction work in the summer of 1958. As the Reservoir was near to Peking, the Chinese Government advised all leading personnel of leading departments to join the construction camp and take part in the manual labour, all had to stay in the Labour Camps with the voluntary workers at least for a week and participate in the construction work. All these personnel of high profile had to stay in the same camp and share same food with the labourers. This attempt of Chinese government was a true experiment of inducting ideals into the lives of the people. It enhanced the spirit of brotherhood and sympathy among the participants coming from different status of society. No doubt there had been some amount of coercion in such type organised labour camps, but the spirit behind these types of effort to eliminate social inequality was noteworthy. The then Prime Minister of China, Chou En-lai, who worked in the labour camp, with the voluntary workers, inaugurated the Camp by saying:

> "The idea that the leading cadres should take part in physical labour was to create a social atmosphere of complete equality and cooperation between the leaders and the rank and file, with no division between them. While working hard to build a socialist society, we must at the same time create conditions for future communism. One of the prerequisites of communist construction is that all members of society ardently love labour and combine mental and manual labour. We must set an example for others by our own work and endeavour to create such social habits."

J. P. was an open-minded man. He always explored new avenues to successfully apply ideals in his own life. He was a great votary of dignity of labour. During the time of his studies in America he worked as a labourer for many days to meet his study expenses. He had never harboured any difference of status between a manual labourer and a 'white-coloured' mental labourer. As a true pioneer of Sarvodaya he believed in equality of status among all individuals, high and low. We have to move towards the ideal of settling down equal wages for manual and intellectual labourers. That would certainly remove the stigma of social and economic inequality. Sarvodaya is not a political organisation but a political philosophy absolutely different from the power-oriented political parties. It is open to all views of human welfare operating in the society through different social and political ideologies. It can extract the cream of humanism from all individuals and institutions. Even the thoughts of Sarvodaya is open to evolution and modification in its process of application. But the fundamentals of building a society of Common Welfare should be taken into account.

Restoration of Democracy

Democracy was so dear to J. P., that he initiated democratic values to all political philosophies. He treated democracy not only as a political system but a way of life. The political norms of the democracy had been fully installed in his mind. To him, democracy is a system which should make the people armed with political power. J. P. discarded that system of democracy which does not function according to the will of the people. The three functions of democracy, i.e., 1. Generating Power, 2. Capturing power, and 3. Exercising power should be conducted according to the collective will of the people. The role of political parties is to involve people with the above functions of democracy. But he was aggrieved to find that no political party is doing this. Instead they make themselves powerful riding on the back of the people and make the people powerless. So, he had in his mind to overhaul the entire system of democracy functioning in India and the role which the political parties are playing in the name of democracy. He had been already engaged in reforming the functioning of democracy within the programmes of Sarvodaya and was already involved in reforming the Panchayati Raj system with the intention to bring administration and power to the hands of the people.

J. P. was an expert in inducting radical ideas to all programmes and philosophies that he had been associated with. Accordingly he was keen of reforming democracy by changing the performance of people and advised the political parties to change their role also. He was feeling that the party in power was jumping over all democratic norms to strengthen its own root of power. Power is the ideal of the ruling party. Autocracy was functioning under the camouflage of democracy. He felt that democratic values were being eroded by that. The government was preparing for changing the Constitution to suit into the unethical performance of the government. J. P. was very much perturbed under this situation. He felt that democracy is to establish its base in India and was driving towards a different type of fascism. Though capturing of power through people's representation is one of the functions of democracy, yet the so called leaders of democracy were drawn towards a misconception that democracy cannot stick to power by illegal and unethical means. That unsound mind of the leaders and their performances had put democracy in the dock. J. P. was intensely observing this gradual fall of the democratic system in India and was very much pained about it. The philosophers have warned thousand times that sticking to power blindly would isolate common people from you. Corruption and other social evils are followed by power. It is one of the most dangerous instrument of degrading human personality.

J. P. was a great lover of democracy. He had always dreamt to make India a true democratic country where people will be made powerful to rule themselves through their representatives who would be efficient, honest, simple and dedicated to the cause of social upliftment. He was very proud to be citisen of the largest democratic nation of the world. He loved to quote from the utterances of the then British Prime Minister Mr. Anthony Eden during his visit to India in 1954:

> "While looking into different systems of administrations those were experimented since ancient days, I feel the system of parliamentary administration experimented by India is most romantic and need to attract the attention of all. The open democracy we are gradually developing in the small island of Great Britain since few centuries, that experiment is being done today by a Sub-Continent like country with millions of population. This effort itself is a deed of great courage. The Indian experiment in this regard is not the modernisation of the experiment done by the Britain, instead we could not ever think of its vastness and its magnanimity. If this experiment will be successful, then its influence will be spread to whole of Asia. Whatever might be the consequence, the people who are carrying on this experiment need to be complimented."

J. P. analysed the remarks of the British Prime Minister and asked the people not to forget about the integrity of democracy in our country. India is having one fifth of world's population. The world has become terrorised and greedy world today. If we apply successfully democratic norms in our life and in our administration, then India will be instrumental in bringing about a new age and show the way to heal miseries of the world. He wanted such a new age where democracy and laws would function with the intensity of desire to serve the people. And the administration would be in the hands of people who are culturally and humanitarianly efficient to take care of each individual of the society efficiently with perfect impartiality. He warned the political leaders to act in such a way that the faith the people placed on us would not be tarnished. Otherwise people will treat us as traitors.

J. P. felt that the foundation of democracy was shaking terribly in India when the then Gujarat government outright rejected the demands of students to eliminate rampant corruption, oppression and inefficiency of the Gujarat government and its elected representatives. And they offered non-violent resistance. They were brutally dealt with by the police, but continued pressing their demands time and again through non-violent resistance. The democratic government of Gujarat did not respond. So the students invited J. P. and sought his advice. J. P. was satisfied with the strategy of the students and was overwhelmed to see the unity of the students. He advised them to paralyse the functions of the assembly which was in session so that the government could come to terms.

But the government was adamant in sticking to its refusal. The Gujarat students appealed to the country for sympathy and support explaining to the country that their demands were justified in all respects. The students of Bihar with the help of J. P. responded, and the student movement spread to Bihar. The entire allegation fell on the government leaders who had been turning deaf ears to the students' demands. The lethargy of the government enraged J. P. and he advised the students to intensify the movement with strict code of discipline of non-violence.

The Congress was in power in both Gujarat and Bihar and did not hesitate to use its method of oppression. In the mean time the student movement had already gained support from the people and particularly from the opposition parties. J. P. made efforts to pacify the situation of turmoil by advising the Congress-led Central government to dismiss those State governments who are tutoring the students and the people supporting them. But the Central government did not pay any heed to J. P.'s advice, nor it showed any respect to the sentiment of the opposition parties. The behaviour of the Central government was highly undemocratic and intolerable. J. P. himself wanted to come forward and take the lead of the movement so long as Central Government mends its attitude by punishing those State governments who were involved in rampant corruption and inefficiency. He came to down to the streets with the masses demanding the dismissal of the inefficient State governments by the Centre. With the joining of J. P. the movement took the shape of a mass movement. Masses were mobilised to raise the protest against the government of Bihar and Gujarat in a strictly non-violent manner. The movement was so organised that it could not be suppressed by the domestic government and the masses boldly faced the oppression of the government. In Patna J. P. himself was manhandled by Bihar Police while leading a mass rally. The whole opposition were united under him and joined the movement.

Indira Gandhi was then the Prime Minister of India. She had already gained popularity by nationalising the Banks, by promulgating Land Reform Acts and other poverty alleviation measures taken in the country. Prior to that her contribution to liberate Bangladesh from Pakistan had made her a world figure and with the full support of her Party she was saddled on power. It was natural for her to be guided by ego with sycophants working around her. She did not give any attention to the mass movement of J. P., nor did she express any concern about the issues taken up the by the masses. He continued to advise the government to change the tactics of administration, but for the reason best known to them the government did not take any initiative in solving the crisis. J. P. showed indomitable patience in restraining the movement to become violent. He was optimistic that Indira Gandhi who was heading the government, would desist from doing anything that could go against democratic ethics.

He was always revolting against the system, not against any particular person. He was revolting against the policies of the government leading to corruption in high places. He gave a call to the people to revolt against the corrupted governments and demanded action to be taken against the criminals who were harbouring corruption inside the government. But the government continued to be evasive in response. J. P. was making efforts to unite the opposition political parties to put pressure on the government. It was difficult task as the leaders of the political parties always keep intact the strategies of their leadership in the party. They too have different political aspirations. But he succeeded in uniting like-minded political parties and groups to fight out the corruption 'in the government. The Congress who was in power adamant in their stand to bring the corrupted political leaders to book. J. P. was touring all over the country to mobilise masses against the corruption in the government.

In the meanwhile an incident happened that created a stir all over the country. Prime Minister Indira Gandhi was found guilty of offences of malpractices in the election by Allahabad High Court and accordingly her election was declared void. No body expected that the Prime Minister would loose her seat in the Parliament. In Congress Party there was no other leader to replace her. It was felt by the leaders of the Party that there was no one other than her who could face the stiff opposition that growing in the country day by day.

The immediate reaction of Indiraji was to step down immediately after the verdict of Allahabad High Court. But a second thought prevailed upon her by her coterie of sycophants who succeeded in convincing her that she should continue as Prime Minister and if possible amend the Indian Constitution. The very though was undemocratic and displayed the ego of power. There might have been some other reasons for her to stick to power, but the world viewed towards it as a blatant oppressive act, as it went against the legal decision of the court. All the opposition parties were at their top of their voice demanding stepping down of the Prime Minister. At last she surrendered to the wish of her sycophant companions and promulgated emergency on 24th June, 1974. J. P. and many others called it a "Black Day of Indian history. The emergency stiffed entire nation. Some of the citizens did not believe that in India, who were the founders of democratic traditions and democratic system could ever impose emergency to shut down the mouth of oppositions. The emergency gave a shock to many leaders who worked for the installation of democracy in India throughout their lives.

It was difficult to conceive that Prime Minister Indira Gandhi, who was nourished under the democratic tradition of his father Jawaharlal Nehru could promulgate emergency and paved the way for dictatorship in India. Some politicians were of view that it was not Indira Gandhi alone who initiated this act of choking the voice of the people. There was a group of her party leaders on whom she used to rely advised her to promulgate emergency for teaching a lesson to the opposition. Whatever may be the reason, the promulgation of emergency was extremely unfortunate and uncalled for which broke India's tradition. The Parliament was functioning as a 'Mock Parliament' without the opposition members. All members of the opposition parties and their sympathisers including the people who raised their voice against emergency were imprisoned without trial. J. P. and his colleagues all over India were put behind the prison in different parts of the country. J. P. who in a precarious health condition was arrested on 26th June, 1975 and was sent to Sohana a place in Haryana. As he was not keeping in good health, he was taken to All India Institute of Medical Sciences in Delhi on 29th June, 1975 and soon after that he was sent to Post Graduate Institute of Medical Education and Research at Chandigarh on 1st July, 1975 where he was kept under medical care.

By that time he was experiencing troubles in his kidneys. But still his mind was active in creating public opinion against emergency. He was a man of chivalrous character. He was never of afraid of death and encountered it many times in his life. That was the supreme quality of his life. Even after the emergency his thinking was not only concentrated on eradication of dictatorship and re-establish democracy, but on total revolution initiated for bringing about basic changes in the structure of society. Emergency brought about a shadow on the political arena of the country. The voice of the people was not allowed to be expressed according to their will. People were apprehensive that democracy may not be restored in near future. So they were disheartened. J. P. was shocked and wrote a letter to Prime Minister Indira Gandhi on 21 July, 1975 from Chandigarh Prison:

> "...;You know I am an old titan. I have completed my work of my life. After completing my education, I have dedicated my entire life to the nation and in lieu of it I have not aspired for anything. Therefore. I can die satisfactorily as a prisoner under your administration. Would you please listen to the advice of such a man? Please do not destroy the foundation

which was laid down by The Father of the Nation and your wide-hearted father. There is nothing on the road on which you have started treading on except sorrow and misery. You have received a great cultural heritage in inheritance, acquainted with rich values of life and an active democracy. Do not live behind the debris of these citadels. It will take a lot of time to arrange and nourish them again. I have not an iota of doubt about the joining of these values again. The type of masses who fought with British Imperialism and defeated it, cannot accept the insult and shameful dictatorship for time to come. The strength of the power of soul of a man cannot be destroyed in any way in spite of various oppressions. Though you have put all democratic values under the grave for your personal dictatorship, it will break open the coffin and come out of the grave some day. In Russia, it is also coming out very slowly."

(Mere Jeevan Yatra)

J. P. was afraid that if autocracy would be imposed then India may enter into the domain of the type of Autocracy of Bangladesh. He referred to the state of Bangladesh after Mujibur Rahman came to power with massive mandate of the people, but cheated them outright by imposing later on one party rule. The purpose of one party rule was to suppress the voice the opposition. Freedom of speech was denied to citizens. All they had to do was to obey the orders of leader of the party in power.

In India, it happened, but for a short period. But there had been a feeling that for the time in the history of the nation people sensed in the air that dictatorship may step in to replace democracy. The first public reaction of Dictatorship was that the humanism was taken away from human beings and they became beasts. He had no right to speak anything according to his desire. The main difference between a man and a beast was, a beast has no language to express his feelings, where as a man has. Language is a precious gift of God to a man. Human language is a powerful instrument of expression. It is the birth right of a man to express his views what he thinks best and acts according to it. But in autocracy this birth right is snatched away from the people. India is a country where people enjoyed the freedom to express their opinion on anything they like. Since the concept of political freedom was born, freedom of speech had been considered as the precious human value. It was through this freedom man changed the destiny of the history many times. Specially in India, freedom to express one's views was linked with our cultural heritage. In ancient days, each individual enjoyed the freedom by his own views. He was free to express his views about religion, about political matters and about functioning of the society.

This was considered to be one of the commendable contribution of Indian culture to the world. The ancient people of India went deep into the thinking process of man and discovered many things congenial to the evolution of mankind. It is the 'instrument that can strengthen the functioning of democracy. Entertaining the views of the opponent is one of the good qualities of democracy. This is not found in any other form of political thought. It is hoped that after so many years of political independence the people of India are well accustomed in pushing the democratic values into their veins. It has gone deep into their hearts.

The promulgation of emergency came as a blessing in disguise as it strengthened the spirit of the people of India to preserve democratic values in spite of their poverty and ignorance. They did not allow their conscience and human values to be bartered for any material prospect. During the time of emergency they demonstrated to the world that it would tolerate any amount of oppression to uphold human values. J. P. was very much relieved to see that the Indian masses were fully equipped with basic human values like freedom of expression and freedom of movement from place to place. They continued to extend support to the movement against the government without his guidance as J. P. was lodged in prison during the emergency.

All wise men of the world, including those of our own country got the opportunity of exploring their genius inside the prison. They all produced thought-provoking and classic literatures. Tilak, Nehru and Vinoba were among them. They utilised then prison term in creating deep-rooted concepts on humanism and dedication that influenced human society for ages to comes. Tilak's Geeta Rhashya, Jawaharlal Nehru's Autobiography and Discovery of India, Vinoba's Geeta Prabachan were the creations they made during their prison life.

The wise men always took advantage of their isolation from the outer world and concentrated on their inner self and discovered their great wisdom that was capable to serve the society for longer period. J. P. was no exception. He wrote his prison diary which was full of emotions, feelings and sentiments, personal and impersonal. He took the full advantage of the isolation and engrossed in developing his concept on Total Revolution. His imprisonment helped to widen his heart and eroded his personal grief gradually and he became a total changed personality. He recharged rich human values which were important to him instead of the material achievements and that was a part of his movement against the government.

By constant introspection inside the prison, he could feel that mere changes in the government may minimise the deprivations to some extent if the future government bears an attitude of humanism. Alike all the wise and enlightened prisoners, J. P. grew amidst physical suffering. His deteriorating health could not stand bar to the evolution of his thoughts. Though he was always in a pensive mood regarding the situation prevailed in India during emergency period, yet he concentrated his thoughts on planning the programmes of Total Revolution. He admitted that the concept of Total Revolution was concealed in Vinoba's Sarvodaya programmes, but his movement did not concentrate on it. J. P. wanted to concentrate all his activities with the object of achieving Total Revolution.

In the prison he contemplated, that through the Total Revolution only democracy could function in a right manner. To make the people truly democratic, we have to change the entire structure of the society. The political system should be completely decentralised, the social and economic inequalities should be removed, the educational pattern should be village industry oriented, the culture of human brotherhood should be inducted into the society with the changing of the attitude of the individuals.

The ownership of the property should be rested on the community followed by the system of equitable distribution. There must be minor difference between the wages of intellectuals and the physical labourers. When these changes would be worked out by the people voluntarily, then the gates of the total revolution will be opened. So, in prison, he was moving towards a higher vision of life with a passion to establish higher democratic values in society.

But one thing hangs in the minds of the common people that was there a situation that emerged out of J. P.'s movement which forced the government of Indira Gandhi to impose emergency? Some other alternatives could have been applied instead. There were thousand and other means to meet the demands of the people and the students. And besides, the movement cannot be compared with an arms uprising. Me wrote defending the non-violent nature of his movement. He claimed that the congregation of All India Janata Rally held at Delhi on 6th March, 1975 where about 5 lakhs people gathered, was completely non-violent in nature, the Kolkata Rally held on 5th June, 1975 was also of the same nature.

The police administration of those states admitted that the rallies were peaceful and non-violent. No doubt, J. P. appealed through the movement to paralyse the functions of the government by non-cooperation and non-violent resistance. The movement was by and large non-violent in nature as though there was some amount of personal hatred against Indira Gandhi, who was heading the government. Had she overrode over her coterie of sycophant advisers, she could have displayed the democratic spirit that she might have inherited from her father, in any case, the promulgation of emergency was a very unfortunate chapter of the nation.

From the beginning J. P. was planning to draw the attention of the government for the various deprivations present in the country. He had organised the masses to put pressure on the government to remove rampant corruption, to remove hunger and poverty, to fix accountability on the bureaucrats who were in change of development, to strengthen the Panchayati Raj by deputing more powers to the Gram Panchayats and many other things. So J. P. went on intensifying the movement prior to emergency and there was plan for a weeklong Satyagraha in all

States from 29th June, 1975. The mobilisation of masses in all these states was complete. The government took a serious view of this situation and thought this could completely paralyse the administration.

The government was also afraid that this seven days Satyagraha may turn violent and may lead to violent confrontation between the administration and the people causing huge loss of life and bloodshed. No doubt J. P.'s movement was based on complete non-violence, but it may be that without his presence the spirit of non-violence may not be retained. So, the administration speculated violence in this seven-day Satyagraha and wanted to ear up the prevention measures accordingly. It might have been that the leaders of the government did not have confidence on their own administration and might have advised Prime Minister to take extreme step of promulgating Emergency without looking into its after effects on the country. However, with the apprehension of violent revolt, emergency was imposed on 25th June, 1975 totally banning all meetings and public congregations.

The government was not then antagonistic to those changes, since prior to that, the government moved on by enacting progressive laws on land reforms, banking insurances, and arranged loans to poor for self-employment with a meagre rate of interest. But still more changes had to be done. With all these measures taken it was felt specially by the people of South India, that the government of Indira Gandhi was heading towards a socialist government. But as we all know, socialism was not that easy a concept to be worked out by the leaders of a Party who did not want to sacrifice for the society, nor believed in elimination of individual ownership. In any case, it was an admitted fact that at the primary stage of Indira Gandhi's government was seriously concerned about improving the conditions of the common people. But the saying goes that "All is well that ends well" never happened. All good deeds of the government was washed away with the promulgation of emergency.

J. P.'s movement was taking shape when he was fully involved in the Sarvodaya movement of Vinobaji. Before embarking upon his movement to paralyse the "corrupt" government, he placed his intention before Vinobaji. But, as Vinobaji was a man of grace and tolerance, he advised J. P. to give a second thought for starting his movement. But J. P. argued that the situation had gone beyond tolerance, and there was no alternative than to launch the movement. It was difficult for both Vinoba and J. P. to go against Indira Gandhi as she was intimately and personally very dear to them. It was more difficult for J. P., because he and Prabhavati were the members of Nchru family and from the childhood Indira Gandhi was daughter to (ban. So, it was natural for J. P. to take a very painful decision of revolting against her and with her administration both. J. P. wanted Vinoba along with all the Sarvodaya workers of the country to abandon their programmes like Bhoodan-Gramdan. Sampattidan, Shanti Sena, etc. and totally join his movement against the government. But Vinobaji did not agree to abandon all programmes of Sarvodaya, but agreed that those who want to join J. P.'s movement may safely go with him and those who want to concentrate in other programmes of Sarvodaya may carry on with it J. P.'s movement would act as a wing of the Sarvodaya.

During the time of reconciliation no body ever contemplated that the movement would one day turn out to be a political movement and join hands with the power-oriented opposition parties with an objective to dislodge Indira Gandhi and capture power. This was because J. P. was aware of the ethics of Sarvodaya that did not approve joining its cadre in power politics. At the time of reconciliation with Vinoba it was never contemplated that the movement lodged by J. P. would one day be diverted to capture power by dislodging Indira Gandhi's government. Probably J. P. was himself not aware of the situation that would come in future and take this shape of the movement. At the outset it was not intended for capturing power.

Because J. P. kept himself away from acquiring any scat of power in the past. He was very sure about his own stand so far as his relation to power politics is concerned. Even when, he was an active leader of either of Congress or Socialist party, he did not contest any election from Gram Panchayat level to Parliament level, though he propagated many times for his party colleagues in elections. That was the secret of ideal and his personality. There was a minor division in Sarvodaya camp. Vinobaji warned

Sarvodaya workers that in whatever programme they want to join they must keep their hearts united. He said that all programmes were emerged out of evolution of Sarvodaya thought. But the entire atmosphere changed alter 25th June, 1975, from the day the Emergency was imposed. Vinoba remained silent advising that the government should function under the guidance of "Reason and Conscience". He was a spiritual man and gave his comments accordingly which was interpreted by his opponents in various abusive and unfair manner. Vinobaji maintained complete silence till 25th December, 1975.

The followers of Vinobaji did not participate in J. P.'s movement, but had great regard for him for his dedicated and value based personality. Vinobaji had to face many calumnies by J. P.'s followers who did not bad the calibre to judge both J. P. and Vinobaji's silence was misinterpreted in many fallacious ways. Some carried on the calumny to the extent that Vinobaji was a supporter of Emergency and therefore he did not raise his voice against it. It would be extremely difficult to judge the purpose of his 'silence' and this point of his view that forced him to maintain silence for a period of six months.

Some did not agree with J. P.'s comment that as Vinobaji was a man of spiritual integrity, as he did not take these issues that affected the day to day life of man so seriously. We have nothing to comment about this remark of great man. But the country had noted that how Vinobaji had always kept his feet on the soil of the earth and treaded 50,000 kilometres by foot only to be acquainted with the day to day life of the people. Since he attained his adolescence, he accepted voluntary-poverty as a way of his life. He survived upon the scanty wages that he earned from the sweat of his brow.

Hence, with all these background, it has been difficult to approve this attribution. Against him, Vinobaji was a man of high integrity and a genius in practising truth in his life second to Mahatma Gandhi. It was impossible for him to harbour either falsehood or blasphemy to uphold his public image to conceal any sort of consistency or truth. He must not be judged through outward circumstances. Let he be judged by his dedication of body and soul for the welfare of the country.

The evolution of the personality of J. P. was the evolution of the Socialism in our country. Again when he stepped into Sarvodaya under the guidance of Vinobaji, he made the concept of Sarvodaya more scientific, more developed and more spiritual in the sense that all his approaches were completely humanitarian. His association with Vinobaji made him more creative and more enlightened. Vinobaji was a seasoned expert in transforming non-violent resistance into Gandhian Technique of Satyagraha of invincible and all well-being-weapon of love and place the same before the society. Vinobaji, thus, in his own way, developed and purified many Gandhian methods to make them more scientific and logical. Through Bhoodan and Gramdan movement, Vinobaji established the concept of Revolution by Cooperation which in itself was a miraculous experiment to modify human attitude towards the society.

The experiment of Vinoba inducted the spirit of compassion into the movement of removing economic inequality. That was one of the most bright and illustrious chapter of our history. J. P. was attracted to this and first shared platform with Vinobaji at Chandil in Bihar in 1953. Since then, J. P. did not look back and moved forward to strengthen Vinobaji's Revollmon by Cooperation. No body, as yet, surpassed the vision of Vinobaji to build up a movement based on the factors of human values. He might have been succeeded fully, but the experiment in itself enriched the vision of humanism. J. P. was drawn towards this enlightened vision of compassionate revolution and took the saddle in his own hands. So, he can be claimed to be the inheritor of Vinoba. There was, not even an iota of difference between the vision of J. P. and Vinobaji. The technique of Satyagraha adopted by J. P. was linked with the experiments made by Gandhi-Vinoba in the field of Satyagraha. There would be no exaggeration in saying that J. P. emerged as Loknayak from the movement of Vinobaji. Vinobaji's movement enriched him and complimented to his talents of non-violent revolution. He was baptised under the care of Vinobaji and attained the captaincy to handle Lokneeti and ultimately become the Supremo of Lokneeti or Loknayak as he was popularly called. Regarding the misunderstanding created in the name of Vinobaji, Dada Dharmadhikari, an exponent of Sarvodaya movement in India said:

> "It would not be out of place to submit regarding the role of Revered Vinoba. One of the symptoms of Satyagraha is that the Satyagraha would place himself on the footing of his opponent and try to understand his situation. Intense tolerance and respect for adversary are identification of a true Satyagrahai. But proper justice was not done to Vinoba in this regard. An atmosphere of disrespect and antagonism was spread through the country. Sufficient efforts were not made to understand his context. This is a matter of great regret that those persons had played a role in it who once loved and placed Vinoba in high esteem. It is a fact that the role of Vinoba during that period was incalculable, but the amount of light to have to harbour difference with Vinoba, at least that amount of right should be given to Vinoba to have difference with us. Why there should he any barrier between difference of opinion and sense of respect? It was a matter of great satisfaction that most of the comrades of Sarvodaya field were not contemptuous in their attitude in spite of their difference of opinion with Vinoba. They were aggrieved owing to their deep love for him, but they harboured love and respect for Vinoba. In the Acharya Conference, when Vinoba expounded his concept of "Third Power " on a non-governmental basis, the whole Sarvodaya family hailed him unanimously from the core of their hearts. In matters of Cow Slaughter also all hailed his role. Probably, we may realise if we look back that in same matters Vinoba was a visionary than any of us. Difference of opinion and friendship should go hand in hand in Satyagraha."

Vinoba has advised us to bum the lamp in our heart and peep into it. Believe in the 'proofless' existence of the Supreme and treat Him as the final 'Proof. He has also taught us that the Supreme displayed thousand heads in His "Viswarupa", but kept one heart. If we respect this indication of Vinoba, then we must understand that all our programmes of the revolution will be activated through

Vinoba's positive programmes. Difference in Jargons do not amount to difference of opinion. It is highly unethical and improper. There had been a minor difference between the culture of Gandhi-Vinoba and J. P.. All the cultures of Gandhi-Vinoba emanated from Indian cultural heritage. And those were reflected in their languages and views.

The words that came out of their mouth spontaneously bathed their culture. J. P. entered into the Sarvodaya field from the cultural heritage of Marxism and Socialism. But the interesting fact was that his entry into Sarvodaya was not initiated through Gandhian concept but through Vinoba's exemplary performance. J. P. went to Paunar Ashram of Vinoba after ending his fast at Puna which he made for self-purification. He joined hands with the inmates in pulling water from the well through 'Persian wheel'. In the process he roamed around the well. He expressed with the completion of every circle, the 'wheel of conscience' was moving inside his head. That was the first day of baptisation to the Sarvodaya world.

In spite of the fact that he won the laurels as the inheritor to Gandhi-Vinoba, he surrendered the laurels to his natural modesty which was one of his great quality. Therefore, he did not claim to be fit in using the conventional jargons such as truth, non-violence. But in practice, he was fully seasoned in applying these values. That was why we saw the character of his movement though radical and progressive in nature, was totally peaceful. The context of Bhoodan-Gramdan movement was different. There was also the objective of eliminating exploitation and oppression from the suffering humanity, and there was more emphasis on self purification and dedication and sacrifice.

J. P.'s movement stood on a different context that demanded immediate confrontation with the State power. The situation was such that J. P. had to go for a different strategy. The words in his movement were used were born out of his Marxist and Socialist cultural background. He had set up "confrontation committees" in many States to raise their voice against the government who was harbouring corruption, misdeeds and exploitation and negligence. He used the word "confrontation" only to make conscious the ignorant people about their rights and liberties. He wanted to infuse the spirit of valour into the veins of the deprived and the underprivileged so that they could raise their voice against these irregularities. Otherwise they had to depend upon the mercy of those who were well to do and established. J. P. wanted to generate the people's power from the performance of the people. This type of life which the common men of our country were living with was full of humiliation and curse. No doubt the technique of his movement was non-violent, but he used the jargon of "confrontation" only to popularise the movement among the youths. He maintained the spirit of complete non-violence so far his strategy of revolution is concerned.

J. P. was famous for his chivalry. In this he stood unparallel to many leaders of India. In the minds of people, chivalry has been always associated with 'confrontation'. One should not underestimate one's chivalry simply because there is some amount of violence had been underlying in the word. Sarvodaya workers should not go by word, instead they should go by spirit. Under this context, J. P. was justified in coining the word 'confrontation' into his movement.

It is a strange coincidence of fact that this language of chivalry is very popular in the field of spiritualism and devotion. Vinoba himself applied the word "Shanti Sena" or Peace Army while pacifying the communal forces and establishing peace in the country. J. P. too led this Shanti Sena movement several times in the country. The word 'Army' used by Vinoba had in it a, bidden sense of violence. But Vinoba did not go by the word only. He went by spirit. J. P.'s word 'confrontation' should be treated accordingly. The hidden objective of J. P. movement was total revolution, which was chiefly a creative movement.

It was not indispensable that confrontation would be continuously carried against the government. That was not the main objective of his movement. Confrontation with the government was just a temporary process initiated under the existing situation. There were probability of confrontation also in cooperation with government in other spheres. After the demise of his dear wife Prabhavatiji, J. P. was really in quest of peace of mind to fill the vacuum of grief. The outward situation spontaneously pushed him towards confrontation as it was against his conscience to digest the challenge thrown to him by the government.

The decision of building up a Man of Revolution did not depend upon any logic or justification. It was the events that built up a man of Revolution. The emergence of the revolutionary personality was spontaneous and came from within one's heart. The outward situation was often instrumental in giving the inspiration to the man to grow with revolution. In case of Mahatma Gandhi, the situation in South Africa was instrumental in inspiring Gandhiji to discover Satyagraha. The situation in Telengana was instrumental for Vinoba for discovering Bhoodan movement. Similarly the Student movement in Bihar was instrumental in inspiring J. P. for Total Revolution. Whatever might be the instruments of application, the main objective of the movement was to inspire the man lying in the lower strata of the society to fight for his own upliftment and at the same time to act as an instrument of social change. Otherwise people's revolution would be a far cry. But J. P. was convinced that the strategy of revolution would be strictly non-violent and peaceful. He had issued directives to all the members of the "Confrontation Committees" to follow up the code of conduct perfectly. He had already expressed several times that since the strategy of violence had reached the point of saturation, it had become obsolete and out dated. It is foolish and unwise to use an outdated weapon as an instrument of revolution. So, he was far away from accepting any form of violence for any form of social change.

The main question before revolution was that how to, make the oppressed and exploited millions crushed under deprivation would be made capable of handling their own revolution. Through revolution J. P. wanted to attain that. This quest of power of making the last man capable of leading his own revolution was still there even after J. P.'s revolution ended. This quest was a continuous process But this experiment in shape of quest is still in infant state. Those who are in need of the revolution are yet to be awakened, they are yet to be inspired. Another objective of the J. P.'s movement was to place democracy on firm foundation and establish the same permanently on democratic values. The sanction for democracy could not be achieved through violence. The sanction for democracy could be generated from the collective will of the people. J. P. strived hard top establish the sanction of the people in favour of democracy. That was a type of cooperation with the process of functioning of the government. It was unfortunate that the men in power failed to recognise this cooperative aspect of J. P.'s movement and went ahead with confrontation, where as this could have been averted through reconciliation.

Election of representatives of people to different public bodies including assemblies and Parliament were conducted after the withdrawal of emergency. No doubt there had been a great display of citizen's power in the election. There was some awakening in the country Lokshakti or the people's power could not be established permanently. People's power took the shape of Party-Power gradually eliminating the identity of the people, and it was a matter of fear that the people's power would ultimately merge in Party power. At the outset, J. P.'s movement seemed to have taken a narrow outlook being chiefly guided by the opposition parties. But this might have escaped the notice of J. P.. It was a matter of great concern for those who believe in founding the people's power.

All must realise that the last man is the source of power. The power must generate from him. It was doubtful whether the political parties carried the same vision as non-violent revolutionaries. The foremost programme of J. P.'s revolution was to create consciousness among the men of the last strata and train them accordingly so that they could be aware of their concealed power. But it was doubtful if the political parties who supported TR's movement was sincere about this goal. J. P.'s movement, no doubt was basically an experiment of generating people's power. But when we look towards its result, it was felt that it was incomplete. Like previous movements, this movement too suffered from many faults. And the lack of decision-making effort had made the movement crippled in the midway. But in spite of its faults, this movement comparatively became successful to the extent that it could be able to arouse the consciousness of the people to a great extent. After the election was over, the opposition who came to power did not attribute much importance to the objectives of J. P.'s revolution.

It had been felt that the forces of communalism subdued for a long time took full advantage of J. P.'s movement and took charge of the opposition of the country defeating secular forces. Secular parties who were in power, were thrown away being over powered by the parties having link with communal forces. J. P. was no longer there to see this political catastrophe. In past, leaders who claimed themselves with pride that they were responsible for the assassination of the Father of the Nation, rallied around J. P. with the single objective to pull down Indira Gandhi from Power and capture power through manipulation.

The Janata Party that was formed with the blessings of J. P. was dismantled and parties with communal intention formed a separate but powerful party. The people of India who aspired to make revolution successful were upset at the result of their revolution in which they so passionately participated. They have to restart again with double vigour the spirit that J. P. inducted in them. They have to pull down the communal forces working in the country and save the country from the onslaught of disintegration. Had J. P. been there, he would have added communal harmony and national integration as a second wing of his movement.

It would not be out of place to mention here that immediately after Mahatma Gandhi was shot dead, Sardar Ballabhbhai Patel banned the communal organisations. Time has again come to take same step to save the country from communal riots, murder, religious hatred and atrocities on the minorities. J. P. was optimistic that the opposition parties who participated in his movement would carry out at least those political reforms essential for preservation of democratic structure of the government and would enhance people's participation. But that was not to be done.

The opposition that came to power did not guarantee J. P. for changing the Constitution by inducting a clause in favour of recalling those people's representatives by the referendum of the electorate if they are found to be inefficient, corrupts, liars and cheats. They placed the argument that constant withdrawal of the representatives by the mandate of people would affect the stability of the government and the process will hinder development work. Delegation of judicial powers to Gram Panchayats to deal with and settle matters pertaining to village disputes of all kinds was another step towards a better form of administration, was also ignored by the opposition parties. In short it did not agree to carry on any reforms to change the fundamental structure of the administration. It seemed the opposition political parties utilised J. P.'s movement for the stability of their parties. So, it was felt that the huge people's consciousness that was created through the movement was fizzled out gradually except some "Confrontation Committees" and "New Development Committees" those are working in some parts of the country in a small scale.

Dada Dharmadhikari who is a great exponent of Sarvodaya revolution and closely associated with J. P. and Vinoba both, suggested few points to strengthen the Satyagraha with the objective to make it perfect and pure and acceptable and easily applicable. These suggestions seemed to be very consistent and appropriate. They were:

- While making efforts for peaceful resistance, the revolutionary himself under no circumstances, would depend on the attitude of counterviolence. But, if at all, violence erupts at non-governmental level, the revolutionary must treat it to be detrimental to the interest of revolution. Under all circumstances violent resistance must be forbidden while conducting peaceful revolution.
- Another important characteristic of peaceful revolution is that if the common men are terrorised in anyway owing to the performances of the peaceful revolution, then the movement will be treated detrimental to peaceful revolution must be withdrawn immediately.
- Our adversary must have full confidence on our integrity and truthfulness. He must relay on us on the method of our resistance. There should not be any act of deception on our part. We must not cheat him in any way. Our movement is not a movement of deceit and anger. This is the border line of a peaceful revolution.
- In this context live have to rethink seriously about "underground movement". From the experience, it has been found that by going 'underground' our adversary looses faith on us as our activities are commenced keeping the adversary in darkness.

Besides, an atmosphere of suspicion and disbelief is created by that. The underground revolutionary is alert about his own shadow. This type of suspicion is compared to poison for any sort of organisation.

- There are some instruments of revolution those seem outwardly non-violent, but inwardly they are more violent than the weapons. Most of the fasts and wrongful confinement of the adversary, though non-violent in nature, cannot be treated purely of non-violent character. When we fail to apply pure logical and justified intellectual discourse and polite requests, then we are compelled to take refuge in superfluous power to purify ourselves and to change the heart of our adversary. This power is not freed from little bit imposition, hut as it harms no body and mind, it may be accepted as a moral pressure. This moral pressure is required to invite the underneath feeling of the adversary. Therefore, it is named as 'moral pressure. The revolutionary should be extremely careful towards its application. To defeat the adversary cannot be the only objective of a Satyagrahi.
- The amount of chivalry indispensable for peaceful revolution must commensurate with the absence of the attitude of animosity. The attitude of adversity may exist for the adversary, but there should not be any attitude of animosity and condemnation towards him. We cannot conceive of any harm to be done towards him.

J. P. himself was an example of this heart-touching character of purity and simplicity. Prior to his departure for America for his treatment he was sinking in his health. He knew that it was difficult to survive for a long time under this health condition. He was unwilling to go to America as the method of treatment adopted at America is available in India. The illness had made him tired physically and mentally. He spoke to Dada Dharmadhikari in isolation.

> "It seems. I shall not live, longer. There is no point in going outside the country for treatment. The treatment that can be done in any part of the world

> can be done here as our doctors have the capability of doing that. Two desires might remain unfulfilled. One is that I could not do "Kanyadan " (Rite of offering the bride in the hands of the groom) and second is that the daughter Indira could not able to understand me. I have not an iota of animosity towards her I had not wanted her sticking to a wrong path. I had not the least intention of doing any harm to her. What was the necessity of removing her? But how can I let her understand this?" (Meri Vichar Yatra-Part II)

The other incident was when Indira sent him Rs. 90,000 /- most probably to meet his medical expenses. He was overwhelmed to receive it. Expressing his spontaneous reaction over this he said:

> "How can I deny it, when Indira has extended her hands to me? My answer would be to that I am accepting your amount with thanks."

The receipt of J. P. with thanks to Indiraji was sent to Delhi by Shri Radhaknishna. But leading friends of J. P. at Delhi thought it better to return the amount. Later on the letter of refusal that J. P. wrote to Indiraji was full of affection and modesty. Whatever might be the situation later, the response of J. P. to his Arch enemy Indira Gandhi was noteworthy, as it was a manifestation of a pure and maliceless heart rarely found in the characters of revolutionaries. J. P. was adorned with the qualities of a true revolutionary in the strict sense of the term. It is extremely difficult for an ordinary volunteer of revolution to fight against an autocratic power and the same time harbouring no personal malice against the person involved in it.

Expressing satisfaction after the election and after restoration of democracy he wrote that he could be able to bring Indiraji back to this track, but the common people have brought back the country into the track of democracy. This situation was created for the first time in the country when it was contemplated that Autocracy would replace democracy. But the poor and illiterate people of India have given clear mandate and saved the democracy. No doubt that the people of India played major role in restoring democracy by unimaginable exhibition of their hidden strength.

The next major role played by J. P. who inspired the entire nation through his sacrifice and dedication and through his commitment towards non-violent revolution. Along with it, even without our wish, there would be no travesty of truth to say that Indira Gandhi was too instrumental in restoring democracy by withdrawing emergency and declaring election. Whatever might be the reason, there was no denial of the fact that she created opportunity for the operation of the parliamentary system allowing the people of India to give their fresh mandate by declaring the election.

Our country is a country' full of wonders. These wonders are happening in India since two centuries. The first wonder was the establishment of British Empire in India. About one and half lakh Britishers who came from a distance of six thousand miles from a tiny island kept in bondage such a vast land and its people for more than one hundred and fifty years.

The entire nation meekly surrendered before the British. The next wonder happened when the Father of the Nation, Mahatma Gandhi liberated India. It is owing to the grace of the Father of the Nation and his associates who fought for the liberation of India, with the help of millions of ignorant and illiterate people. Now, India is acclaimed as the most powerful democracy in the world. These millions of people suffering from all types of deprivations have shouldered the burden of democracy and showed that they are capable of offering guidance to democratic functioning of the nation.

The literate and so called elite of the world often express their amazement that how these people without any academic knowledge of the democratic system run the administration of the nation as per their will. It is fact unimaginable to most of the elites. The wonder really happened when these simple and ignorant Indian folk overthrew one hundred and fifty years of British slavery by winning courageously the battle of liberation under the leadership of Mahatma Gandhi with the help of weapons of non-violence and peaceful non-cooperation. Such a weapon was used for the first time in the world in a fight for liberation. No doubt the fighters of liberation faced batons and bullets and gallows voluntarily without acting upon any vengeance on the Britishers. Mass non-violent resistance was offered by the people against all violent actions. This became another wonder that happened in India. Another wonder occurred in the Province of Kerala where communist government was established through ballot not through bullet. Never before in any corner of the world communists came to power through electioneering process and adult franchise. The communist leader EMS Namboodripad was perhaps the first communist in the world who accepted and applied ballot that never practised earlier in any communist nations of the world. It was in India that this wonderful event occurred and all the credit goes to the people of Kerala who unexpectedly and smoothly transfer the administration to the hands of communists. The next wonder occurred when the Congress Party who ruled the country continuously for twenty nine years since independence was overthrown in March 1977 facing complete and unprecedented defeat. J. P. played the leading role in putting an end to the Congress rule by successfully organising the opposition political parties and by initiating a revolutionary process. The old revolutionaries believed that social changes could not be brought about through parliamentary system of democracy. But J. P. established the notion that social changes can be done through parliamentary democracy. This event established the fact that parliamentary democracy if effectively and ethically implemented could be able to initiate social change.

The greatest of all wonders is the exhibition of people's power in India. In all events mentioned above proved that the hidden power that lies in the docile, meek, poor, ignorant people can change governments one after another according to their will. They have shown to the world that when required they can rise up from their slumber and meet the challenge and change the fate of the nation. History must take note of the bravery of the Indian masses and should not treat them awkwardly.

4

J. P.'s Thought

Renouncing Party - Politics

Some time back when I decided to withdraw from party politics I felt it necessary to explain my action to my colleagues of the Praja Socialist Party and to the public generally. The statement that follows is intended to do that. It begins with a few words addressed specifically to my friends of the PSP, followed with an elucidation of my position and the evolution of my own ideas which are meant not only for them, but for all those who may be interested in the matter.

—Jayaprakash Narayan

Calcutta

21 December. 1957

"A few words addressed specially to my friends at party." Dear Comrades After long deliberation I have decided to write you this letter. It has not been easy for me to do it. Because it is never easy to cut oneself away from an association of a lifetime. We have worked together, and together have we suffered imprisonment, lived through the adventures of the underground, and tasted the ashes of independence. We have all far to travel yet.

But I, on my part at least, find myself at a point of the journey where I must decide to part company and walk it alone. It would have gladdened my heart beyond measure had I been able to persuade you to come along with me but I realise that that is not possible—at least for the present I hope, however, that our paths will often meet and that at the journey's end they will merge together. We may not live to see that consummation ourselves, but I feel confident that if the world were ever to reach the port of peace and freedom and brotherhood, socialism must eventually merge into *sarvodaya.*

It was four years ago at the Bodh Gaya Sarvodaya Sammelan that I decided to give up politics. But I had continued to be a member of the PSP; though, apart from attending an occasional meeting or offering an occasional advice, I took no part in the activities of the Party. Some time before the last General Election, I came to the decision that I should give up even the sleeping membership of the PSP. But Acharyaji was ill and I did not want to take the step without discussing the matter with him. To the great misfortune of this country and of the socialist cause. Acharya Narendra Deva passed away. It was a staggering blow to the PSP, which had already been weakened by a split Leading comrades, therefore, pleaded with me not to announce my resignation till the elections were over. I agreed, but it was understood that soon after the elections the announcement would be made. The delay in doing this has been due entirely to the fact that I was anxious to place before you and before the country generally the reasons that led me to take such a drastic step—i.e. a step that was natural to me but that appears so drastic to others. Almost everyday some one or another raises the question with me why at all I should have given up politics. The faith and hope that people seem to repose in politics appear pitiable to me, but I find it difficult to explain to every one individually the rationale of my action. I am attempting to do so here.

The hold of politics on the minds of people is such, and its alternative is in such an incipient state yet, that I shall not probably be able to persuade many of those who may read the statement, but I do hope there will be more mutual understanding and also a quickening of interest in the ideas herein propounded. There is also another aspect of the matter. Everyone views things from his own particular background. Those who have not gone through the experiences which I have passed through, nor pursued the ideals which have been mine might fail to appreciate my reasoning. A new enthusiast for socialism, or the class struggle, political action, or parliamentary democracy, may not perhaps be able to follow me until he has come to enquire how the drawbacks that he has discovered in his particular enthusiasm can be remedied. I am not for a moment suggesting that I have arrived at a flawless solution of social problems or that *sarvodaya* is the last word in social philosophy. Man is ever progressing towards the truth, for he is by nature an enquiring being. He will never be able to reach the ultimate truth, but by gradually eliminating untruth, he will be able slowly to approach the truth. There is no doubt that many flaws in *sarvodaya* thought and practice will be discovered and removed in the future and thus the human mind will keep up its ascent to the truth. But I do believe that *sarvodaya* represents a distinct advance over the existing social philosophies and systems. I shall try to explain the process through which I arrived at this conclusion. What follows is by no means a full statement of the *sarvodaya* philosophy, for which task I have no adequate equipment in any case, but a narration of the evolution of my own thinking that led me finally to renounce politics.

From Non-cooperation to Communism

The past course of my life might well appear to the outsider as a zigzag and tortuous chart of unsteadiness and blind groping. But as I look back I discern in it a uniform line of development. The groping undeniably was there, but it was certainly not blind; there were clear beacons of light that remained undimmed and unaltered from the beginning and that led me on to my apparently tortuous path. I, at least, am not sorry for having made this zigzag journey, for it has made me the surer of the path that I have now decided to tread.

As a boy, like most boys of those days, I was an ardent nationalist and leaned towards the revolutionary cult of which Bengal was the noble leader at that time. But even then the story of the South African *satyagraha* had fascinated my young heart.

Before my revolutionary leanings could mature, Gandhiji's first non-cooperation movement swept over the land as a strangely uplifting hurricane. I too was one of the thousands of young men of those days, who, like leaves in the storm, were swept away and momentarily lifted up to the skies. That brief experience of soaring up with the winds of a great idea left imprints on the inner being that time and much familiarity with ugliness of reality have not removed.

It was then that freedom became one of the beacon lights of my life, and it has remained so ever since. Freedom, with the passing of the years, transcended the mere freedom of my country and embraced freedom of man everywhere and from every sort of trammel — above all, it meant freedom of the human personality, freedom of the mind, freedom of the spirit. This freedom has become a passion of life and I shall not see it compromised for bread, for power, for security, for prosperity, for the glory of the State or for anything else.

Strangely enough, it was in the land of resilient and successful capitalism, in the United States of America, which was my home from 1922 to 1929, that I became a convert to Marxism, or more precisely, to Soviet Communism as it was then. It was at Madison, Wisconsin, the home of La Follette progressivism then, that in the company of Jewish and European-born fellow students I drank deep at the fountain of Marxism, I think we left nothing unread of Marxism that was available in the English language then and with the help of a brilliant student of German even read some of the untranslated Marxian classics. The pungent writings of M.N. Roy that found their way from Europe into the communist cells, particularly of Asian students, completed the conversion to Marxism.

Freedom still remained the unchanging goal, but the Marxian science of revolution seemed to offer a surer and quicker road to it than Gandhiji's technique of civil disobedience and non-cooperation. The thrilling success of the great Lenin, accounts of which we consumed with unsatiated hunger, seemed to establish beyond doubt the supremacy of the Marxian way to revolution.

At the same time, Marxism provided another beacon of light for me: equality and brotherhood. Freedom was not enough. It must mean freedom for all — even the lowliest — and this freedom must include freedom from exploitation, from hunger, from poverty. I cannot say what were the early experiences that had laid the foundations in the subconscious mind of sympathy with poverty and suffering. But the latent sympathy certainty was there, and it was awakened and brought to the surface of conscious living by Marxism. This process was reinforced by the mode of my life in the United States. Coming from the lower middle class, I hardly received any help from my family and had to work as an ordinary labourer in field and factory to earn my upkeep and the expenses of university education. At that time I was not very certain about Gandhiji's stand on the vital question of equality which captivated me as much as the ideal of freedom. As a matter of fact, Roy's writings of those days (though Roy, too, later travelled far from those positions) persuaded me to believe that Gandhiji was against the social revolution and would at a moment of crisis hasten to uphold the system of exploitation and inequality. I did not understand then that Gandhiji had his own conception of the social revolution and of the means to achieve it.

From Communism to Democratic Socialism

The end of 1929, when I returned to my country, was not a propitious time for Marxism. Nationalism was reaching white heat and when, in December of that year, Gandhiji failed to persuade Lord Irwin (as he then was) to agree to full 'dominion status" for India, in terms of the Calcutta Congress Resolution, the stage was set for a gigantic leap towards national freedom Complete independence was set as the goal of the nation, and early next year Mahatma Gandhi launched his celebrated Salt *Satyagraha*. Naturally, I plunged into the fray with all my heart. But I did not find the Indian communists anywhere on the battle lines. Some of them, no doubt, were in prison in connection with the Meerut Conspiracy case. But there were many who were outside and the underground organisation of the CPI did exist in some form or another. But even in the underground of the national movement, where I soon found myself, the communists were nowhere in evidence, though subterranean channels could have easily connected the two undergrounds. Worse, I came to know that they were denouncing the national movement as bourgeois and Mahatma Gandhi as a lackey of the Indian bourgeoisie. I do not wish to recall that whole story of folly and shame. I have made a reference to it here only to indicate how my differences arose with the Indian communists and their brand of Marxism. The communists in India were only following, of course, the policy laid down by the Third or Communist International which by then had come completely under the leadership of Stalin. The patently mistaken policy that the Comintern had been following since 1928, and which had resulted in the division of the labour and socialist movements throughout the world and in the isolation of the communists from the national movements in all the colonial countries, appeared to me, as indeed it was later acknowledged to be, contrary to Marxist theory generally and specifically to the famous colonial policy enunciated by Lenin. My differences with the CPI thus marked the beginning of my ideological alienation from Soviet Russia itself, which to me was till then the paragon and exemplar of all communist virtues. The ideological conflict and struggle for power that had gone on in Russia for some years prior to this had not yet produced any positive reaction in me, apart from a suppressed anxiety. Indeed, there was not much information available yet regarding those matters. But when at home I was face to face with a Soviet-dictated policy which my Marxism just could not be reconciled with, I could not help being somewhat alienated.

Congress Socialist Party

I naturally kept away form the CPI and joined the ranks of the soldiers of freedom. But freedom or *swaraj* had come by then to mean much more to me than mere national independence. Free India to me meant socialist India and *swaraj* the rule of the poor and downtrodden. Congress policy and programme on this score, in spite of the famous Karachi declaration, seemed vague and inadequate. Naturally, with other like-minded fighters for freedom, we formed the Congress Socialist Party so that the social policy of the Congress might become more definitely socialist and the fight for independence itself might be conducted in a more revolutionary manner—which meant in Marxian terminology the linking of the movement for national freedom with the movement for economic and social emancipation of the masses. The Congress Socialist Party played a notable part in giving shape to the socio-economic content of Congress policy and a hard edge to the struggle for freedom. By and large, the Congress Socialists were among the most uncompromising and undaunted soldiers of freedom.

Marxism Re-examined

Howsoever that may be, all these events and experiences compelled me to re-examine the basic postulates of Marxism. Most of my colleagues in the Socialist movement are acquainted with that painful process of rethinking because we passed together through that phase. The whole course of development of the CSP and then of the (old) Socialist Party was vitally influenced by this process of ideological re-education.

The CSP had started as a Marxist-Leninist group: and we always claimed during the earlier years that both the CPI and the Kremlin were misapplying Marxism-Leninism to India particularly and to the world situation generally. But now I came seriously to question if Marxism-Leninism, no matter what its interpretation, was itself a safe guide to the social revolution and to socialism. If the theory of violence as a midwife of revolution was not challenged in its entirety, at least this much became clear to me (a) that in a society where it was possible for the people by democratic means to bring about social change, it would be counter-revolutionary to resort to violence and (b) that socialism could not exist nor be created, in the absence of the democratic freedoms. As a logical corollary, I rejected the theory of the dictatorship of the proletariat, which in effect meant the dictatorship of a bureaucratic oligarchy.

The Russian revolution had started as a people's revolution that had the active support of the broad masses of Czarist Russia, but Lenin converted it into a minority revolution when he forcibly dissolved the Constituent Assembly in which he was in a small minority and seized power with the help of rebel soldiers and the urban working class. The subsequent miscarriage of the revolution and distortion of socialism to my mind was the direct result of the forcible seizure of power by a minority.

Thus I was led to the conclusion that even where the people lacked the democratic freedoms, a violent revolution must have popular support and the revolutionary government must have the backing of the majority of the people. It is easier during a revolution for the popular will to be expressed than during constitutional elections. A social revolution must be allowed full freedom to find its own democratic expression. The people's instinct is always in favour of freedom and democracy, and it is never natural for them deliberately to subject themselves to a dictatorship. The communists everywhere, under Lenin's brilliant inspiration, have tried by devious methods to clamp down upon the people their minority and dictatorial rule. Perhaps we have an exception to this in China where a larger section of the people seems to have been with Mao Tse Tung than with Chiang Kai-shek, though that does not mean that the Chinese Government is not a dictatorship. Perhaps it is dictatorship of the majority over the minority. Perhaps again, this is so in Yugoslavia. Elsewhere communist rule is a minority rule; the communists, wherever in power, have invariably established a dictatorship which in their usual 'double talk" language they call people's or even socialist democracy. All this drove me to the conclusion that the path to socialism did not pass through dictatorship of any kind.

The Soviet experience made it further clear to me that socialism was not merely the negation of capitalism; that it was possible for capitalism to be destroyed, for industry, trade, banking, agriculture — all to be nationalised and collectivised and yet for a country to remain far from socialism: nay, not only to remain far from socialism, but even to go counter to it. In Soviet Russia we saw not only the denial of "formal" freedom, but also the denial of social justice, of equality, we saw the growth of a new class of bureaucratic rulers, of new forms of exploitation. All this was not only the absence of socialism but also its negation.

Western Socialism

Since Asia regained her political freedom from Europe (the process is yet to be completed). European socialists have been visiting us and giving us all manner of advice. All this advice and friendship are welcome but there is one little matter which the European socialists must not forget. If European communism has failed, European socialism has been no conspicuous success either.

It was Germany whose Social Democratic Party was a pride of international socialism and which had been nurtured by some of the greatest names in the history of socialism—Engels himself. Bebal, Kautsky, the elder Liebknecht and many others. And yet German Social Democracy, when presented a chance by history after the First World War, foundered hopelessly. The record of French socialism has been most depressing, the crowning infamy being the association of the Guy Mollet Government with the British Conservative Government in the imperialist attack on Egypt. British Labour under Attlee — particularly during Attlee's first government — no doubt, set a fine record both at home and aboard. And during the Egyptian interlude Gaitskell's leadership doubtlessly raised high the prestige of British socialism. But there are many skeletons yet in the cupboard of British socialists and Great Britain is far away yet from a socialist democracy. The welfare state, which is constantly under Conservative fire, is a poor substitute for socialism, and that too seems to be in the danger of being converted into the "opportunity state" of Mr. Macmillan. True, in Scandinavia, particularly in Sweden, democratic socialism has achieved a larger measure of success, but there, too, it cannot be said that the socialist ideals have been fully realised. Perhaps the comparative success of socialism in Sweden has been due, among other things, to the small size of the Swedish community and the relatively greater emphasis, on the non-state forms of socialism, such as cooperation; both factors, as we shall see, are of great pertinence to the evolution of socialism into *sarvodaya.*

European socialism, both Marxian and non-Marxian, is, among other things, the picture of an industrialised society. Socialism, according to Marx as much as to other European socialist thinkers, was a stage of society that came after the maturing of capitalism. In Asia industrial capitalist development is in its infancy and Asian countries are overwhelmingly rural and agrarian communities. The task of building up socialism in such an environment is not familiar to European socialists, so there is little guidance that can be obtained from their experience. The communists have no doubt been successful—in the sense of capturing power — precisely in backward and rural communities, such as Russia and China. But the "socialism" that they have built up is a far cry from the brotherhood of the equal and the free, which to me is the essence of true socialism.

Contours of Asian Socialism

Asian socialists, therefore, are left very much to their own devices. I am not suggesting that we have nothing to learn from Western socialism or Russian communism, but the main bulk of our work of thinking, experimenting, innovating, we have to do ourselves. I am afraid this process of original enquiry has been halted for the past few years in the Indian socialist movement. It is time that the thread of enquiry is picked up again. This process should be facilitated by two different trends of development: one the unfolding of the Gandhian technique of social revolution and reconstruction as exemplified in the *bhoodan, gramdan* and *gramraj* movement and the accumulating experience of state ownership and bureaucratic management of economic enterprise which is being misconceived as socialism.

This process of re-examination that I have briefly traced above was a collective experience of those who were working in the CSP and the old Socialist Party. The conclusions that I have indicated above were also collective in nature. The emphasis on democracy, the need for decentralisation, the realisation that means must be morally consistent with the ends—these were the common conclusions drawn from a common experience. Thus the Marxist-Leninist CSP, through several incarnations, developed into the democratic-socialist PSP.

From Socialism to Sarvodaya

Thus far I travelled together with my colleagues in happy comradeship, the memory of which will sweeten the remaining part of my life. But some years back my journey took a turning where we parted company. That parting began with what has come to be grandiloquently known as *jeevandan*, but which was no more than a decision on my part to withdraw from party-and-power politics and to devote the rest of my life to the *bhoodan* and *sarvodaya* movement.

The same old beacon lights of freedom, equality and brotherhood, that had guided the course of my life and brought me to democratic socialism, drew me onwards around this turning of the road. My regret is that I did not reach this point in my life's journey white Gandhiji was still in our midst. However, some years back it became clear to me that socialism as we understand it today cannot take mankind to the sublime goals of freedom, equality, brotherhood and peace. Socialism, no doubt, gives promise to bring mankind closer to those goals than any other. But unless socialism is transformed into *sarvodaya*, those goals would remain beyond its reach; and just as we had to taste the ashes of independence, so future generations may have to taste the ashes of socialism.

Materialism and Goodness

My final break with Marxism, though not with politics, had come during the three weeks' fast at Puna. It was then that a long process of questioning started by the Russian purges came to an end, and it became clear that materialism as a philosophical outlook could not provide any basis for ethical conduct and any incentive for goodness.

If man and his consciousness and the society and culture which he has built up are mere manifestations of matter — howsoever dialectically active — I can see no reason why in such a society, anyone should try to be good, that is, be generous, kind, unselfish. Why should then one feel sympathy with those who are weak, poor or sick? What is matter will dissolve into matter after death. So, what incentive can there be for moral behaviour? Lust for power or wealth, or desire to win the acclaim of the people or the regard of one's peers, may be an incentive to action. But such an incentive can have no concern with valuations of right or wrong. Ethical ideas have no doubt a history and a social origin, but when the individual begins to question his inherited standards of conduct and asks himself why he should act ethically, materialism offers him no answer. A person may have grown up with the ideals of social service, sacrifice, freedom, equality and the rest. But if he begins later to ask himself why he should subscribe to those ideals at all and put himself to trouble and loss on their account, the philosophy of materialism, dialectical or otherwise, would not be able to give him any satisfactory answer.

I am not suggesting that among philosophical materialists, there have not been examples of great sacrifice for noble causes. What I am suggesting is that their action was not consistent with their philosophy.

A way out of this difficulty may be the assumption that the human being is an automaton, that his behaviour is wholly conditioned and that he has no freedom of will. On this assumption, of course. Marx and Lenin could not help working and suffering for the exploited peoples of the earth. But I doubt whether even the most bigoted Marxist would be prepared to reduce man to such a mechanical entity. Indeed, the whole Marxian theory of revolutionary leadership is based on the assumption of free will.

A great debate has raged in philosophy whether matter came first or consciousness. The point is that no matter which came first, there are today modes of existence that may be described as matter and consciousness. The mistake Marxism made was to assume that consciousness (whatever its origin) could be understood in the same manner as matter. It did not realise that the laws of matter cannot be applied to the realm of consciousness. The study of matter is an objective exploration, whereas that of consciousness is subjective realisation. The study of matter, the objective exploration, science in short, is necessarily amoral. The Marxists (and the materialists generally), having reduced consciousness to a behaviour of matter, naturally knocked the bottom out of ethics. They talk a good deal no doubt of revolutionary ethics, but that is nothing more than the crassest application of the theory that the end justifies the means. Once an individual persuades himself, sincerely or otherwise, that he is on the side of the revolution (or the Party or the People), he is free to commit any infamy whatsoever.

Not only the Marxists and materialists, but also those who differ from them in philosophy attempt to understand consciousness by the methods of science. Mental science also, therefore, provides no basis for moral behaviour. Nor is it ever possible for science to understand consciousness, which can only be subjectively experienced, Subjective experience is by its very nature incapable of being expressed in material categories. Therefore, all the mystics and *yogis* who had experience of subjective reality, or absolute consciousness, have been unable to express it in any language. As Roger Godel has said: 'The philosopher *thinks* his philosophy: the sage *lives* his wisdom."

Modern science has reached a point where the dualism of matter and consciousness becomes too tenuous to be real. Says Godel in his essay on The *Contemporary Science and the Liberative Experience of Yoga:*

> But now suddenly — around a bend of quantum mechanics — exploration of the objective field brings the theorist of the physical sciences to a most disquieting position; before him appears an ambiguous universe where the observer and the phenomenon observed are inextricably commingled. So close is their confrontation that each is reflected in the other, powerless to separate or to fuse.

In this realm of indetermination, all the symbols and formulae familiar to our experience of things vanish. Notions of energy and of matter require so profound a transformation as to lose their original meaning; energy condenses into matter, matter dematerialises into radiation. The waves associated with the propagation of light quanta need no substratum in order to propagate in space-time: they undulate neither in a fluid, nor in a solid, nor yet in gas. Only the unreal thread of analogy links them to the image of a wave rippling the surface of water. They are in fact waves of probability, waves of consciousness which our thought projects afar: curvilinear variation of an abstract function."

Science cannot resolve this dualism completely, because in objective study the seer and the seen must remain different, no matter how 'inextricably commingled'. It is only in the ultimate spiritual experience that this dualism is shed and the seer and seen become one.

The root of morality lies in the *endeavour of* man to realise this unity of existence or, to put it differently, to realise his Self. For one who has experienced this unity, the practice of morality becomes as natural and effortless as the drawing of breath.

To some all this might appear to be irrelevant to the political and economic struggle. In all humility, I would demur. All actions, personal or public, political, economic or other, should have an integration and the centre of this integration must be a philosophy of life.

Limitation of Wants and Socialism

This leads me at once to an aspect of the task of social and economic reconstruction that both socialists and communists have neglected. Socialism and communism both lay great emphasis on material prosperity, on ever-growing production and on an ever-rising standard of living. Since socialists and communists are always the advocates of the poor and downtrodden, their emphasis on material progress and happiness can be appreciated. It is also true that in poor and backward countries like India it is the main task of social reconstruction to raise quite considerably the people's standard of living. But it would not do here or elsewhere to apotheosise material happiness and encourage an outlook on life that feeds an insatiable hunger for material goods. There can be no peace in the minds and hearts of men, nor peace amongst men if this hunger gnaws at them continuously. That would necessarily set up an uncontrolled competition between individuals, groups and nations. Everyone would be trying to outdo his neighbour and every nation not only to catch up with other nations but to leave them all behind. In such a restless society violence and war would be endemic. All values of life would be subordinated to this over-mastering desire for more. Equality, freedom, brotherhood would all be in danger of being submerged in a universal flood of materialism. There would be no poise in human life, no real satisfaction because the possession of more would only whet the appetite for still more.

I am aware that there have been and are quite a number of socialists who have been aware of the danger of a purely materialistic view of life, but nevertheless the main concern of socialism has been and is with the material aspects of life. The socialist or labour parties and the trade unions do not educate the people about a balanced or whole view of life. If the socialist movement became conscious of the issue I am raising, its whole attitude towards science, industrialisation and social organisation and international relations would be revolutionised.

Disciplining of the bodily appetites is essential for a moral life and growth of the human personality and the blossoming of all human qualities and values. This is true particularly of socialist values. The socialist way of life is a way of sharing together the good things that common endeavour may make available. The more willingly this sharing is practised the less tension and coercion in society and the more of socialism. I believe that unless members of society learn to keep their wants under control, willing sharing of things may be difficult, if not impossible, and society would be bound to split into two divisions: (i) comprising those who are trying to discipline others and (ii) comprising all the rest.

Such a division of society always leaves the question open: who would discipline the discipliners, rule the rulers? The examples of the communist countries and the experience of socialist governments show that the answer to this perennial question is extremely difficult.

The only solution seems to be to restrict as much as possible the need and area of disciplining from above by ensuring that every member of society practises self-discipline and the values of socialism and, among other things, willingly shares and cooperates with his fellow men.

Cooperative Politics

As a way out of the faults and failures of the party system, I toyed for some time with the idea of a cooperative, rather than a competitive, system of parties, I realised, however, that in the first place, there was no climate for such a political experiment, and in the second place, the experiment could not succeed within the given framework of struggle for power and the system of parliamentary' democracy, except for limited purposes and limited periods. I still believe, however, that given the psychological climate for it, such a political experiment might yet be made. But for that the frame of reference will have to be changed from parliamentary democracy to something different. Be that as it may, my disenchantment with the party system kept on urging me to seek a better substitute for it. Gandhiji's non-partisan constructive approach towards people's self-rule seemed to offer one hopeful line of exploration.

Place of the State

As questioning about politics was net confined to the party system alone, a fundamental question arose in my mind as to the place and rote of the state in human society, particularly in relation to the goals of social life that had fixed themselves before me Perhaps my schooling in Marxism, with its ideal of a stateless society, made these questions more pointed and troublesome. Though I had given up the basic postulates of Marxism, because they did not promise to lead me to my goals, I continued to feel strongly that human freedom could be fully and wholly realised only in a stateless society. I was, and am, not sure if the state would ever wither away completely. But I am sure that it is one of the noblest goals of social endeavour to ensure that the power and functions and spheres of the state are reduced as far as possible. I became at this time, and still am, an ardent believer, like Gandhiji, in the maxim that that government was the best which governed the least. The test of human evolution for me became man's ability to live in amity, justice and cooperation with his fellowmen without outward restraints of any kind. That is why I have considered the human and social problem to be at bottom a moral problem.

With this conception of the role and place of the state in society at the back of my mind. I viewed with very deep apprehension the march of the state to greater and greater glory. Democratic socialists, communists as well as welfarists (not to speak of the fascists) are all statists. They all hope to bring about their own variety of the millennium by first mastering and then adding to the powers and functions of the state.

The bourgeois state had monopoly of political power. The socialist state threatens to add to that the monopoly of economic power. Such a great concentration of power would require equal, if not greater, power to control and keep it in check. There would be no such power at hand in a socialist society. Paper Constitutions could hardly be expected to guarantee freedom and sovereignty to the citizen. The economic and political bureaucracy would be entirely at its mercy.

I am aware that democratic socialists are conscious of these dangers and are trying to devise 'checks and balances'. The independent trade unions are supposed to be a great bulwark of freedom, though it is recognised that the great trade unions are themselves becoming more and more ridden with bureaucracy. Plans for industrial democracy and public accountability for state enterprises have been drawn up. Consumers' associations and cooperatives of all kinds are rightly supposed to function as balancing and restraining factors. Even decentralisation of authority and functions has figured of late in socialist thinking. But after all is said and done, the democratic socialist state remains a Leviathan that will sit heavily on freedom of the people.

People's Socialism vs State Socialism

The only remedy for that I could think of took me further away from politics and towards *sarvodaya.* The remedy obviously is, as I have said above in the context of internal and external discipline, to make it possible for the people to do without the state as far as practicable and to run their affairs themselves directly. Speaking as a socialist. I would put it thus: the remedy is to create and develop forms of socialist living through the voluntary endeavour of the people rather than seek to establish socialism by the use of the power of the state. In other words, the remedy is to establish *people's socialism* rather than *state socialism. Sarvodaya* is people's socialism. Whether every socialist agrees or not with *sarvodaya,* he should agree that the more of people's or voluntary socialism and the less of state-enforced socialism, the fuller and more real the socialism, Unfortunately, there are very few socialists who are giving much attention to people's socialism. Speaking of British socialists. Mr. Jack Bailey, the British Cooperative leader, says: "In Britain the concentration of most socialists upon the capture and use of state power has tended to blind them to the validity of non-state forms of socialism." (Quoted by Harold Campbell in *Socialist Commentary.* July 1957.) What is true of Britain is true of all the world It should be obvious that in order to develop non-state forms of socialism, it should be unnecessary for any one to function as a party or to engage in a struggle for the capture of power. Both power and party have no relevance in this context. What is needed rather is a band of selfless workers prepared to live and move in the midst of the people and help them to reorganise their lives on a self-reliant and self-governing basis. One cannot help being reminded here of Gandhiji's *Lok Sevak Sangh* again.

Community of Future

The question now arises: What will be the form of that society in which it will be possible for the people to run their affairs directly and develop all those values of life that characterise a socialist society: cooperation, self-discipline, sense of responsibility? This is a question to which socialists have paid the least attention so far. Human society has so grown that we have the complex industrial civilization of today, with great human forests that are called cities, with economic and social relationships that are utterly impersonal and non-life giving, with modes of work that are irksome and bereft of joy and opportunities of creativity and that have the sole criterion of productivity and efficiency to recommend them. Science has shrunk the whole world into a neighbourhood, but man has created a civilization that has turned even neighbours into strangers. Such a complex and top-heavy society cannot but be a heaven for bureaucrats, managers, technocrats, statists. Such a society cannot be a home for brothers to live together as brothers. Socialists, in the name of science, production, efficiency, standard of living and other hallowed shibboleths, have accepted this whole Frankenstein of a society — lock, stock and barrel — and hope, by adding public ownership to it, to make it socialist. I submit that in such a society the very breath of socialism would be hard to draw. Self-government, self-management, mutual cooperation and sharing, equality, freedom, brotherhood — all could be practised and developed far better if men lived in small communities. This is beginning to be realised by forward-looking thinkers even in the West.

Further, man is a product both of nature and culture. So, for his balanced growth it is necessary that a harmonious blend between the two is effected. This blending, in spite of parks and green avenues, is not possible in such centres of modern civilization as London. Paris. New York. Moscow. As a result, modern man's development is warped and one-sided. A harmonious blending of nature and culture is possible only in comparatively smaller communities. Let me quote Aldous Huxley from his *Science. Liberty and Peace:* "Now it seems pretty obvious that man's psychological, to say nothing of his spiritual, needs cannot be fulfilled unless, first, he has a fair measure of personal responsibility within and towards a self-governing group, unless, secondly, his work possesses a certain aesthetic value and human significance, and unless, in the third place, he is related to his natural environment in some organic, rooted and symbiotic way."

It was for these reasons that Gandhiji insisted that the Indian village and village self-government *(gram raj)* were the foundations for his picture of society—the society of equal and free beings living as brothers in peace.

Science and Small Production

Living in small communities and producing mostly for self or local consumption on small machines may be regarded by some as setting the hand of science backward. Science and centralised large-scale production and large conglomerations of human habitations are thought to go necessarily together. Nothing could be more absurd. Science is of two kinds: (a) pure science and (b) applied science. I would call pure science alone science and the other technology. Now, the application of science does not depend upon science itself but upon the character of society. Large-scale, big machine production was profitable to the money makers, so technology took the course of that particular type of production. The money makers were the dominant class in society and their will had to be done. Government also—irrespective of ideologies—preferred centralised, big-scale production because that was necessary for war making (or defence, if you please), and — no less important — because it also concentrated great economic and, therefore, political power in their hands. Thus governments and profiteers combined to create the Frankenstein of modern society. Pure science had no say in the matter, Rather, had the scientists their way, many of them. I believe, would be happy to smash many of the engines of production and destruction that their discoveries had helped to create. But supposing, society had pursued not the aims of power, profit and war, but of peace, goodwill, cooperation, freedom and brotherhood, science could have been equally applied to evolve the suitable technology. If that were to happen, it would be not regression of science, but progression in a creative rather than destructive direction. It should be pointed out that atomic energy has made more possible than ever before the dispersal of production and the development of small technology, that is, technology appropriate to production in small units and by small-sized machinery. Let me quote Huxley again:

> "My own view, which is essentially that of the decentralists, is that, so long as the results of pure science are applied for the purpose of making our system of mass producing and mass distributing industry more expensively elaborate and more highly specialised, there can be nothing but ever greater centralisation of power in ever fewer hands. And the corollary of this centralisation of economic and political power is progressive loss by the masses of their civil liberties, their personal independence and their opportunities for self-government. But here we must note that there is nothing in the results of disinterested scientific research which makes it inevitable that they should be applied for the benefit of centralised finance, industry and government. If inventors and technicians so chose, they could just as well apply the results of pure science for the purpose of increasing the economic self-sufficiency and consequently the political independence of small owners, working either on their own or in cooperative groups, concerned not with mass distribution, but with subsistence and the supply of a local market. The Sabbath was made for man, not man for the Sabbath; and the same is true of applied science."

Small Communities and the Great Society

I am not suggesting that the whole picture of this new society is clear to any one or that all its problems have been thought out and resolved. How, for instance, would these small self-reliant, self-governing communities be related together is a major question that immediately springs to the mind. There is, of course. Gandhiji's grand conception before us:

> "In this structure, composed of innumerable villages, there will be ever widening, never ascending circles. Life will not be a pyramid with the apex sustained by the bottom. But it will be an oceanic circle whose centre will be the individual, always ready to perish for the village, the latter ready to perish for the circle of villages, till at last the whole becomes one life composed of individuals, never aggressive in their arrogance, but ever humble, sharing the majesty of the oceanic circle of which they are integral units."

Gandhiji's words give us direction, but much thought and experience will be necessary before the picture becomes more clear. However, one warning must be sounded.

While it is undoubted that life in small communities, permitting and promoting personal relationships, will be more suited to the realisation of *sarvodaya* ideals, it should not be imagined that small communities, by virtue merely of their size, will necessarily be *sarvodaya* communities. Had that been so, we would have encountered *sarvodaya* in every village of India today. The outward forms of living have relevance only when the inward forms are given. Men must understand and accept the *sarvodaya* view of life before they can proceed to investigate in what environment and social framework they could live that life best.

The fear is often expressed if self-reliant and self-governing communities will hold together, and the unity and integrity of nation will abide. In a *sarvodaya* world society the present nation states have no place. The *sarvodaya* view is a world view, and the individual standing at the centre of Gandhiji's oceanic circle is a world citizen. But let us leave for the present the world picture of *sarvodaya* There is no reason to suppose why self-governing small communities will be hostile to one another or isolationist or selfish in their interrelationship. If the internal life of a community is laid on sound foundations, its external life cannot but be equally sound.

Non-violent Social Revolution

Vinoba's movement thus supplied an answer to the question that I had long been asking: Could Gandhiji's philosophy offer a practical method to accomplish the social revolution? In a brilliant extension and development of Gandhiji's work. Vinoba demonstrated that there was such a method.

As I see it, is a two-pronged method. One prong of it is a mass campaign of what Gandhiji termed "conversion". In other words, a widespread campaign is launched to persuade men — irrespective of class, creed and other differences — to give up those ideas, ways and values of life that have been found to be wrong and harmful and to accept in their place certain others, Thus a revolution in ideas and values is set in motion. At the same time, the new values and ideas are so chosen that they have a direct bearing on some major social problem, and their acceptance and practice are expected to lead to a solution of that problem and incidentally to a radical change in society.

The change, let it be emphasised, takes place as a result of individuals beginning here and now to live the values of the future society. Other revolutions failed because those who brought them about used means that were inconsistent with their ends.

For instance, if the end was a stateless society, the means were the coercive powers of the state itself; if the end was brotherhood, a fratricidal war amongst brothers, called class-war, was the means used; or, again, if the end was rooting out of selfishness as the driving force in life, the selfishness of certain sections of society was used as the driving force for the social revolution. In the *sarvodaya* method of revolution, the ends and means become one. If in the new social order property is to belong to society and the property-owner is to be a mere trustee, the revolution begins by individuals converting themselves here and now into trustees.

Another important feature of the method is that though the new ideas and values appear difficult to practise, a phased programme is so contrived that even ordinary persons are able by easy steps to advance towards the seemingly difficult goal. To illustrate, Vinoba through his movement is propagating the idea that we are only trustees of "our" properties and therefore entitled to no more than what society gives us as our share. Therefore, he is exhorting us to live as trustees and share what we have with others. In the present circumstances, this appears to be a very difficult road to travel.

Therefore, Vinoba has made the pilgrim's journey easy by asking him first to share only a small part of his possessions. Even this should have been difficult for the individual if he were asked to do it alone. The moral life is difficult to live in the midst of immorality. It requires greater effort and higher moral resources. But when all around one are making a similar effort, it becomes easy even for weak characters to raise themselves. Therefore, the programme of "conversion", though directed to the individual, has a mass character; that is to say, whole groups and masses of men are sought to be touched and moved by it.

The other prong of the method is to devise a programme of self-help and self-government through which men — first those living in small communities — may learn to manage their own affairs and, *moved by the new ideas and values,* cooperate together to create new institutions and forms of social life.

To illustrate, side by side with *bhoodan* there is the programme of production for self and local consumption; of *gramdan,* which is a new agrarian economic order; and of *gramswaraj,* which is village self-government. The revolution in ideas as represented by *bhoodan, sampattidan* and *gramdan* and the revolution in the outward organisation of society represented by community ownership of land and community self-government together constitute a full revolutionary programme that is different both from revolutions of violence and revolutions made by law.

This is a new technique of which the world has had no experience yet It is common for new ideas to be treated with suspicion and reserve. But for us in India who have had the privilege of witnessing the miracle of national freedom being won with radically new ideas and methods, which too had been met first with doubt and derision, it should not be difficult to appreciate the new ideas and methods of Vinoba that are after all in the nature of an extension and development of the earlier ones used by the Father of the Nation. We in India have also the additional privilege, as one of the youngest nations of today, of being in a position to benefit from the successes and failures of others.

After the achievement of freedom it was perhaps natural for public spirited persons to rush towards the newly conquered seats of power in order to be able to serve the country, but I hope in the last ten years there has been enough experience accumulated about the inadequacy and futility of service through power for large numbers of patriotic individuals to rally under the banner of *sarvodaya.*

Already hundreds of *satyagrahi lok sevakas* have rallied to that banner. There is need for hundreds of thousands of such.

A Positive Decision

I hope it can now be seen why I decided to withdraw from politics. I hope also that it will be appreciated that it was not a negative decision. It was not the ugliness of politics that repelled me, but the attraction of the new politics of *sarvodaya* that drew me. For, as I have tried to show above, *sarvodaya* also has its politics, But it is politics of a different kind: politics of the people as I have called it, as distinct from the politics of party and power. *Lokniti* as distinct from *rajniti.*

The politics of *sarvodaya* can have no party and no concern with power. Rather, its aim will be to see that all centres of powers are abolished. The more this new politics grows the more the old politics shrinks. A real withering away of the state.

I should add that there can be no question of any hostility between *rajniti* and *lokniti,* nor can the two be kept apart as two unmixable castes. *Lokniti* is but the child of *rajniti.* Between the two there must be constant contact and cooperation.

Democratic *rajniti* cannot possibly ever resist the idea that the people should practise self-government as far as possible. All democratic parties should, by definition, be prepared—nay, anxious — to hand over power to the people as soon as possible, in the same manner as every good father is anxious to hand over to his sons when they are of age. If pressure of work permits me,

I shall try some time later to place before the country my humble suggestions in regard to the evolution of our polity from *rajniti* to *lokniti.*

I should also add that though all my energies would be bent towards developing *lokniti, I* shall not shut my eyes to what happens in the sphere of *rajniti.* For good or ill, *rajniti* does to some extent influence the lives of the people. It shall be my concern from the outside to see that that influence is as salutary as possible. I am aware of the risks involved in that, the risk, for instance, of being misunderstood and charged with "playing politics". I would regret very much if anything like that happened. But perhaps one cannot always avoid misunderstandings in public life. I wish, however, to assure everybody that for my part I cannot but view every issue from a detached non-partisan point. If my intervention at any time causes annoyance to any one, the misfortune will be entirely mine.

5

Important Writings

The Wisdom Grows

Jayaprakash was sent to Patna for better school education by his father He was only nine years then. At the out set the shy village lad felt like a fish out of water. The atmosphere was noisy and active. People were engaged and struggling for their survival for a living. There was no serenity in the town like at the village. There was commutation between his own village and Patna. People coming to Patna from the village had to use bullock cart. Jayaprakash too travelled by a bullock cart to join his new mission of education. There were no friends, no pets, no natural beauty in Patna town. He felt lonely and forlon. He could not pick up friendship with the town children of the school. So, he was forced to confine himself to his lessons and the books became his only friends. He prepared his lessons with full sincerity and became a good student of the school. He passed Matriculation in 1918 with good marks and got a scholarship for his good proficiency. He joined Patna college for higher studies. With good academic knowledge, he developed political consciousness within himself. The country then was in a state of turmoil. A critical situation prevailed in India. The freedom struggles had already taken shape. The freedom struggle was gaining momentum. People of India had started dreaming about a Indian free from British yoke. The Indian atmosphere was charged with a National feeling of liberation.

The Indian National Congress was established by a Britisher David Octavio Hume with the help of intellectuals loyal to the British regime. The objective of the organisation was to look into the welfare of the people of India within the framework of British government. When the organisation was conceived, there was no intention of liberating the Indians from the British subjugation. But as time rolled on, the behaviour of the Britisher turned into tortures and oppressions. By that time Jayaprakash joined school and Mahatma Gandhi had already appeared in the scene of Indian Politics. He appeared to every Indians as an angel and a saviour. It was extremely difficult for every Indian to ignore his clarion for Indian freedom. Mahatma Gandhi appeared as a ring master to transform the Indian slave into lion-hearted human beings. To quote Jawaharlal Nehru in Discovery of India: *"And Gandhi came*

The emergence of Mahatma Gandhi changed the face of National Congress organisation. He made Congress as a revolutionary organisation. He invited the people of India to Indian liberation movement and paralysed the British government with the instrument of non-cooperation and Satyagraha. He charged a new life in Indian people. Through Mahatma Gandhi, the meek and docile Indian people became hungry-hearted fighters. The people of Bengal under the leadership offered stiff resistance to divide Bengal. The whole Bengal revolted against it. It had set forth an example before the entire country. The evil design of the Britishers were foiled. The whole of India was united in saving Bengal from division. The public opinion against partition of Bengal forced the British government to give up its nefarious intention. The political giant of India, Bal Gangadhar Tilak was so moved by the spirit and unity displayed by the people, that he declared that "Freedom is our Birth right". The voice of Lokmanya Tilak (as he was popularly known), generated new awareness and spirit of sacrifice among the Indian people. The spirit to non-cooperation with the British in all spheres had spread among the people and they boycotted all England made commodities. The volunteers of the Congress vowed to use only those goods produced in India.

The magnitude of oppression of the British continued to grow with time as they felt that they had their grip over the Indian people. All leaders of the Congress including Lokmanya Tilak were put behind the bar. But still the spirit of liberating India continued to grow with the common people. The British oppression was so severe that some younger people and their organisation vowed to put an end to the British rule by eliminating British oppressors from the soil of India. They did not believe in non-violence, but started violent fight against the British. They succeeded in killing certain British officials and faced the gallows. These brave young men laid down their lives for the liberation of their motherland. This was the time when Jayaprakash had just entered to study in the Patna college.

Those young patriots who believed in violent method linked the liberation movement with the Hindu spiritualism. It teaches the body is perishable, but the soul is immortal. The soul is the real being who dictates the actions of body. It never dies nor it can be killed by any body. So the wise should not ponder over their body, because the immortal soul exists even after the destruction of the body. This wisdom made them fearless and they willingly jumped into death to rescue their motherland from bondage. The martyrs like Mangal Pandey, Ram Prashad Bismal, Anant Singh and many others sacrificed their lives in the battle of liberation. The stories of these great sons of our motherland made Jayaprakash restless. His heart was searching for an outlet to breath the air of a Free India. The student Jayaprakash thought that the spiritual scriptures would help him to build his steadfast wisdom that may help him to gather courage and stamina to fight for the liberation of India. Alike many great sons of our country he started reading Bhagvad Geeta daily and learned ethics and philosophy of life and death and about the duty of every human being towards the society. These situations of the country ignited the invisible flame that was burning within him since so many years. The shy and docile young man was turned into a vibrant patriot inwardly who was eagerly waiting for an opportunity to plunge into freedom movement. He was even prepared to give up his studies and take active part in the freedom movement. But his parents wanted him to complete his education. With hesitation

Jayaprakash continued his college education at Patna. But inwardly he had grown already as a political thinker.

By the time Mahatma Gandhi began his Satyagraha in India, Jayaprakash had gathered his political wisdom. Mahatma Gandhi was leading the Satyagraha movement. The Mahatma had already won many battles in South Africa before he came to India. He fought and won the non-violent battle against racial humiliation of Indians in South Africa. The victory over the British colonialism was an amazing achievement. Mahatma Gandhi's satyagraha had already drawn world attention. To defeat an oppressive colonialist government with the weapon of non-violence and peaceful resistance was not a joke. The Britishers were then the powerful colonialist in the world. Rudyard Kiplings boasting lines of the poem described Britishers.

Dynamics of Sarvodaya

During Gandhiji's life time, in spite of the fact that I was gradually drawing close to him, as I have recounted above. I could not see how this non-violent technique could bring about a social revolution. I had seen how that technique worked during the national revolution, but how feudalism and capitalism could be abolished by the same means and a new society created was not at all clear to me. I had, no doubt, read Gandhiji's writings on revolution through change of heart. But in the absence of a direct demonstration, those ideas seemed impractical in the extreme. During my Marxist days, I had written a vehement critique of the theory of trusteeship, and though I had moved considerably away from Marxism by the end of Gandhiji's life, I was not prepared to accept that trusteeship could be a social, as distinguished from individual, norm of behaviour As I have indicated above. Gandhiji, soon after independence, was evolving in his mind a national programme for launching upon the second and greater phase of his unique career. His proposal to transform the Congress organisation, which he had fashioned as a non-violent army of freedom into a *Lok Sevak Sangh* was no doubt a sensationally bold stroke of genius. But as I have said earlier, its significance was entirely lost upon me. So, having already rejected the use of violence under democratic conditions as counter-revolutionary. I was naturally left only with the traditional socialist methods of bringing about the social revolution. At the same time the gaping inadequacies of that method and the poor quality of the results achieved through it—some of which I have discussed above — put me in a questioning mood.

Birth of Bhoodan

I was in this frame of mind when an event of great significance took place. In a remote village of Telengana, *bhoodan* was born. My first reaction to the event was of the usual sort; it would take hundreds of years in this manner to redistribute all the land in the country, I thought. But there were two factors in the situation which arrested my attention and forced me to give it serious thought One was the author of *bhoodan* himself. I had known Vinoba for years and often when I had occasion to visit Wardha I went specially to see him. I always found him unusually stimulating and original. Some of his writings that I had read had an exhilarating freshness. I recalled how Gandhiji had selected him as the first *satyagrahi* in 1941. I remembered again his clear-sighted lead at the first conference of Gandhian constructive and political workers convened at Wardha after Gandhiji's death. When a person like Vinoba. I thought, had started something, it could not just be brushed aside as a stunt or futile gesture. The other factor was the steady growth of the movement. It was found that whenever and wherever a serious band of workers took it up, it produced results. The method was not impractical. It appeared that if as much effort was put behind it as behind the usual political movements, the results would be far quicker and sounder.

About this time, the old Socialist Party had decided that it should turn its urgent attention to the question of redistribution of land which it considered to be the most vital question of economic reform before the country. In a resolution on this subject which I had sponsored, the Pachmarhi Party Conference had made a brief reference to *bhoodan,* welcoming it and promising support. Some time afterwards, I went to see Vinoba when he was in the Banda district of U.P. to discuss this question of land redistribution. I saw that he was serious about the problem and his economic outlook was revolutionary in a basic way. I decided to join Vinoba's movement. But I had a three weeks' fast impending, which completed. I plunged into the *bhoodan* "Ganga" in the Gaya district of Bihar. My brief experience was exhilarating beyond expectation. Within a week nearly seven thousand acres of land were obtained as gifts—most of them spontaneous and from small holders—announced at my meetings.

First Gramdan

As the movement progressed it took on new forms. Already in 1952 it had disclosed an aspect which was startlingly attractive. In the village Mangroth of the district Hamirpur in the U.P., *gramdan* had been announced. Vinoba has a great talent for coining words and investing old words with new meanings. Thus *dan* in his vocabulary does not mean gift, but "sharing together". That is his rendering of Shankar's definition, *danam sam vibhagah. Gramdan* was equitable sharing together of the lands of the village by the people of the village. *Bhoodan* signified distribution of land to the landless; *gramdan,* on the other hand, meant communisation of the land: institution of community, in place of individual, ownership of land. It became evident that *bhoodan* had within it the germ of total agrarian revolution.

And, how beautiful a revolution, how different from all others! Private ownership of land (including *zamindari* and peasant proprietorship) has been abolished in other ways in other countries, namely, by the compulsion of law or direct physical violence. The social resultants of these "revolutions" have been uniformly unhappy— such as bitterness and hatred; misery and tyranny; growth of an agricultural bureaucracy and reduction of free peasants to the status of serfs; concentration of power and dictatorship. In the beautiful revolution of *gramdan,* ownership was not abolished by force of any kind, but freely surrendered to the community. The outward social change was accompanied with inward human change. It was an example of what Gandhiji meant by a double revolution. In place of social tensions, conflicts and tyrannies, there were freedom and mutual goodwill and accord, making it possible for an unprecedented output of free and collective endeavour. (It may be remarked parenthetically that production of foodgrains in Mangroth has trebled in the course of a little over four years.)

Sampattidan

A little after the announcement of Mangroth *gramdan. I* made a special trip to the village to see for myself what had happened there. What I saw opened a new vista into the future. It was thrilling to visualise the great moral, economic, political and social revolution that would sweep over the country if Mangroth were repeated in every village. And I could find no reason to suppose that what had happened in Mangroth could not happen in all the villages of India. The people of Mangroth were by no means angels.

In due course Vinoba added a new item to his programme: *Sampattidan.* On a superficial view it appeared that this was another trick for raising contributions. In reality it was the beginning of a programme of converting proprietorship (not only of land but of all property) into what Gandhiji called trusteeship. *Sampattidan* demonstrated that the mythology of the new revolution was not restricted to the problem of land, but could be applied to the entire social field.

Bihar Movement

The Bihar movement is working for removal of corruption from the fields of social life, such as business (blackmarketing, hoarding, etc.), industry, education, and lastly, but most important of all, it is for basic social, economic, political, cultural and educational changes. Thus this struggle in Bihar is not just a flash in the pan of history but a continuing process of revolutionary changes. That is why I have called it a struggle for *total revolution.* In this revolutionary process governments and political parties will certainly play a role, but the main moving force will be the direct action of the youth and the people. This action, in order to succeed in its objectives, has to be peaceful, and also constructive while being combative.

Some of us, including political parties, might have helped, but in its basic character the Bihar movement is something that has welled up from the ground. The people, who have been suffering, have awakened and are trying to improvise ways to help themselves. They are rebelling against all sorts of conditions they find irksome or intolerable. This is a phenomenon that should put great hope in our hearts.

In their fight against all-around corruption they have realised, and some of us helped in this realisation, that if a remedy has to be applied, it has to be applied at the roots of corruption which lie in political and administrative corruption.

Things can't be perfect As some scientists say, some impurities have to be there to make things move. But political corruption has to be eradicated and the relationship with the people of those who are charged by the people to represent and lead them must be clean. Some institutional framework will have to be built and some instruments have to be forged and created through struggle for this purpose. The Bihar movement also wants the 90 per cent population made up of the poor and the exploited to win against the 10 per cent who belong to the exploiting and privileged classes and castes.

It has aimed at freeing us from the evil effects of misrule and laying the foundation of a truly democratic and just society. We are particularly struggling to make the members of our legislatures accountable to the people, not only at the time of the elections, but also throughout their tenure. We are also trying to make the elections genuinely free by curbing money and creating people's power in its place by giving the people of the constituency the dominant role in the selection of candidates for these elections.

We are also keen to reorganise the educational system with a view to making it more purposive and freeing it from the evils of nepotism and corruption.

Last, but not the least important, we want to reshape the economic policy and administration of the State so that youngmen, both educated and uneducated, may secure gainful employment; peasants acquire ownership over the land they till and also get adequate facilities, like water and fertilizers, to improve the yield from it; and people working in offices, factories, and mines become free from the scourge of inflation and also secure their due place in the management of the concerns in which they are employed.

A Common Struggle

Acceptance of the British proposals will loosen many forces Of national disintegration. It is commonly supposed that one positive contribution that the British have made to Indian polity is to unify the country: and it is a common lament that they foolishly enough are bent today upon destroying that monument of their noble work. Nothing could be greater folly than this view. Far from creating unity in Indian life the British have always done their host to divide us: to divide Hindus and Muslims, to divide Harijans from other Hindus, to create a Sikh minority, to detach princely India from the rest of the country, to set the Princes against the people, to bolster up the Zamindars into pillars of the British rule, to bribe Capital and the middle class to turn into enemies of their country. That is in their hundred years rule they have done all that was possible to briny about a situation in which weakening of British rule was sure to mean chaos and disintegration. The only unity under British rule is the unity of a dictatorial regime and not a people's or a nation's unity. Such positive unity, has been created by the Congress: and this unity today is in jeopardy. Therefore, the struggle for notional unity IN bound to acquire a special importance with the acceptance of the British proposals.

Secondly, the impending constitutional changes are hound to bring to the fore economic and class issues. The form of Swaraj, the question. "Swaraj for whom? will no longer remain academic or remote questions, but will become matters of immediate and urgent importance demanding immediate answers and affecting all our politics not theoretically but practically. That is, the struggle for bread, always on integral part of the struggle for freedom, will move up to the front line and acquire an importance no less than any other.

I should make it clear that these are not three separate struggles, but aspects or parts of one common struggle of the people. At different stages, one or the other aspect receives a greater or less emphasis, but as the present constitutional plans develop, all these are likely to assume equal importance.

As matters stand, this common simple of the people would have to be waged in the context of a Constituent Assembly, possibly of interim government, and later on in the context of a union government, group and provincial governments.

The Congress, of which we are a part, seems likely to be associated with all these developments. As such, it seems certain, that the Congress Straggle for liberty, unity and bread will be conducted, if at all through the constitutional and state machinery. Already the Congress is being converted into a parliamentary party. If this process goes on to its logical conclusion, there can be little doubt that the Congress must fail to achieve much success in this threefold struggle. A constitutional and administrative machinery might be of use in certain circumstances, but situated as we are the people's struggle must be carried on mainly outside the legislatures and the portals of government departments.

To carry on this struggle is our job today - the job of all the fighters for freedom.

Mass Sanctions

How shall we wage this struggle? By terrorism? By sporadic violence? By fratricide? By dacoities? By incendiarism? Obviously not. At the present moment the only manner in which we can wage this struggle is by forging mass sanctions. The creation of mass sanctions includes, first, the psychological preparation of the masses of a struggle; second, the building up of organisations of the masses, such as peasants and labour unions, volunteer corps student and youth organisations, village republics, weaver' cooperatives and myriad other organisations which would help in different ways to develop the collective strength and consciousness of the people. To all this must be added the overall task of strengthening and vitalising the Congress urbanisation and renewing and extending its effective contacts with the people. A full picture of the task of creating mass sanctions in so far as it relates to the present phase of our struggle, is laid out below in the section dealing with our programme.

Here let me illustrate my meaning of the term "mass sanctions" in the context of national unity. National unity cannot be imposed from above. It must be based on unity at the bottom. Such unity can be brought about, or at least a considerable success be gained in the task, by patient political work among the Muslims, by the development of economic or class Organisations such as labour unions. Kisan Sabhas, weavers' cooperatives, by social reform among the Hindus, by encouraging common cultural and recreational activities, by strengthening those forces in society that by their very nature work for national unity, such as the need for a strong frontier, the need for a coordinated plan of economic development, the need for a common economic system, the need for a common medium of speech, etc. and in many other ways. The first requirement. I need hardly stress, is for every freedom lighter to be completely free from communal or caste prejudice or arrogance, and to practice in his personal life the principle of the equality of all human beings.

The mass sanctions for national unity are particularly weak at the moment. Their development is a foremost priority on the list of our present tasks.

Lest there should be misunderstanding I must point out that the work of developing mass sanctions cannot be split into compartments and sanctions for each objective created separately from the others. The political, economic and social, sanction, overlap, interpenetrate and supplement each other and form part of one broad movement of the people.

Problem of Organisation

Before I proceed to explain our prevent programme of work, it is necessary to place before you my views, which I am glad to say are also the views of most of my colleagues, regarding the form of organisation through which fighters for freedom could function today. During the August revolution all of us functioned in the name of the Congress. That was as it should have been, because it was the policy of the whole Congress then to fight Any Congressman who kept away from the fight or opposed it opposed and betrayed the Congress. Today the position is different. The official policy of the Congress today is not a policy of struggle or preparation for a struggle, it is rather a policy of compromise and constitutionalism. Therefore, it is not possible for us today, who still adhere to the policy of struggle and revolutionary action to function in the name of the Congress.

But at the same time I am very clear in my mind that it would do the greatest possible injury to the cause of freedom in this country if we were to leave the Congress and form a parallel mass organisation. There is no doubt that there is going to be a growing divergence between our line of work and that of the present Congress leadership. But the leadership is not identical with the organisation. The present Congress is as much the result of your labours and sacrifices as of any other group within it. You have as much right to speak in the name of the Congress as any one else. The Congress represents the greatest organised national and social force in the country and exercises unprecedented power over the mass mind. As such it is an instrument par excellence for a mass struggle.

It would be foolish to give up this instrument as long as the possibility exists of its being utilised for a revolutionary purpose. I believe that this possibility still exists today. Therefore I have no doubt in my mind that we must continue to work within the Congress, doing our most utmost to strengthen it, trying by active work and service of the people to convert it to our view v II the present Congress leadership persists in its attempt to transform the Congress into a mere parliamentary body with no constructive programme, relying entirely on governmental machinery to verve or rule over the people, turning more and more bureaucratic, keeping its hold over the Congress organisation by the distribution of patronage and largesse, we shall no doubt be unavoidably drawn into conflict with it. But at the same time if we carry on our work among the people with energy and devotion, we shall undoubtedly he in a position to rally the Congress masses around us and resurrect the Congress from its parliamentary debris.

We arrive then at two important conclusions: (1) It is not possible for us now as during the August uprising to work and act in the name of the Congress: (2) we must continue to work within the Congress. The problem now arises, how are we to function so that we may act in an organised and coordinated manner and provide all fighters with a political and ideological focus. This question assumes an added importance when we remember that our activities are not confined to our work within the Congress alone. We have to function in trade unions, Kisan Sabhas and many other organisations which are outside the Congress. It were possible perhaps had we to work in the Congress alone to function as a loose group, but it we are to fulfil our present tasks efficiently, of organised locus of the type described above has to be created.

I have thought earnestly over this question and consulted with my colleagues and have come to the conclusion that we have in the Congress Socialist Party a ready-made basis for an organisation of the type we require today. I believe that after proper overhauling and reorganisation the CSP, would serve our purpose admirably. The CSP has a fine record of political work, and the contribution it made to the August Resolution was, even hostile critics agree, worthy of commendation. The old Party had certain organisational weaknesses, part of which was due to the experiment it had made in socialist and left unity. These weaknesses can and will he removed. My recent contacts with August fighters has shown me that while there are a few who cannot rid themselves of old prejudices, the vast majority do look upon the CSP with hope and show a great deal of good will towards it. I therefore came to the conclusion as I said above that the C. S. P. should become the organisation of all fighters for freedom.

I should mention here an additional reason that supports (his conclusion The CSP includes in its platform the objective of national freedom as well as of socialism. I believe ninety-five out of hundred fighters for freedom have today a strong inclination towards socialism. National freedom without socialism can never satisfy them. Therefore the CSP becomes doubly acceptable to them.

6

Significant Speeches

Panchayati Raj as the Basis of Indian Polity

During the freedom struggle, because of Gandhiji's formative influence upon the political thinking of those 'who fought for freedom, it was more or less taken for granted that *gram raj* would be the foundation of *Swaraj*. In other words, the concept of political and economic decentralisation was axiomatic with the fighters for freedom. But when the Constitution came actually to be constructed, that concept somehow was forgotten or, to be more precise, remembered only as an afterthought. The present widespread practice in the ruling circles of showering seasonal, fulsome praise on Gandhiji and neglecting him in practice seems to have had its beginnings right at the outset of our freedom, when Gandhiji was still present in flesh and blood.

There was, perhaps, a subconscious thought in the minds of the political leaders who followed Gandhiji that while in the enforced condition of disarmament of the Indian people, Gandhiji's technique and philosophy of *Satyagraha* were useful in the struggle for freedom, his ideas were not relevant to the tasks of post-freedom reconstruction. This thought was never clearly formed in the minds of the political leaders, who would have most indignantly rejected any such suggestion. I suspect, however, that from the beginning that subconscious thought has influenced the practical policies that the new rulers of the country have followed since independence.

Be that as it may, it is rather remarkable that it should have been believed at the time that Constitution-making was the job of lawyers and constitutional experts All Constitutions that were framed after successful revolutions, had been the work of the revolutionary leaders themselves, the experts doing no more than giving their ideas a legal framework Unfortunately, in our case, even the distinguished lawyers to whom the task had for all practical purposes been entrusted seem to have performed their functions rather perfunctorily, as is evident from Shri T.T. Krishnamachari's lament.

Since the report of the Balvantray Mehta Committee and inauguration of what is now known as Panchayati Raj in Rajasthan in 1953, there has been a quickening of interest in the subject of decentralised economic and political democracy. It is to help in this process of rethinking that this material is being published It should be found refreshing to be reminded of sentiments and ideals expressed when the glow of a unique revolution still lighted the minds of the people and their leaders.

I should like, as adding a sort of a footnote (this is not the appropriate place for elaboration) to the old debate, to emphasise that the question involved is not only that of decentralisation. As I look at it, there are two entirely different concepts of society involved here. Even though not clearly expressed, this is implicit throughout Gandhiji's discussion on the subject. One concept is that put forward by Dr. Ambedkar, and accepted as the basis of the Constitution, namely, the atomised and inorganic view of society. It is this view that governs political theory and practice in the West today The most important reason for this is that Western society itself has become, as a result of a certain form of industrialisation and economic order, an atomised mass society. Political theory and practice naturally reflect this state of affairs, and political democracy is reduced to counting of heads. It is further natural in these circumstances for political parties, built around competing power-groups, to be formed, leading to the establishment, not of government by people, but of government by party: in other words, by one or another power-group.

The other is the organic or communitarian view, that puts man in his natural milieu as a responsible member *of a responsible Community*. This view treats of man not as a particle of sand in an inorganic heap, but as a living cell in a larger organic entity. It is natural that in this view the emphasis should be laid more on responsibility than on right, just as in the inorganic view it is natural that it should be the opposite. When the individual lives in a community with others, his rights flow from his responsibilities. It cannot be otherwise That is why in Gandhiji's sociological thought, the emphasis is always laid upon responsibility.

Now, a community in order to be real, that is, in order that it might be infused with the sense of community, must emphasise in its internal life such ethical values as adjustment, harmony and cooperation. Without these there can be no community. The community can never bear war with itself: one part of it fighting the other (albeit democratically) and the majority ruling over the minority. Such kind of political battle is possible only in the mass society, where there is no community. This does not mean that within the community there can be no difference of opinion or of Interests. But they must be adjusted together and harmonised so that the community and its individual members live and grow and evolve materially and spirituality The job is to discover the political and economic institutions and processes that can accomplish this task. It is time the protagonists of Panchayati Raj looked beyond the hackneyed phrases of political and economic decentralisation, and stopped thinking that local self-government would perform the trick and usher In people's democracy of their dreams.

It is necessary to point out that according to the communitarian view, the community does not begin and end with the primary community: the village or the small township. Gandhiji's concept of concentric circles of community might be recalled in this connection, the outermost circle, which Gandhiji termed 'oceanic', embracing the whole world community of human beings; just as within the primary community adjustment, conciliation, harmony and cooperation are the aim so, the relations between different 'circles' of community have to be adjusted and harmonised in the interest of all concerned. This objective and the means to achieve it should be expressed in the polity of society The representative political institutions, for example, should be so constituted as to represent not individuals, but their communities, beginning with the primary community and going outward to embrace wider and wider circles. In this system, the community thus takes the place of the party — the difference within and between communities being adjusted and harmonised at every level.

In the sphere of world relations, this concept of adjustment of the interests of national communities, even of the USSR and the USA, is being considered to be a practical proposition But it is remarkable that within the national community this is no yet thought to be possible, or to be possible only on the basis of the majority in numbers imposing its will democratically upon the minority. In the United Nations it is inconceivable that the majority of the nations should seek to impose their will over the minority It would lead immediately to the break-up of the world organisation For the good of each, it is imperative that the nations should discover ways to adjust and harmonise their interests. It is true that this imperative is accepted not because of moral conviction, but because of the threat of destruction from the new weapons of war Nonetheless, the mental acceptance of the imperative is real There is no equally clear imperative at work within the national community In the West, where the community has almost wholly ceased to exist the frustrations of the mass society resulting in a new moral consciousness will perhaps in time replace the present political system based on the struggle for power with a system based on harmony and cooperation.

In India, and perhaps in all the developing countries of Asia and Africa, however, the situation is more favourable. The small primary community, the village or the township, still exists True, there is little of true community life found at present in the village, but at least, the physical makes shell the villages and townships real communities But if a political system is introduced into the village that further disrupts the already largely disrupted community, the result would be not the development of a feeling of community and harmony but just the opposite. The polity of Panchayati Raj, or communitarian polity, must not copy the polity of the mass society It is for this reason that Gandhiji rejected parliamentary democracy, which he termed the tyranny of the majority, laid stress on gram ray {which logically embraces *nagar raj)* as the basis of *swaraj,* and also why he commended the process of decision-making through a process of consensus-making and emphasised the role of a detached moral force based on popular sanction and derived from selfless service as a unitive and corrective force in the democracy of his conception

There is a last point which I should like briefly to touch upon. It might be urged, as is actually done, that in the organic or communitarian society the individuality of man would tend to be submerged in the community and he might not be able to enjoy that freedom which is essential for the dignity and development of the human personality. Contrarily, it might be urged that it is only in the society that treats the individual as a unit in the political system and bases the political structure on individual votes, that there is the highest possible freedom enjoyed by the individual. Nothing could be farther from the truth. It is exactly in the mass society, which falsely proclaims the sovereignty of the individual, that the individual is alienated from himself and becomes a nameless digit which the political and economic masters manipulate for power and profit and glory The individual in the modern society is a victim of social and economic forces over which he has little control. On the other hand, it is in life in the community, in which the sense of community has developed, that the individual is a distinct personality living with other personalities and has the possibility to develop to the highest as a human being. The relationship between the individual and the community, as Gandhiji has expressed it, is the readiness of the individual to die for the community and of the community to die for the individual To the extent to which this attitude is developed on both sides, to that extent there is individual and social development The task is to discover the best social, political, economic, cultural and educational processes and institutions that would achieve that objective.

Class Organisation, Class Struggle and Social Change

In the past I took objection to forming of class organisations. But I have no such objection now. There is a need for such organisations. We should, however, make it a rule that these class organisations have the right to nominate or co-opt members belonging to Muslims, tribes. Harijans and backward castes. When we talk about backward castes, we should also keep in mind that some of the backward castes have remained backward only in name.

Indeed, I have used the term 'class organisation because I have the background of Marxism. But I have not used this term in the Marxian sense. I have the impact of both Gandhi and Lenin on my thinking, I firmly believe that the people's movement can only be non-violent. This is now testified. *Satyagraha* is non-violent class struggle.

Generally the youth constitutes the revolutionary force in India. But to me working class has no significant rote to play. As a matter of fact, I consider it more or less part of the petty-bourgeoisie. But the landless is a real revolutionary force. To arouse and organise them is a tremendous task. They have been suppressed due to caste and economic reasons.

Sarvodaya methodology has no answer to this problem. It may be effective to some extent But it ultimately proves unsuccessful.

Let me make my position dear. There is no difference between caste and class in the village today. Even among the upper castes there is higher class One may find it difficult to persuade them to forgo their special privileges, which they are now enjoying, and to establish unity among different castes. There is no option left but to bring this change Unless the downtrodden assert their organised strength and cultivate the sense of self-respect, those who are on the top will not change. It is true that there are poor men even among the upper castes When we go to the village, we find that the Rajputs generally sit on the cot whereas persons belonging to the lower castes take lower positions and the Harijans remain even far behind them To make them sit together with the *baboos* need a good deal of effort I wonder how many years it will take to create the situation of equality. If we have to depend on the methodology of change of heart in the upper castes, it will take a millennium This one fact warrants the downtrodden to rise and to display enough strength.

There is a danger of violence. But I believe that the struggle for social and economic equality should be peaceful Why should it be violent? This struggle is to organise the poor and to assert their rights. Where does the theory of permanent struggle which has obsessed the communists arise?

But if violence occurs, the struggle of the downtrodden will suffer One should take caution If once violence is committed, it leads to a chain of violence and counterviolence I myself do not approve of violence by the downtrodden as retaliation to one by the higher castes. For, it is the poor who suffer most. We must avoid violence at any cost.

My statement has caused much confusion in *Sarvodaya* circles. But one need not be taken by surprise but take it as natural Many of the *Sarvodaya* leaders hold that my statement smacked of class struggle and, therefore, of violence. *Sarvodaya* movement prohibits class struggle or for that matter any class organisation. If there is a class organisation, there is bound to be class struggle. For many years, I followed the *Sarvodaya* view. But I have begun to feel that beyond a certain point it becomes ineffective and there is no way out except class struggle Those who suffer humiliation, injustice and exploitation must develop the capacity of resistance. How can this strength be inculcated? If class struggle is inevitable. I said, let it be. But it will not be the same as the Marxian *one.* In my scheme of class struggle there is no question of violence. Nor will there be ill-feeling against the opponent We may not even consider them our enemies We will maintain compassion and poise This will be a new thing, which is unfortunately lacking in the Marxist ideology of 'class struggle".

How can we avoid violence, particularly in Bihar? This state had been under permanent settlement I sometimes become sceptical We should, however, give serious thought to it When we take steps in this direction, we should be very careful and cautious. There are a hundred ways of bringing about a revolution. We have seen enough of the struggle in this world between the rich and the poor, the powerful and the week. But how to carry out this struggle through non-violent means is the question.

Vinobaji has replaced class struggle by class harmony. We were active in making this experiment in the past But what was the result? If one makes a statistical analysis of our work in the

Sarvodaya movement, our performance seems to be wide off the mark. How much of land was redistributed? How much land has now been left under the possession of the landless? Is there any change in their social relations after land was redistributed? I have no intention to undermine the achievement of the *Sarvodaya* movement during the last several years by raising these questions. But let us ask ourselves: have we left some impact on society?

I wish to examine all these questions afresh. There are two forces in society: One, the weak, and the other, the powerful. In *Sarvodaya* we have thought only of the strong and we wanted to change them through persuasion and change of heart. But we never took those who are weak or backward into account. There may be some individuals who have changed. But whether they have changed as a class is doubtful. How many of us have changed since independence?

Those who belong to higher castes are also economically affluent. They are not prepared to grant even ordinary status of human beings to the lower castes. Bosses abuse the workers. In the villages the Rajputs will always sit on cots. But the backward castes, whether they are Ahirs or Harijans, will stand before them This has been the practice in our country. They were not even told to sit together with the higher castes. The Harijans will always shudder to sit with them. They are the remnants of feudalism.

There is the law of demand and supply in operation in the villages. Where there is scarcity of labour, a worker may get better wages and also better treatment. But on the contrary, where there is a plenty of labour, the wages are low and also the labour gets inhuman treatment How will this situation change? Let us think over it. It is not enough to say that we should not wage class struggle for it is contrary to *Sarvodaya* ideas. While on the one hand there is no change of heart taking place, we on the other have not been able to create the necessary condition for such a change. If such is the situation, what is the way out? Should we go on raising polemics about ideologies? Or, should we do something to bring about a change in the situation?

Since the idea of class harmony was mooted, there have been several experiments going on in this direction But there is no one in the *Sarvodaya* movement to carry forward this idea Even Vinobaji has now renunciated social work. Neither Dhirenbhai nor I have enough talent to take his place. I am not obsessed with the idea that those who are making this experiment should eschew it Those who want to propagate such ideas are welcome to do so. But as far as I am concerned, I have lost my belief in it. Nor do I feel that it may lead us anywhere Personally speaking. I am no longer a believer in such ideas. Nor do I think that the *Sarvodaya* movement of for that matter, even some voluntary organisation has enough strength to change class struggle into mass harmony. There is no other way left.

The Marxist ideology of class struggle has no relevance to us A great quantum of energy might have been deployed to develop this concept. Both communists and socialists made planned efforts to intensify class struggles. But have they been able to make any progress in this matter? There might be some small achievement Marx's ideas about class struggle are applicable only to an industrial society. India being predominantly an agricultural country, there is no distinct class stratification. Nor is there any possibility in the future. A landholder is both a small peasant as well as a labourer He earns his livelihood from land. But is his interest in land different from that of a big land holder? How can there be class struggle in such a situation? There are villages where the percentage of the landless is negligible. The communists and also the socialists have tried in the past to unite small peasants and the landless together. But that attempt too has failed. Small peasants see in the landlords their own image.

I have, therefore, come to this conclusion that one cannot escape from class struggle It is inevitable. Those who will the land have no land of their own. Is this not injustice? It is their right to own land It sounds natural that they should assert their right There is no other way out The tower class has as much the right to have the sense of self-respect as the upper class. I have thought of a twofold pressure. One, the pressure of the toiling masses, and the honest and the selfless youngman should take up the task of educating the masses. Two, the pressure of network of class organisations and intensive class struggles by the downtrodden. This twofold pressure will break the social structure that symbolises the feudal tradition of exploitation.

When I speak about class struggle. I know that the people point out the danger of violence I was cautioned about this even earlier, particularly when the Bihar movement for total revolution was going on. If this fear is there, how can we struggle for social change? It is true that we should not allow any kind of violence to erupt on our part it's better to improve our methods than to submit to violence. For it proves fatal to the cause of those for whom we are waging class struggle. I also hold the view that violence can be avoided in class struggle. It can be launched as a peaceful struggle as non-cooperation or as *Satyagraha* If the working class have their own strong organisation and there is unity among them, they can make use of non-cooperation as an effective weapon against their employers. How long will the bosses stop taking work from outside. India is yet to be completely mechanised and the bosses are dependent on the working class There is no question of the bosses ignoring the workers.

As you know, the struggles have been going on in society. But they are unilateral. Those who hold land also hold some power and position either in the *panchayat* or government or any other non-official organisation and they wield authority. But our effort should be to organise these exploited and downtrodden people and see that they develop their own strength.

We must take out from our mind the thought that violence is an inevitable part of class struggle. It all depends on the leadership and the organisation. If all this is right, my conception of class struggle is a comprehensive *Satyagraha.* In brief an all-embracing peaceful *Satyagraha* is my class struggle.

Concept of Total Revolution

My objective has not changed. It remains the same as it *was* when I was young. It is the same as that of socialism or communism—a society free from exploitation, a classless society, a stateless society. Complete elimination of inequalities appears to be impossible but they must be minimised, one to five or one to three. Critics of partyless democracy, which I advocate, who claim to be Marxists have forgotten Marxism Marx envisaged a society in which the state would, with time, wither away. Political parties are instruments for the exercise of power. There can be no parties in a stateless society.

For years I was groping to find a way out In fact, while my objectives have not changed I have all along been searching for the right way to achieve it. I wasted two years trying to bring about a politics of consensus.

It came to nothing. I also spent quite some time with the opposition parties to prevent the splitting of votes, However, I do not know what is wrong with them but opposition parties go on splitting into smaller and smaller groups. I came to the conclusion that the people must become their own saviours But how to bring that about ? How to activate the people was the problem? Then I saw students in Gujarat bringing about a big political change with the backing of the people and the moral support of Ravishankar Maharaj and I knew that this was the way out.

I was however, not involved in the student movement in Bihar in the beginning. However, at the instance of students and their action committee. I agreed to lead them on condition that they remained peaceful and acted in a non-partisan manner. By and large the Bihar movement has remained peaceful The occasional acts of violence were committed against agents provocateurs

What you see happening in Bihar is a struggle between "*Chhatra Shakti*" (youth power) and "*Jan Shakti* (people's power) on the one hand and "*Rajya Shakti* (state power) on the other. And the struggle is not for the capture of power, in other words, for replacing the Congress government with the opposition, but for purification of government and politics, including those of opposition and for fashioning instruments and conditions for taming and controlling power, irrespective of which party or parties happen to be in power for the time being.

Two new forces have been created in the country: one. *Jan Shakti* (Force of the People), and the other *Yuva Shakti* (Force of the Youth) The organised form of these two forces in Bihar is *Jana Sangharsh Samitis* (People's Struggle Committees) and *Chhatra Sangharsh Samitis* (Student's Struggle Committees). Similar committees are springing up all over the country.

These Committees have to be coordinated, nurtured, strengthened and guided. This is a new political development which everyone has to reckon with. All the old ways of political and social analysis will have to change in order to take into account the working of these two new forces.

The instruments of youth and people's power have to be permanent in order to be effective. If it arises from a movement and then disappears later, nothing remains.

Socio-political-economic Ideas

My socio-political-economic ideas have also been expressed from time to time in my writings, but I may not be able, just by personal influence, to persuade those who may come to power after the next ejections in Bihar to accept and implement them. I cannot hope to succeed where Gandhiji failed. But there is one historical factor to be taken into account, namely. Gandhiji's assassination less than six months after independence. There is no doubt that had he lived even for only five years more, he would have awakened and mobilised the masses and the youth to compel the new rulers of India to cut out their high-sounding but empty verbiage and face the reality of India that lived and still lives in her villages and stinking urban slums

Without wanting to draw comparisons. I might say that if my life is spared for a few years, it might be possible for me to compel the new rulers of Bihar to come out of their comfortable homes and officers to face the reality of poverty-stricken and backward Bihar. That could be done only if the students' and people's struggle committees were to continue to function and exercise enough influence over the representatives, not only to make them carry out their promises but also to participate actively in the peoples continuing revolutionary struggle. Accordingly, the present attempt is to strengthen the struggle committees so that they do not have to depend upon any leadership from above and can continue to function and march forward on their own.

I have been at some pains in the past months to explain that the Bihar movement is a people's movement and not a movement of a united front of opposition parties. What could the objectives of such a movement be? Obviously they could only be fulfilment of the people's desires and needs, their freedom from exploitation, oppression poverty and a host of similar injustices.

What would the people want except fulfilment of their needs, aspirations, and a drastic change in the condition of their life? For instance, where they do not have water to drink, they want water, they want work for their idle hands, land to till or gainful employment or in the absence of both, at least a subsistence allowance; cloth to cover their body and keep out the cold in winter; habitable homes; thorough reform of the caste system; eradication of social evils like tilak and dowry; education, which they find is meant only for the upper few, to be made available cheaply or free to all of their children, and also education which is meaningful for their young so that it develops their mind and heart and equips them for jobs, professions and gainful self-employment; break-up of the power structure in the rural and urban society so that the domination of a few over many may end and it may be possible for the people to order their lives and carry on their government directly and freely; a complete overhaul of the administrative system so as to bring it under their (people's) control and make it less expensive, dilatory and overbearing; drastic measures to deal with corruption in politics and in government, which is the source of all corruption. This list can be multiplied if we are thinking of the objectives of the movement in terms of the people and not in terms of *ism* or political, economic and social theories.

The key question obviously is how all this can be done ? It is the question which I am expected to answer when I am asked to define the objectives of the Bihar movement. It is in the search for the answer to this question that I have journeyed from Marxism to Democratic Socialism and from Democratic Socialism to *sarvodaya* I have briefly described this pilgrimage in my little book *From Socialism to Sarvodaya*.

I am of the view that the answer to the question facing me and the Bihar movement cannot be found within the framework of any single ideology, no matter how radical sounding. There is all the evidence in the current world history, which has witnessed intense ideological feuds leading sometimes to assassination of one another to show that ideological systems have a way of changing their basic character when faced with social realities and the practical task of revolution-making and post-revolutionary reconstruction, even though their adherents might continue to swear by the ideological Gods.

Critique of Marxism

Marxism itself is a good illustration of this. How flexible or if you like, how vague and ill-defined this ideology has been found to be is illustrated by the fact that Lenin. Rosa Luxemburg. Trotsky. Bukharin, Zinoviev, Stalin. Khrushchev, Brezhnev, Tito, Imre Nagy, Kadar, Dubcek, Husak (in Europe). Mao, Liu Shao-Chi, Lin Piao (in China), Castro (in Cuba) and, coming nearer home, Dange, Ranadive, Rajeshwara Rao, Sundarayya and a host of Indian Marxists, ideologically tearing one another apart have all sworn and are swearing by the name of Marxism. This is no disparagement of Marxism nor repudiation of my own debt to it, but only an illustration of the fact that isms are capable of being differently, even contrarily interpreted. What is true of Marxism is true of all other *isms*. The word Gandhism has been bandied about and likewise interpreted differently.

I consider that given certain value commitments and certain goals, problem-solving and social reconstruction are serious scientific tasks. True, scientists also have their differences, but their objectivity is a guarantee that they will not be limited by the blinkers of ideology. Some scientists too have ideological commitments, but in that case they have forfeited their right to be considered scientists. Value commitments should not be confused with ideological commitments. The fault of an ideology is that it insists that certain values, such as social and economic equality, can be achieved only within its own framework and no other. Whereas my contention is that once the goal is fixed and the values defined, it is a question for science to determine how the goal can be reached within the given value framework There can be no dogmatism about the means, provided the goal and the values are kept clearly in view, These means can be altered by experience

Problem of Non-Implementation

As I have said, the people are interested not in promises but in their implementation So far implementation of socio-economic programmes of parties and of promises made at election time has depended entirely on the sincerity and seriousness of those in power. It has been my effort to create people's organisations in the constituencies so that they may keep a watch over those voted to power.

In our Constitution and the democratic institutions and processes established thereunder, there is no provision to ensure the accountability of the people's representatives to their constituencies In the absence of any such safeguard, especially in a backward society that is woefully lacking in the infrastructure of a developed democracy, the representatives of the people behave as they please in complete disregard of the people's feelings, interests and wishes. Such a state of affairs leads to the present kind of unprincipled politics.

At least in Bihar, *Sangharsh Samitis* will be there. They can speak on behalf of the *Janata*. The *Jana Sangharsh Samiti,* and the *Chhatra Sangharsh Samiti,* are the two powers are that have developed into, as I keep on saying, the *Jan Shakti* and *Yuva Shakti.* They represent the people.

The Bihar movement is trying to educate and organise the people so that they might by their own action change and better their condition of life. This is one aspect of social change to which traditional politics has paid little attention. It has depended entirety on legislation and the processes of administration, planning and development But there are laws in the statute books which cannot be fully implemented without the people actively participating in the implementation process. *Benami* and fictitious settlement of land so as to evade the *Ceiling Act* cannot be undone by merely passing a law or by administrative action; nor can surplus lands be distributed to the landless people in that manner.

Lack of Political Will

There is another serious problem. It there had been a will, the land reforms already on the statutes could have been implemented. The political will was missing. The administration was also not very keen because its members were tied up with landed interests and so on and so forth. One of the first laws passed by the

Shrikrishna Sinha Government was the *Privileged Persons Homestead Tenancy Act,* making homestead tenancy secure. The landless labourer, who had built a hut on somebody's plot of land, could not be evicted and this kind of security was given to him and in lieu of that he was supposed to have been given a ticket, a piece of paper from the revenue department, saying that so much land is in the occupation of" this man, he cannot be evicted. If you go even now to the villages of Bihar after so many years, if the landless people are asked whether they have received the *parcha* the answer is in the negative.

Likewise, laws regulating sharecropping, under-tenancy, minimum agricultural wages, homestead land, moneylending, etc. cannot be enforced through the legal or administrative machinery alone. Unless the people are made conscious of their rights and organised to fight for them, the benefits conferred upon them by law cannot be realised by them. The Bihar movement through the struggle committees and the *Janata Sarkans* trying to achieve this very end.

There is another set of socio-economic changes that legislation or administration can hardly bring about. For instance, take the problem of high and low castes, of *dwijas* and *shudras,* of untouchability, of dowry and *tilak,* of the status and treatment of intercaste and interreligious marriages, and a host of other social evils Laws exist to curb or remove many of these evils, but they are helpless unless the people themselves, particularly the young people, take it upon themselves to cast them out from their own life and the life of the society These changes are the most difficult to effect Yet, they are an important part of the total revolution that the Bihar movement is aiming at.

Power Structure

The social distinctions of high and tow castes in rural society have hardly changed since Independence. The social-economic-political power structure in the village is much the same as before: a few high castes and landed families holding sway over the rest The *Harijans* live in segregated *bastees* beyond the pate of the so-called "village community". The *Harijan* is an outcast, an *avarna* Untouchability is still rampant, and in most of the villages *Harijans* cannot draw water from the wells of *savarnas.* Even elderly *Harijans* are treated with disrespect. The least assertion of human dignity on the part of a *Harijan* leads to dire consequences, even burning alive.

The system of *tilak* and *dahez* has reduced marriages, particularly among the so-called higher castes, to commercial transactions, causing economic ruin to many families and leading to corruption of every sort. Even the slogan shouting youth are not immune from this disease. The pomp and show exhibited at marriages by ministers and the well-to-do is an affront to the poor.

In many of the fields discussed above there is legislation to regulate the concerned activities. For instance, a law of the state legislature lays down that no one can take *tilak* and dowry of an amount higher than Rs. 250. There is a *Minimum Agricultural Wages Act.* There are laws for protection of sharecroppers. There is a law to regulate money lending. There is a land ceiling law. There is a *Privileged Persons Homestead Tenancy* Act for the benefit of the landless. There is a Vigilance Department. But most of these laws are on paper or have been most unsatisfactorily implemented.

A total revolution in the social sphere, particularly Hindu social sphere, would mean eradication of caste. But it is easier said than done From days immemorial social reformers, religious leaders and revolutionary activists have tried to break up the caste system. But there is something in it which holds it together. I have advocated intercaste marriages as the only method by which the system, the barriers, the walls could be broken down.

During the movement I found that a number of intercaste marriages took place. But I feel that the intercaste marriage by itself is not a solution. It must be an accompanying part of a larger revolution; a larger social revolution within the context of which or within the meaning and sphere of which the caste system would also undergo a change.

Administrative Reforms

A great deal of fundamental change is required to bring the administration near the people. By this I mean that the people have a say in the running of administration. Now at the people's level there are branches of the organised parties. They are interested in their own parties and they are not so much interested in programmes as in propaganda in order to win the votes at the next elections.

Then again, the structure of local government, in both urban and rural areas, has been systematically destroyed out of political considerations and there is a total lack of commitment to democratic decentralisation. Most of the municipalities are being ruled (or ruined) by administrators. It is well known that the three-tier Panchayati Raj *System* was not even given a full trial in the State.

I find that one of the most difficult spheres which has resisted change is administration and bureaucracy though many committees were formed to look into their working. The recommendations of the *Administrative Reforms Commission* have really not been seriously carried out because the very people who are to carry them out are the people who would be affected by the changes, i.e. the bureaucracy.

I think it needs a very strong political leadership and a very well-knit organised political party with a mass base and its following among the intelligentsia to bring about a total revolution in view of the vested interests in our bureaucracy. This, as I said, is the hardest nut to crack.

Ironically enough, the bureaucracy grows after some time even in a violent revolution. In Soviet Russia, there had emerged a new bureaucracy of party managers So also in China. A social revolution is not social welfare and economic well-being There is as much need for social revolution in the USA or the USSR as in India A social revolution is a fundamental change in the economic, political and social power structure, so that power comes to be exercised "at the work-place". This implies fundamental change in property relationships, in respect of ownership, management, and disposal of profits It implies end of exploitation, employer-employee relationship and socio-economic inequality. This also implies universal freedom and a radically different set of values governing individual and social life. Without these it will be impossible for the people at the ground level to exercise power Indeed, the very concept of power would change radically.

You cannot get rid of bureaucracy wherever there is centralisation Simplification of this whole system of administration more decentralisation, more devolution of authority and decision-making, and so on is the only answer.

Nevertheless. I have been often asked to define the socio-economic aims of the struggle, or as some call it, 'its frame'. I do not think a detailed socio-economic programme such as that of a political party, particularly of the left, is advisable for the movement.

However, the continued interest of the masses in the movement belies the view held among some elite circles that unless the objectives of the movement are clearly spelled out, it will gradually lose the support of the people Framing of programmes and policies has been the concern of the political elite in the country. But the history of the past years has shown that the mass support does not depend upon detailed policies and programmes of political parties, but entirely on other factors As a matter of fact, there is hardly a political party aspiring to win elections which has not put forth an attractive socio-economic programme. But what the people want is not promises, but their implementation, From their sad experience of the last 27 years, the people have come to regard honesty to be a much greater virtue than radical programmes. And honesty, alas, has rather a low priority in the country's politics. That is why the people's mood today is one of distrust of politicians and political parties.

But I do think that I and my colleagues in Bihar have a fair idea of the broad social, economic, political and cultural frame for the movement.

Gandhian Frame

This, broadly speaking, is a Gandhian frame laying emphasis on agricultural development, equitable land ownership, application of appropriate technology to agriculture such as improved labour-intensive tools and gadgets, of which the *gobar* gas plant is a fine example; development of domestic and rural industries; aid to the widest possible spread of small industries; regional planning and development; political and administrative decentralisation and devolution qualitatively and materially different from the present bogus decentralisation that we have in the shape of *Gram Panchayats, Panchayat Samitis* and *Zilla Parishads,* etc.; drastic educational reform to destroy its elitist character and relate it to the problems of socio-economic development and to the lives of the students themselves; dismantling of the hierarchical caste structure of Hindu society, dismantling also of the economic hierarchical structure in a manner that did not discourage production and create a privileged class of managerial bureaucracy linked with the political and administrative as we have today Nationalisation in our country has not achieved any of the aims of socialism except converting private ownership into state ownership. Indeed, it has militated against socialist aims and values.

Well. I suppose in such areas as oil and steel, modern technology will have to be applied, but I suppose there is also a limit I do not think we are in the stage of push-button technology, whole factories being run by computers and so on but as modern as possible, taking into account employment and the cost of production, etc. The rest of it, I would want, may be small, medium and rural. The smaller industries, may be cooperative, may be even private I would encourage employment as much as possible. In Bihar, because the cooperative department and the cooperative movement are in a very bad shape, I have been advising that informal groups be formed comprising six or seven small marginal farmers to get together and pool their land, maybe 20 acres, without going to the cooperative department where so many papers have to be signed and so much bribe has to be given for anything to be done. The ownership question is not so important as far as I can see unless the ownership is of political significance, that is, the owning of some economic institutions or organisations which lend political power to manipulate. Then, of course, to that extent I would like to break this political power.

But if they work well merely as economic institutions. I would like them to be more on the pattern of a responsible company I would not use the word 'trusteeship' because that is not a current coin But a private firm which is responsible to its proprietors and shareholders, and also to its producers, workers and employees, and also to consumers who buy the goods so that they do not sell shoddy goods or overprice them There has to be some sort of control by the workers on management. There should be some responsibility to the community also, the responsibility being defined. Maybe some ceiling on profits, too. Open books and enquiry into balance sheets and accounts by workers' representatives, and so on. This. I would say, should apply to the public sector also. The public sector should also be responsible not only to Parliament but in an respects. Unfortunately, this part of what I have said received so little attention from the traditional communists and others because it does not fit into any ideology. It is Gandhian more or less but also certain experiments made in Europe have been of great value as far as my own thinking is concerned. Some experiment in England, France and Germany, even in Switzerland, has been made. I had an international seminar here in 1965, which was concerned with the responsibility of business.

Genesis of Total Revolution

The movement for total revolution is not a political party. It started with 12 demands. Eight of them were related wholly to student issues. Four others dealt with issues of wider interest to the people—fight against corruption, high prices, blackmarketing, hoarding, artificial scarcities, etc. and fight against unemployment and against the present educational system. That is why it could get the cooperation and involvement of the people after it started.

Now, these are basic demands and they have given me the opportunity to raise the question: How is it possible to fulfil them without a complete political, economic, social transformation in society? You cannot keep every thing as it is today and say that you will remove corruption, remove unemployment, and so on. Therefore you must think in terms of social change, economic change, political change, administrative change, cultural change, and so on. In fact this is the beginning of a social revolution that will touch all aspects of social life and even individual life. For example, in the course of the struggle I think the boys are undergoing a change. Boys, who in the past, would have gone to beat up a principal, are now offering *satyagraha* and going to jail. This is a the kind of change that is taking place.

I hope that the leadership would come from the people to sustain a revolution of this magnitude, any revolution for that matter. I can only stimulate the leadership, but the urge for a change must throw up the right leader at the right time and at the right place.

I am aiming at a people's movement embracing the entire nation. Such a movement cannot have a clear-cut programme. The main purpose of a movement is strong, it will see that the people's will is carried out. If not, the Government goes out and a new Government comes.

Nevertheless, there is an urge among the people for a revolutionary change. But as you know from history, the gestation period of any revolution has been long and beset with a number of difficulties. It cannot be otherwise in India. The people's revolutionary movement is not over and whether Jayaprakash lives or dies, he has no doubt that the movement will eventually succeed It is inconceivable that countless millions of human beings will be content for ever to live an animal existence. In fact it is wrong to suppose that the Bihar movement is finished and is now only a matter of memory.

If there were a Total Revolution of my concept, the individual man would also undergo a revolutionary change. So it is the totality that undergoes the change including the individual I think the specific nature of a total revolution at any particular time would be governed or determined by the needs of the time, the situation that obtained in the country arid the forces that were contending for power. So at different times a total revolution might take different forms, even different meanings, in the sense that its contents might also be different.

In the present context, a total revolution in India should mean a revolution from the village upwards to the largest urban concentration There must be a total change in civic life, civic relationship, civic institutions, and as we go beyond the sphere of civic life we enter larger spheres of the state or the national life; we have innumerable spheres in which the changes will have to be brought about.

Which individual or which political party should or should not be in power was and is not the main concern of total revolution.

The latter is far more interested in revolutionising the political institutions and processes.

I believe only in two kinds of militancy There is the Gandhian non-violent militancy and there is the violent militancy Anything in between makes for chaos and can only lead to a dictatorship It invites retaliation in kind and the government has far greater resources of that kind than anyone else. There is no political party today which can organise a violent revolution. Maybe, ten years from now there will be but not today. So the only way is the non-violent militancy.

Violent *versus* Non-Violent Revolution

On this I made up my mind long time ago. I have been through all these phases I started out by advocating violent revolution after my return from the US in 1929 and continued to be a revolutionary in that sense until I saw that independence was achieved by the Gandhian way. I then told Gandhi that there was no room in independent India for violent change because we have our own and not a colonial government.

I haven't changed since then I don't believe that you can change man with violence, that change will be only superficial The only way to achieve permanent social change is through non-violence. I have made up my mind on the basis of my experience and I do not argue with anyone who comes to me and says that violence is the only way.

I say that I have decided for myself, but if you want, you go your way Nobody can accuse me of encouraging violence. A lot of people have told me that had it not been for me the situation would have been difficult to control on June 5. 1974, in Patna when the Indira Brigade people tried to provoke us by shooting at the procession.

When there is the situation of despondency and despair, and when the institutions and processes of democracy are focused to be so woefully lacking, is there any wonder that discontentment frustration anger and want should turn the minds of some towards violence as the only possible saviour ?

But while all this is understandable, it is relevant to ask if violence will prove to be the saviour it is promised to be It is not as if we were at the dawn of the first violent revolution in history that is to usher in the first day of deliverance for the 'wretched of the earth' There have been quite a number of such revolutions already that have rubbed off a good deal of their shine and brought disenchantment in their train. This is not the place to go into a detailed examination of this issue, but a few points may be noted to put the matter in perspective.

We, the levers of revolution, are not in the Parliaments of the world, but in the hands of the people. Whether the revolution is brought about through violence or non-violence, it is the people always who bring it about.

But a violent revolution by its logic turns out every time to be half-a-revolution. The illusion of success is created by the fact that a "successful" violent revolution does succeed in destroying the foundations or the old power structure, be it of feudalism (France), feudalism-cum-capitalism (Russia) or other.

Violent Revolution

But the remaining half of the revolution—the building up of a new social order in accordance with the revolutionary ideals — gets lost in the new power-structure that comes into being. This is never the structure of people's power. The reason is not the betrayal of the leaders, but the logic of violence. The mass violence that breaks out in a violent social revolution has to be brought under control once it has achieved its destructive purpose. In this an instrument of organised violence—a Red Army, a Peoples Liberation Army — comes into being. Whoever come to control that instrument power rests in their hands and not in the hands of the people There may be a struggle at the top—like a palace revolution — as to who (individuals, groups, parties or factions of parties) will control that instrument, but that is irrelevant to the question of people's power.

A violent revolution is generally considered to be swift and sure. It is neither. It takes a long time, sometimes centuries, for a violent revolution to succeed, and when it does, the aims of the revolution are thrust into the distant future to be achieved no one knows when. Witness France and Russia. Therefore. I reject the violent way. If the Naxalites want power for themselves, I have nothing to do with them; but if they want power for the people, they are following the wrong road.

I believe a non-violent social revolution may lead to power at the ground-level. I also believe that a non-violent revolution can be quicker than either a revolution by constitutional means (if at all possible) or a violent revolution.

Two, it must be noted that political violence can be both revolutionary and reactionary. There is no certainty that a violent revolutionary movement will always lead to a social revolution. It might very well produce a reaction and end up in a fascist dictatorship. (Naxalite violence is already generating counterviolence). Or it might just end up in chaos, mass misery, and disintegration and enslavement of the nation Those who preach violence must reckon with these possibilities.

Three, revolutions do not just happen at the will of revolutionaries. Social and historical conditions have to be ripe before a revolution can succeed. That may well take a century, as history has often shown In India, the advocates of violence have been at it since the Telengana days. But how far have they progressed in these twenty-two years? Nothing can be more untrue than the facile belief that a volent revolution takes little time to engineer.

Four, even when a revolution, after a long period of incubation, does ultimately succeed, what does its "success" mean? It means no more than that the old social order has been torn up and destroyed But for no revolution is destruction an end in itself. The end is always a new social order. But how long does it take the revolutionaries — whose first occupation after success is invariably to plunge into a bloody fight for power among themselves—to establish the social order of their dreams, or such of their dreams as have not been washed away in the fraternal blood-bathing? Was there a single social revolution in history which had achieved its purpose? Think of the French Revolution and the ideals of Equality, Liberty, and Fraternity. Think of the Russian Revolution and of Lenin's slogan of "all power to the Soviets'—workers' Soviets, soldiers' Soviets, peasants' Soviets. It is 53 years since the Russian Revolution and there still happens to be party dictatorship tightly clamped down upon the Russian people No one can tell how long that dictatorship will last before the Soviets really come to power after all.

Five, though the central issue in all revolutions is that of power, and though they are all made in the name of people's power, power comes invariably to be usurped by a handful of the most ruthless among the erstwhile revolutionaries. Nor can it be otherwise when power comes out of the barrel of a gun and the gun is not in the hands of the common people but in the hands of those of the organised instruments of violence that a successful revolution always throws up — the 'revolutionary" army and its auxiliaries. Whoever controls those instruments controls power. That is why a violent revolution has always brought forth a dictatorship of some kind or other. And that is also why after a revolution a new privileged class of rulers and exploiters grows up in course of time to which the people at large are once again subjected.

No, violence has not proved to be the saviour that the oppressed and exploited are led to believe. To alter slightly Tolstoy's famous remark, the revolutionaries have done everything for the people but get off their backs.

In that connection I often point out which is a fact of history, that a violent revolution does not succeed unless the existing state of the ruling class begins to disintegrate and the bulk of the armed forces, particularly the army, either remains neutral or goes over to the side of the revolution. I point out further that in a peaceful revolution there is no need for any army to do that. But if the rulers do venture to use the army to suppress a peaceful revolution, the army should not allow itself to be so used. On such occasions the leaders of the revolution may call upon the army to come over to their side.

But I have always made it clear that it was certainly not such an occasion I have also decried sometimes the use of armed personnel to deal with civil disturbances for which the civil armed forces, like the armed police and paramilitary forces should be enough. If all this amounts to committing treason. I shall not mind being prosecuted for this offence.

Class Struggle: Its Limitations

Marxist ideology of class struggle is applicable essentially to the industrial society, where there was or is an owning class who owns the means of production and the other class more or less the tools of production. They are human beings but nonetheless they are the tools. Now in our society we don't have that kind of classification. We are an agrarian society. In the countryside in which 80 per cent of the people live, there are larger numbers, maybe they form the majority, of very small peasant proprietors. But the land that they own is not sufficient for their livelihood. So they have also to work as labourers and there you have the class distinction breaking down.

As a landowner he belongs to the possessed labouring class and as a labourer he belongs to the dispossessed labouring class. But he is the same person Yes, in the case of bigger landlords who do not work with their own hands in their fields, a division like that can be made But how many big landlords are there in this country, particularly after the operation of the ceiling acts, etc.? There has been redistribution of land. Landed proprietors voluntarily have done it They have distributed the land among their relations to save themselves from the operation of the *Ceiling Act.* So in a way the land revolution has taken place in India, quietly and silently, over a number of years. But the countryside is not what it was ten or fifteen years ago The caste hierarchy is there but that also, I think, is breaking down There is both *levelling up* and *levelling down* Surely, the depressed is more depressed But the middle castes, such as the *Ahirs* in Bihar or the Jars and the *Gujars* in the U.P. and Haryana who form the peasant proprietory class, are the labourers as well as the owners of their fields and no class analysis applies to them. This, I think, is a picture that probably will last and Marxists' hope that Indian agriculture will also in time become a capitalist industry I don't think is going to be fulfilled It will remain, more or less, a peasant proprietory form of class

Role of Revolutionary Leadership

As history records, not even the greatest revolutionary leader could create revolutions at will. The secret of their leadership lay in the fact that they were able to recognise the signs of the times and skilfully exploited the historical opportunities. There was undoubtedly a revolutionary climate in the country last year (1974).

You know that it is a truism that everything in the world is changing ceaselessly. In human society there is an automatic Change as children grow into adulthood and then into old age, so the cycle goes on revolving. When one generation hands over its culture to a new one, there is automatically a change. This you might call the unconscious process of change in human society. But there is also a conscious change because everyone likes to better his condition. I believe that in the material sphere, particularly in the toots of production, changes are consciously and constantly sought to be brought about. At the other end of the spectrum, changes in customs, manners and beliefs are comparatively much slower. But there also changes are taking place both consciously and unconsciously.

Those changes, conscious or unconscious, might be considered to make up the permanent revolution. But there is one distinction which I should like to make here.

Change might be either revolutionary or reactionary The motive force for changes of the former kind naturally comes from the deprived and unprivileged sections of society. The task of revolutionary leadership is to channelise the revolutionary urges of the people and to give them direction, an objective and an ideal.

7

Select Letters

To All Fighters of Freedom

Letter No. I

Revolutionary Greetings,

Comrades,

Let me first of all offer you and those comrades who have been made prisoners of war my heartiest congratulation on the magnificent battle already given to the enemy. Nothing like it ever happened or was expected to happen in this our long suffering and suppressed country. It truly was the "Open Rebellion" envisaged by our incomparable leader Mahatma Gandhi.

The Rebellion, no doubt, seems to have been suppressed for the moment. But I hope you will agree with me that it has been suppressed only for the moment. This should cause us no surprise. As a matter of fact, had the very first assault been successful and had it completely crushed imperialism, that in reality would have been a matter for surprise. The very fact that the enemy himself has admitted that the Rebellion came pretty near destroying his power, shows how successful was the first phase of our National Revolution.

And how was the first phase suppressed? Was it the Military power of the enemy, his unmitigated reijn of goondaism looting, arson and murder that did the Job? No. It is wrong to consider the "Revolt" as having been "suppressed". The history of all Revolutions shows that a Revolution is not an event. It is a phase, a social process. And during the Evolution of a Revolution, tides and ebbs are normal. Our Revolution it at present going through the period of low water. SO soon rather than rise to higher heights and go from Victory to Victory, not because the superior physical force of the Imperialist aggressors intervened, but because of two important reasons.

Firstly, there was no efficient organisation (of) the national Revolutionary forces that could function (and) give effective lead to the mighty forces that were released. The Congress, though a great organisation, was not tuned to the pitch to which the Revolution was to rise. The lack of organisation was so considerable that even important Congressmen were not aware of the progress of the Revolt, and till late in course of the rising it remained a matter of debate in many Congress quarters whether what the people were doing was really in accordance with the Congress programme. In the same connection should be mentioned the regrettable fact that quite a considerable number of influential Congressmen failed to attune their mental attitude to the spirit of this "last fight for Freedom". The earnestness, the urgency, the determination that marked the attitude of leaders like Mahatma Gandhi, Dr. Rajendra Prasad and Sardar Patel failed to reflect in the minds and hearts of all congress leaders.

Secondly, after the first phase of the Rising was over there was no further programme placed before the people. After they had completely destroyed the British Raj in their areas, the people considered their task fulfilled, and went back to their homes not knowing what more to do. Nor was it their fault. The failure was ours: we should have supplied them with a programme for the next phase. When this was not done, the Revolt came to a Standstill and the phase of the ebb began. This situation was created many days before the British soldiers arrived in sufficient numbers to push back yet further the receding works of the revolt. What programme should have been placed before the people in the second phase? The answer is suggested by the nature of Revolutions. A Revolution is not only a destructive process, it is at the same time a great constructive force. No Revolution could succeed if it only destroyed. If it should survive, it must create an authority to replace the one it has destroyed. Our Revolution loo having accomplished over large territories of the country the negative task of destruction, called for a positive programme. The people who destroyed the objects and means of administration of the foreign power and drove away its agents should have set up in their areas their own units of Revolutionary Government and created their own police and militia. Had this been done, it would have released such an unprecedented volume of energy and opened up such a vast field for constructive work that the waves of the Revolution would have mounted higher and higher till—if the rising was countrywide—the imperialist power had been broken and the people had seized supreme authority throughout the land.

The lack of efficient organisation and of a complete programme of National Revolution these were two causes of the downward course of the first phase of the present Revolution.

The question now is what are our present tasks? First, to banish all depression from our minds and those of the people, and create an atmosphere of joy instead at the success achieved and of hope for success in the future.

Second, we must keep steadfastly before our minds and of the people the nature of this Revolution. It is our last fight for freedom. Our objective can, therefore, be nothing hut victory. There can be no halt way houses. The efforts that men like Rajagopalachari are making I'm the establishment of National government are not only fruitless but positively harmful in as much as they distract public attention from the real issues. There is no compromise, between the slogans of "Quit India" and of a "national government". Those who are running alter the slogan of Congress-League unity are merely Serving the ends of imperialist propaganda. It is not the natural unwillingness of imperialism to liquidate itself. Mr. Churchill left no manner of doubt about it when he declared recently that he had not assumed the office of the King's first minister to preside over the liquidation of the

Empire. He would be a foolish student of society indeed who expected Empires to wither away of their own accord. Those erstwhile "revolutionaries"' who are attempting today to wish away the Indian Empire by the cataclysmic force of humble memorials are making of themselves the most pitiable fools of history.

It is not the unity of all the important elements in Indian life, to quote the imperialist jargon, that is the need of the hour but the unity of all the national revolutionary forces. And these are already united under the flag of the Congress. Unity between the League and the Congress does not foreshadow the growth of these forces, but their absolute relation, for the League cannot conceivably tread the path of revolution and freedom.

The complete overthrow of imperialism, then, is our objective and we must keep this steadfastly in view. There can be no compromise on this issue. Either we win or we lose. And lose we shall not. Not only because we are determined ceaselessly to work for victory, but also because powerful world forces are drawing the doom of imperialism and fascism ever nearer and nearer. Do not believe that the formal results of this war settled laboriously at the Peace Conference would settle the fate of the post-war world. War is a strange alchemist, and in its hidden chambers are such forces and powers brewed and distilled that they tear down the plans of the victorious and vanquished alike. No peace conference at the end of the last war decided that four mighty Empires of Europe and Asia should fall into dust—the Russian, the German, the Austrian and Ottoman. Nor, was the Russian, the German, the Turkish Revolution decreed by Lloyd George, Clemenceau or Wilson.

Throughout the world where men are fighting, dying and suffering today, the alchemist is at work, just as he is in India, where he has already let loose a mighty social upheaval. Neither Churchill nor Roosevelt, neither Hitler nor Tojo will determine the fate of the world at the end of this war. It is force such as we represent that will fulfil that historic task. Can we doubt that revolutionary forces are stirring everywhere'. Can we believe that millions of people are undergoing unutterable suffering without a thought for the future? Can we believe that millions are satisfied with the lies that their rulers daily feed them with. No, it cannot be so.

Having therefore definitely fixed our vision on the goal of total victory, we have to march ahead. What concretely must we do? What does a general do when he loses or wins a battle? He consolidates and prepares for the next battle? Rommel stopped at El Alamcin after his great victory to consolidate and prepare. Alexander too prepared and he turned his serious defeat into a resounding victory Ours was not even a defeat. We really won the first round of the fight in as much as our large territories of the country the civil rule of the British aggressor was completely uprooted. The masses have not learnt from experience that the imposing edifice of the police and magistracy and law courts and prisons which goes by the name of British Raj is but a house of cards when they hurl against either collective power. This lesson is not likely to be forgotten and it constitutes the starling point or the next offensive.

Out third and most important task then at the present moment is to prepare tor the next major offensive. Perhaps organisation, discipline ourselves—these are our present watchwords.

The next offensive? When do we expect to launch the next offensive'.' Some people think that the masses will not rise again for the next five or six years. This estimate might be true of peace time hut it does not hold good for a stormy war torn world of last moving events. The savage tyrannies of the British fascists—the Linlithgows the Hallets, the Stewarts and the myriads of others and theirs base Indian Lackeys— may has compelled the people to lie low for the present, hut they have nowhere converted them into friends of the oppressors. The whole country side, where this British type of Nazi hell was let loose, is seething with the most intense discontent, anger and thirst for revenge. The people haw merely to understand that powerful preparations are afoot to lake courage again and to enter the plans and schemes of the next offensive, with active, coordinated and disciplined work; it would be wholly favourable for the next assault. International events may come to our aid. Then there is Gandhiji's ever impending fast unto death, a constant reminder to us and to the people not the slacken, not to waver, not to rest on the oars.

The question of the next offensive is linked up with the question of the positive task of the Revolution—i.e., the establishment of the units of the Revolutionary governments. With the latter question is bound up the question of violence and maintained firmed forces. I wish, therefore, to place before you my view on this question, as to my mind it affects vitally the future of our Revolution.

First of all. I feel I must say a few words about the noise the British authorities have made about the violence committed in the course of this revolution. There was some violence indeed under extreme provocation, but it was remarkably little as compared with the magnitude of the Rising and the staggering manifestation of individual and collective non-violence It is not realised, perhaps, that thousands of British and Indian employees of the foreign power were for some days literally at the mercy of the masses, who took compassion on their foes and spared them their lives and properly. And what of the cool, sublime courage of those thousands of young and old who received the enemy's bullets on their chests with the flag revolution in their hands and "Inquilab Zindabad" on their lips?' Have the British a word of praise for this godly courage?

In any case is it not remarkable that the British power which is soaked in violence, which is based on violence, which daily commits the most pitiless forms of violence, which grinds down millions of people and sucks their lifeblood should make so much noise about the violence that others commit? How are the British concerned with what weapons we choose to fight them with? Have they pledged non-violence if the rebels adhere to it? Have they not already shot down thousands of our non-violent soldiers? Whatever weapons we use the British have only bullets for us and looting and rape and arson. So let them keep quiet as to how we fight them, it is our business entirely to decide that.

Coming to the question as it affects us. I would first remind you of the difference between Gandhiji's views on non-violence and those of the Working Committee and the A.I.C.C. Gandhiji is in no event prepared to depart from non-violence. With him it is a question of faith and life-principle. Not so with the Congress. Then Congress has stated repeatedly during this war that if India became free, or even if a national government were set up, it would be prepared to resist aggression with arms. But, if we are prepared to fight Japan and Germany with arms, why must we refuse to fight Britain in the same manner? The only possible answer can be that the Congress in power could have an army, whereas the Congress in wilderness has none. But *supposing a revolutionary army were created or if the present Indian tinny or apart of it rebel,* would it not be inconsistent for us first to ask the army to rebel and then ask the rebels to lay down arms and face British bullets with bared chest?

My own interpretation of the Congress position—not Gandhiji's—is clear and definite. Congress is prepared to fight aggression violently if the country became independent. Well, we have declared ourselves independent, and also named Britain as an aggressive power: we are, therefore, justified within the terms of the Bombay revolution itself to fight Britain with arms. If this does not accord with Gandhiji's principles, that is not my fault. The Working Committee and the A.I.C.C. themselves have chosen to differ from Gandhiji and to reject his conception of non-violence as applied to the war. Nor was Gandhiji allowed by the British power to lead and shape this resolution: so, in following interpretation we should in no manner he false to him. We should only he discharging our duties in the light of our own reason. As far as I am concerned, I feel that I should be completely justified as an honest Congressman, without in any manner intruding my socialism upon the question, in repelling the British aggression with arms.

I should add that I have no hesitation in admitting that non-violence of the brave, if practised on a sufficiently large scale, would make violence unnecessary, but where such non-violence is absent. I should not allow cowardice, clothed in Shastric subtleties, to block the development of this revolution and lead to its failure.

With the implication of the last phase of the revolution clear in our minds, we have to prepare, organise, train and discipline our forces. In everything we do, we have constantly to bear in mind that ours is not to be merely a conspiratorial action. It is total revolt of the masses that is our objective So, along with our immense technical work, we must do intensive work among the masses—peasants in the villages and the workers in the factories, mines, railways and elsewhere. We must do ceaseless propaganda among them and help them in their present difficulties, organise them to fight for their present demands, recruit from them selected soldiers for our various activities and train them technically and politically With training a few may succeed where thousands foiled before. In every fiska and taluka and thans in every considerable factory and workshop or other industrial centres, we must have a band of militants, mentally and materially equipped for the next rising.

Then there is our work in the Indian Army and the services. There is agitational and demonstrative work. There is work in the schools and colleges and in the market place. There is the work in the Native Stales and *on t*he frontiers of India. It is not possible for me here to describe our preparations more concretely. Let it suffice to say that there is tremendous work to be done and work for every one. Much is being done at present, but vastly more remains to be done.

Who but youth can accomplish all this? Is it loo much to hope that our students who have set such *a* brilliant record already will follow up their achievements and vindicate the promise they have given? It is for the students themselves to answer.

I should make it clear that preparation does not mean that fighting entirely ceases for the moment. No "Skirmishes", "frontier activities", "minor clashes", "sniping", "patrolling"—all this must go on. These are in themselves a preparation for the offensive.

With full confidence in the people and devotion to the i let us, then, march ahead. Let our steps be firm, our hearts resolute and our vision undimmed. The sun of the Indian freedom has already risen above the horizon. Let not the clouds of our own doubts and disputes, inaction and faithlessness, obscure that sun and drown us in our self-created darkness.

In the end, comrades. I should like to say that it has made me inexpressibly happy and proud to be able once again to place my services at your disposal. In serving you, the last words of our leader, "do or die" shall be my guiding star, your cooperation my strength and your command my pleasure.

Somewhere in India Jayaprakash Narayan

Letter No. 2

I

After a close contact with the progress of the Revolution for the past half year, I find no cause to change the views I had formed at the very beginning, nor do I find that the analysis made in my last letter requires any vital modifications, except in one respect, not of a vital nature, yet important.

In December last it appeared to me that it might be possible within a few months for another mass uprising to take place. That rising has not yet materialised, and it has to be ad-milled, does not appear to be immediately imminent. The question naturally arises how this fact affects our present policy and the course of our struggle. In order to be able to answer this question, it is necessary to probe a little into this failure of the masses to rise again.

First of all it seems to me that it would be a mistake to deduce from this that the spirit of the people has been crushed or that there is no fight left in them. The people never hated British rule as they do today and were never more determined to get rid of it. A certain amount of demoralisation undoubtedly exists today, but it is found largely. I do not say wholly, in the cities and among the higher strata of the society. In the countryside, the areas where the repression had full away, are far from having been cowed down, they are on the contrary filled with a burning desire for vengeance. At the first suitable opportunity they will rise and tear up British rule to pieces. It is rather the people of those villages who escaped British goondaism that sometimes show symptoms of fright and a tendency to save their skin at any cost. But I believe these people too could be persuaded to march abreast of their brethren when the final hour approaches. The students who played a notable part in the first rising are, it is true, back at their schools and colleges. But from what I have been able to gather, they are far from being dispirited, and would be ready again to place themselves at the head of a rising. The growing severity of the food situation, the increasing hardships of living, and the steadily falling real wages have not induced labour to look kindly at the so-called war efforts, and were another 'open rebellion' to break out, labour's contribution to it might not be less, but mote than it was in August-September last. The lower ranks of the Police forces, though apparently won back to loyalty to the super regime, are far from satisfied with it and would prove much less reliable in the event of another rising than they did in 1942. The discontent among the officers and ranks of the Indian Aimed forces has grown rather than lessened with the progress of the war: nor the new schemes regarding salaries, etc. of the new Commander-in-Chief are likely to allay it.

It may be asked why, if this picture be true has not a second rising broken out and why is it not even an imminent possibility. The reason, to my mind, is to be found in the intangible psychological factors. These factors are often unpredictable though it is one of the tasks of leadership to assess them properly. One of the essential conditions, though not the only one is the rise of a belief in the mass mind that the ruling class or power is played out and at the end of its tether. The course of the world war in the months immediately prior to last August had been such that the Indian people had come to believe that the British Empire was crumbling and they had but to deal it a blow for it to totter entirely to the ground. At the present moment and for some time past, this psychological background has been absent, or rather altered so as to become an inhibiting instead of a stimulating factor. To all appearances the Americans seem destined to save the British Empire and piece together the fallen pails. As a matter of fact, the dissolution of the doomed Empire goes apace as certainly as ever -and strange though it may appear, the Americans are not without their share in it, for they cannot fail to acquire the first mortgage over the territories they 'liberate'. But this process is not visible to the naked eye and so an inhibition is created in the mass mind.

This inhibition can be removed under two conditions either when the international situation improves, i.e., when it goes against the British Empire, or when an organised revolutionary force by dealing sustained and continuous blows at the enemy assures the mass mind that the British in spite of a huge army, are powerless in the face of a Rebellious India and arouses in it the hope that an uprising would possess a powerful leadership and a fair chance of success.

In August last not only did the war situation contribute to the creation of a suitable psychological atmosphere but also the fact that the Congress stood in all its power at the head of the people. The people had faith in their leaders and when the call went in forth they responded with confidence and enthusiasm.

Today these leaders are in prison and they must present an appearance of helplessness to the people. Thus the second element in the creation of a mass psychology of the rebellion is also absent today.

But while it is not in our power to provide the first clement, we can and should remedy the situ alien in respect of the second. A tendency is growing amongst fighters to take shelter from activity behind the idle complaint that the masses do not move, do not respond. This is defeatism. The masses cannot move till there is force in us to move them. They cannot respond, they cannot follow us till we are able by our activities, and the strength and efficiency of our organisation to win in their confidence The masses did their duty once. It was we who were found wanting. They shall do their duty again provided we do ours. In August last the masses had before their eyes the concrete power of the Congress and the leadership of Mahatma Gandhi. Today if they are made to feel that they are left alone, that there is no organised force in the country, which remains undefeated continues the struggle, they would naturally sink down into despair and resign themselves to their Kismet.

The present, therefore, is a stage primarily for the enlisted soldiers of Revolution, the irreconcilable fighters of freedom to act in. They must strengthen their organisation and carry ceaseless war unto the enemy. No suffering, no sacrifice should be counted too great; no controversy, no temptation, no false hope should deflect our course. All avenues of struggle are open to us. Whatever be our faiths and creeds, whatever our methods and weapons, our course is clear. We must keep on lighting. Whether we fight a year or ten years should make no difference to us. The Americans fought their war of Independence for seven years, the Chinese have just entered the seventh year of their war of liberation. We have but completed our first year of fighting. During the American and Chinese wars there were moments when all seemed to be lost, but the leaders and men held on, and victory was eventually with the Americans, as it will be with the Chinese. The present is far from being the darkest moment of our struggle, and yet weaklings and cowards have dared raise their voice. These are traitors to their country and we must chuck them out of our way and march on. Worse times in as be in store for us, but let hardship and suffering not deter us but harden us. Then shall we be worthy of the people's confidence, then they shall respond to our call.

II

For some months past, particularly since the correspondence between Gandhiji and the Viceroy was published, a controversy has sprung up among fighters on the question of violence and non-violence. My views on this question have been clearly stated in my first letter to you and I still adhere to them. There is no need to repeat what I have already said, hut I should like to say word or two about this controversy. To me a controversy on this issue at this stage seems meaningless, livery fighter for freedom is free to choose his own method. Those who believe in similar methods should work together as a disciplined group. And the least that those who follow a different path should do is not to come in the way of one another and waste their energies in mutual recrimination. Where 'do or die' is the mantram of action, there is no room for recrimination whatever. Those who believe in non-violence may harbour the fear that those who practise violence might compromise the position of Gandhiji. That fear is unfounded. Gandhiji's adherence to non-violence is so complete, his position in respect to it so clear, that not a hundred thousand Church ills and Amerys will be able to compromise him. Also, we must remember, that whatever we do, however we try, we can never prevent British statesmen whether Tory or Labour, from telling lies; for lies are one of the central pillars of the Empire. Remember also that if there is violence in India no one but the British Government itself is responsible for it.

Another controversy that has been Started since the publication of the Gandhi-Viceroy correspondence is whether the present struggle was started by the Congress and whether it can he called a Congress movement. It has been claimed by some, who have gone so far us to suggest that a rump A.I.C.C. should meet to withdraw the Bombay Resolution, that since Gandhiji and other Congress leaders were arrested before they could make a formal declaration of war, this struggle is not a Congress Struggle at all. According to the logic of this argument no struggle, if the British were to arrest the leaders in time, could ever have the formal authority and sanction of the Congress. What is it that those who deny the authority of the Congress to the struggle would desire to have happened on the 9 August after the cowardly attack on our leaders? What do they think was the desire of Mahatma Gandhi and the Working Committee in the event of their arrest Would the detractors of the present struggle have been happy if there had been no reaction to the arrest of the leaders, if the country had calmly bowed its head before the imperialist jackboot? Or was it expected that only protest meetings should have been held demanding the release of arrested leaders (as was advocated by certain erstwhile Revolutionaries), and when they were not released, further meetings should have been held, till the audience became too disgusted to attend, after which the "protestants' could have gone to sleep with a clear conscience? If this be so, where was the sense of that brave revolution and those brave words that were poured forth from the lips of the greatest in the land at the Bombay A.I.C.C? If on the other hand this be not so, and if the people were expected to rise in answer to the British offensive, if indeed the arrest of the leaders was a signal for a mass struggle, then where is the grace and fairness in decrying the present struggle as un-congress and unauthorised? When you are on the war path, it is foolish to expect the enemy to allow you the leisure to complete all the formalities required by a peace-lime Constitution. It therefore appears to me to he mean and cowardly to attempt to show that the national struggle that started on 9 August 1942, has not the authority and sanction of the Congress.

It is a different matter when we turn to the question whether the programme of the present struggle was authorised by Gandhiji or the Working Committee. Here we are in the realm of facts and not principles, and political ethics. And about the facts there is no dispute. It is well known that the Working Committee had not prepared a plan of action but merely requested Gandhiji to assume command of the struggle. Gandhiji in his turn had also no plan of action. He had sketched the merest outlines in his address to the A.I.C.C. That outline and his articles in the *Harijan* were all that the people had before them and they formed the basis of that detailed programme which was prepared by those Congressmen who were left behind, and who hastily met in Bombay to lay foundations of that 'illegal' Congress organisation which has functioned since then. That programme still in the framework of the National Struggle. There is no room for murder in it nor for any form of violence to the person. If murders were committed in India as they were. 99 per cent of them were acts of the British fascists and hooligans and not more than 1 per cent were of an infuriated and sorely tried people. Creation of deadlock and paralysing and dislocation of British rule by all non-violent means was and remains the sheet-anchor of that programme and 'to the fullest extent under Ahimsa the star to steer it by'. While it is true that there are some who in the name of non-violence are attempting to disown certain parts of the programme, which they had themselves sanctioned previously and which even such a high authority as Shri Kishorilal Mashruuala did not have the heart to condemn or ask the people to desist from, there is no doubt that the conscious basis of the programme which the Congress organisations have followed since August 1942 has been non-violence, as interpreted by the people in authority during this period. They who prepared the programme have never disowned the responsibility: and when the time comes they will no doubt appear before the tribunal of the Congress and receive its commendation for having discharged their duty at a most critical moment.

Be that as it may to fasten the August programme on Gandhiji is a piece of perjury of which only the British ruling class can be capable.

III

In the past couple of months there has been in evidence a symptom which bodes greater mischief than these controversies. Since the beginning of the struggle there has been a group of Indians who have deplored the step taken at Bombay and attempted in their wonted manner to 'resolve the deadlock'. I do not think Congressmen were ever concerned about them, nor need they be now. Every time India launches a fight for freedom this- group sets out to 'resolve the deadlock'. The fact that men like Shri Rajagopalachari, Bhulabhai Desai, K.M. Munshi, whose rightful place was in the midst of fighters, have joined the association of saboteurs of the freedom movement, should make no difference.

But, as time passes and fighters are released from prison, some among them - a very few now doubt - show signs to fatigue and demoralisation. They too have taken up the slogan, 'resolve the deadlock': and different proposals to effect this are set afoot by them

First, it is highly disloyal of these Congressmen to initiate a policy of retreat when the generals are in the firing line. A real sense of discipline is tested in action. At the stage of discussion, criticism and difference of opinion are the law of the democratic life. But at the time of action, particularly in war, the strictest discipline is necessary And discipline requires in the present instance that every Congressman should remain in the firing line and give no thought to retreat or surrender. It is for the generals to consider these issues. Mahatmaji and Maulana Azad are in jail, but in the matte of peace and war the initiative is still with them, as it always is with either side at war. Mahatmaji could easily resolve the deadlock' whenever he wanted by surrendering. He has not elected to do so. This means that he wanted the fight to continue or to put it at the worst, the deadlock to continue.

Secondly, let us go a little deeper into this question of the so-called deadlock. It would he conceded by everybody that ending of the deadlock is not an end in itself. It must mean and advancement of the national cause; it must lake us a step further towards the goal that is unalterably ours.

Keeping this in mind we may proceed to examine the ways to bring the deadlock to an end. There are three possibilities: either we force the British Government to concede our demands, or we surrender, or there is a 'negotiated peace' between India and Britain - a compromise. The first would mean a complete victory for India and could clearly be brought about only by the method of struggle. Those who have lost all hope of victory and feel suffocated by the stalemate and yearn for the freedom of parliamentary play-acting have the option of surrendering. But they would thereby most effectively kill the Congress and extinguish the spirit of resistance for at least a generation. That would be a complete victory for Britain.

We are left with the possibility of a compromise the superficial attraction of which draws many well-meaning people into its snare and the path to which, as to a well-known place is, already paved with a great many excellent intentions. A compromise implies give and lake on either side. Now, the lost gains on the side of the Congress can be the release of all those imprisoned in connection with the national struggle and restoration of the status of 'legality' to the Congress and its ancillary bodies. The least that Britain can gain is removal of the terrible strain that British administration has to bear due to the continuance of the struggle. It is my conviction that in this sort of a compromise British stands to gain everything and the Congress to lose much.

Let us picture the implications of such a compromise. What would be the Congress position with regard to the war? Nothing has happened since August of last year to cause Congress to change its views of the war or to induce it to join it unless it is in a position to wage the war in the interest of the Indian people and on their behalf. On the other hand, an awful deal has happened in the past year that would make it impossible for any self-respecting Congressman to be associated in any manner, official or Otherwise, with the goondas and cutthroats who rule India and who let loose such a hell over the heads of the people - a hell the fires of which have not yet been extinguished. It is inconceivable to me how Congressmen can ever offer the plan to men who have murdered and pillaged and burnt and raped and tortured lender boys in the stillness of prison cells. Tor this reason and for the reason that Congress cannot accept office in the present circumstances without power. I cannot imagine that the Congress would agree to work the 1935 Constitution again. Congress had once agreed to work that Constitution in order to wreck it and had nearly wrecked it sell in the attempt. That wretched fraud has, however, been most effectively wrecked by the war and as the memorable statement of Maulvi Fazul Huq to the Bengal Legislative Assembly showed, not a shred of provincial autonomy remains to hide the ugly nakedness of bureaucratic rule.

(Parenthetically let me remark that it is a pity that after so ably exposing the hollowness of provincial autonomy Maulvi Huq and other nationalist members of the Bengal Assembly, including those who sail under one or the other Congress flap, should persist in playing at futile parliamentaism. To my mind the only manly and patriotic course open to them after that great statement was to walk out permanently of the present Assembly and have recourse to extra-parliamentary methods to seek to overthrow the monstrous Herbert regime.) To return to my point. Provincial Autonomy being what it is, it would he the height of political imbecility to expect the Congress to resuscitate that fraud by installing its ministers again in the provinces. The Act of 1935 is dead and there is no going back to it: let this be well understood. Nor can India live at peace again with those who have heaped unspeakable indignities and beastial cruelties upon her: Let this loo he well understood.

A compromise with such implications would put the Congress in a most embarrassing position. The Congress would be restored to 'freedom': but would continue to be opposed to the imperialist war and to all the measures — economic and political, that the usurper power might adopt to prosecute the war in the interest of British capitalism; it would be unable to take a hand in the administration of the country and to democratise in the least the ordinance, or to use the modern phrase, fascist rule: it would be helpless to alleviate the sufferings of the people, to provide food for the hungry, cloth for the naked, shelter for the homeless. In short, if the Congress took its principles seriously it would find itself drifting into opposition to the usurper authority at every point. The deadlock would have been resolved in vain.

The Congress would suffer another great loss. As soon as Mahatma Gandhi, President Azad, Pandit Nehru and others are out of prison the world would forget India. The pressure that the deadlock exercises over those who guide the destinies of the world would be suddenly relaxed and the Churchills and Amerys would go peacefully to sleep - lightly thinking that the India question was settled for the time being and would not become pressing again till the mad Gandhi look into his head to march his flock once more to the prison. Pandit Nehru released from the jail might make statements which American correspondents might lap up with avidity, but there would be no strength behind those statements, despite the beauty and grace of their expression. Nehru imprisoned is a greater problem for the Roosevelts and Church ills than Nehru proliferating nobly worded statements and casting his spell over the envoys of treat nations.

It might be suggested that the basis of compromise might be more advantageous to the Congress than that pictured above. Let us see what this basis can be. Britain is not prepared to offer anything more than the Cripps plan – that is, no power during the war and a fraudulent promise of it at its end. The Congress rightly rejected the British offer, and no one in his senses would expect Congress to accept it today. The most moderate demands of the Congress, with which I personally am not in the least in agreement and which I doubt if the Working Committee would be prepared to father today, were placed in the hands of the 'Devil's advocate in April 1942. They were rejected by the British Government. How do those, who are anxious to break the stalemate, propose to enforce those minimum demands, supposing the Congress would be satisfied with them? Could anything but a struggle succeed? So it appears we are back to the deadlock again.

The deadlock is thus inescapable. Its resolution, except on the terms of the Congress, spells disaster to the country, It however, does not mean that we are static. We remain at war, we continue to resist, to exploit every- shift in the national and international position. The very continuance of opposition to the British rule, the very fact that India's best men are in prison is a guarantee that India remains unbeaten, the spirit of resistance remains unbowed, that the Indian question remains a crying world problem, that the subject peoples of Asia and Africa draw inspiration from India's struggle, that the working classes of Britain and the allied nations are constantly made aware of the nature of 'democracy' for which they are said to fight, that the possibility of a better post-war world is brought near, that India gains the leadership of the third camp of the common men of the world for whom neither Allied nor Axis-victory holds any prospects of liberation and happiness. I shall therefore be content even if the deadlock continues till the end of the war. None can tell how long the war may last and what turn it may take and what forces it may release. The longer the war lasts, the more the internal situation deteriorates, not only in India but in every country of the world. A turn in the war the release of a new social force may alter the situation so completely in India that the deadlock may become the starling point of a great leap forward, whereas if we have gone back to 'normally' again the normalcy itself might become for us a deadly fetter. The deadlock is the best guarantee of our success in the future.

It might be urged that by keeping alive the deadlock we are playing into the hands of Britain, for Britain too desires that there should be a political deadlock in India. This is a misreading of British policy. Britain does not desire a political deadlock but a political blackout. She wants to crush the Congress and still its voice, to break the peoples spirit of resistance and will to freedom. A deadlock in which the power of the Congress grows, the spirit of resistance remains unbroken, the right for freedom continues: a deadlock as a result of which British prestige and authority daily dwindle and those of the rebels grow -such a deadlock would defeat Britain's purpose and turn her weapon into an instrument of her own defeat.

IV

Closely connected with the above discussion is the question of a national government and Congress-League agreement. A national government all means. Hut the most amusing thing is that while Congress fights for such a government and suffers others merely talk. If a national government is not the same thing as coalition ministries under the Act of 1935 or a glorified Viceroy's Council, it cannot be won by holding conferences. The Congress left that futile path years ago and if communists expect to establish such a Government In petitioning to their imperial masters, they are welcome to their loading. But they will achieve nothing but the ridicule of the people and the contempt of their pay-masers.

The agitation for a Congress-League agreement as a precondition of a national government is not new and there was no reason for me to touch upon it here. But the depression that has caught some Congressmen who have been seeking a way back to constitutionalism has led them anew into this barren agitation. Becoming weary of direct action, they are eager to fall back on this easy nostrum, forgetting that the author of the agitation. Mr. Rajagopalachari is still cooling his heels before the gates of Mr. Jinnah's mansion, and that Mahatma Gandhi's letter to the League leader still remains undelivered. (Though we have had the rare fortune of reading the reply to an undelivered and unread letter.) I have for this reason considered it desirable to touch upon this subject briefly,

One is compelled to pay a tribute to the skill of British propaganda when one observes how intelligent men fall a prey to it. Either that, or one must acknowledge the depth of national degeneracy which we have reached. If British propaganda 'takes in' the innocent Americans (though even among them there are quite a few who see through it), one can understand, but when it bamboozles Indian, you have to regard it us one of the world's wonders. Recent events in India have born Britain's every pretence to shreds. Not even a fig leaf hides now the true shape and purpose of British Imperialism. Yet, there are Indians who believe and want their countrrymen to believe that nothing but the absence of a Congress-league settlement stands in the way of India achieving her independence.

If the course of British policy in the past few months has established anything it is the grim determination to hold on at any cost to their Indian Empire. If any point emerged with undimmed clarity from the Cripps Negotiations it was the firm resolve of Britain not to hand over real power to India during the war, no matter what measure of unity was achieved in the country. Cripps stated categorically that even if the Congress and Muslim League jointly demanded a real National Government, responsible to the people, it could not be grated during the war. (And who was or its interested in British promises for the future?) In view of this clear statement of British policy, to agitate for a Congress-league agreement serves no Other purpose but to lend strength and respectability to the lies which the Church ills and Amerys tirelessly peddle around the world. The agitation for Congress-League understanding he-comes in these circumstances a part of the imperialist offensive against nationalist India.

It might be asked: even if Congress-League settlement does not by itself compel Britain to grant India a National Government, would it not at least strengthen the forces of freedom and, as such, is it not desirable in itself and worth working for? The conclusion would be true were so the premise. But the premise is entirely untrue. In our country the only forces of freedom are those that are ready to fight and suffer for freedom. The Muslim League during its entire career has not once taken the path of struggle and suffering, nor is it ready to take the path today. India cannot win her freedom without fighting for it. And when the Muslim League is not prepared to participate in the fight a settlement with it in no way strengthens the forces of freedom. Pandit Nehru was not using empty word when he stated that it would have been easy any day to settle with the League were it prepared to join the struggle for freedom.

So much for the Congress-League unity. A word about the real politics of the League. It is necessary to grasp clearly that the League is in league with Britain. Mr. Jinnah is a deliberate traitor to his country, a Mir Jaffer of the present day. He believes that he can get what he wants from Britain. But Britain is not accustomed to handing over parcels of her Empire to its tools. There is no doubt that after she has made the full use of Mr. Jinnah she will throw him into the dustbin of discarded tools as surely as she has thrown others into it before Mir Jaffer included. Let Muslims remember that it is not the sons of Mir Jaffer who rule Bengal today but the dirty kin of Clive. Mr. Jinnah no doubt considers himself a very clever person, but for all his conceit and Fuchrerian attitudes history will show him to have been made a historic fool.

Mr. Jinnah wants his Pakistan. Rut if he is serious about it, he must fight for it, he must make sacrifices for it, possibly die for it. But there is the rub: it is exactly these things which Mr. Jinnah and his followers are never prepared to do. Therefore. Mr. Jinnah shrieks his demand for Pakistan in the face of Mahatma Gandhi. But poor Gandhi is not in possession of Jinnah's sacred homelands. It is the blood-soaked heels of imperialism that possess and trample upon them that defile and desecrate them. The Congress can have no objection if Mr. Jinnah takes his 'homelands' from the British at least a part of India would then be free. But he will not take them, for he is not prepared to pay the price. He therefore wants to get along by blackmailing the Congress. But in the end it will be Churchill who will have blackmailed Jinnah. If India is ever partitioned under the auspices of the Mother of Parliaments it would be in the interest of imperialism not to bestow a separate freedom upon the so-called Muslim nation of Hindustan. Ulster does no good to the Irish, but it is a British knife thrust into the very heart of Fire.

The League's real polity is the ugly issue of imperialist machination and national treachery.

V

You probably know that Shri Subhas Chandra Bose has formed a free Provisional Indian National Government at Shonan (Singapore) which has been recognised by the Japanese Government. Me has also organised an Indian National Army which is said to he growing rapidly. These events have some significance for us. Parenthetically I may add for your information that one of the first act of the Subhas Government has been to offer to send us as much rice us may be required to feed the starving people of Bengal, but the British Government prefers to let the native vermin die.

It is easy to denounce Subhas as *a* Quisling. Those who are themselves quislings of Britain Find it easiest to denounce him. But nationalist India knows him as a fervent patriot and us one who has always been in the forefront of his country's fight for freedom. It is inconceivable that he should ever be ready to sell his country. No doubt it is true that all the necessary resources of money and equipment that he has, have been supplied to him by the Axis Powers. But in the first place the men he has in his Government and the National Army are Indians who hate British rule and burn with a desire to free their Motherland. In the second place, it is well to remember that the resources of all the fugitive Governments of Europe which bask in the patronage of the United Nations come from those Nations. Thirdly, no one can tell what concessions the requirements of global strategy may force a great power to make to a weak and prostrate nation. The conferment of 'independence' upon Burma by the Japanese has received some advertisement and a report says that the Soviet Government has been so much impressed as to congratulate the Tojo Government upon their act of generosity. Be that as it may there seems to he

no doubt that the Burmese today enjoy much more freedom under the overlord ship of a fascist state than they did under British 'Democracy'. Turning to Shri Subhas Bose, it is clear that he has permitted himself to accept aid from enemies in accordance with an age-old political maxim - older than Machiavelli and older than Kautilya. In thus accepting help from a third party he may be deceived in the end but there can be no question as to the honesty of his purpose and scale of his resourcefulness. His success or failure in assisting his country to achieve her freedom will depend on the course of events over which neither her nor any other political leader of any country has much control.

Recognising the importance of the Shonan Indian Government and the National Army, I must emphasise that our freedom largely depends upon our own strength and resources. Hopeless inaction which feeds upon the hope of outside help is suicidal politics. No outside help by itself can free us. It is fantastic to believe that Subhas' army, no matter how large, can defeat the Allied Armies in India. If any army can defeat them it may possibly be the Japanese. But if the Japanese defeat the British in India, they would not quietly hand over India to us - whatever the understanding between Tojo and Subhas. We must he ready in the event of an Axis-Allied clash in India to seize power ourselves. Only if we are ready to make this attempt can outside help, such as Subhas National Army be of value to us and Tojo be prevented from annexing India. It is difficult to say how far Subhas himself is conscious of this aspect of India's national strategy.

This brings me to the question, what should we do when the war enters our doors. British policy has made the average Indian so anti-British that he is prepared if not to welcome the Japanese, it least to remain indifferent to the Anglo-Japanese conflict. This indifference will be our death. We must endeavour to remove it and in its place develop a positive policy of action. In the areas where war is waged or which the Japanese occupy or where they infiltrate, the foreigner's civil rule will weaken or come to an end. In these areas we must establish a Swaraj Government. In the name of this Government we must appeal to retreating units of the Indian Army to stay behind and become the people's army. From this day we must prepare to establish such a Government

in the Eastern Province which in the course of time might embrace the entire nation. This preparatory work raises many questions which cannot be discussed here. It is sufficient to point out the broad policy and invite the attention of fighters to it as well as of the people generally.

VI

A word or two about the war before I conclude. The futile controversy about the character of the War still goes on merrily in the backwaters of Indian life. The fifth-columnists still insist - naturally enough - that it is a peoples war. And those to whom controversy is the beginning and end of politics gel terribly excited about it and argue with words and sometimes with blows. But the Indian people have no doubts about the nature of Britain's War and about those of their countrymen who support it. They do not require any longer to be told what fascism is or that this is their own War. British fascism has revealed itself to them in all its horrid brutality in the last year. Those who rot in prison, those who lost their dear ones in the countrywide murder by which the British re-established their 'law and order', those whose homes were burnt and looted, whose women dishonoured, those who starve and die like rats on the streets - all these people know too well what sort of a people's war this is. A British general bill the decapitated heads of the Shahzadas of the House of Babar on a tray and sent them to the last Mughal Emperor, the father of the hapless Princes as a gift form Queen Victoria. A century and a half later Tottenham boasted to American correspondents, that he had bought enough sandalwood to burn the remains of Gandhi India knows of these deeds and of other black deeds that fill the period from the beginning to the end (for the end is near) of British rule and she does not need to he told by traitors, masquerading as Marxists, what fascism is.

The war has entered its fifth year. The destruction of life and happiness that it has caused can never be repaired. The interests of the common man of both sides demand that the war end immediately. But it cannot be ended by Churchills and Roosevelts, Hitler; and Tojos. Even if they cried halt to the present butchery, it would only be to prepare new and more terrible weapons for more terrible butchery in the future. Allied plans for the post-war

world, of which the barest glimpse has been vouchsafed to the common man picture the same old world of privileged class and national tyranny, capitalist rivalry and chaos which brought two devastating wars in a generation and will surely bring a third

The war can be truly ended by the common people of the world. But their voice is stifled. Russia which could have become the champion of the common man has herself suppressed him at home and disowned him abroad by truckling to the imperialists and super capitalists of Anglo-America. Lahour throughout the world has become the camp-follower of the capitalist class and has thus sold its conscience and forfeited its leadership of society and of the new world.

In these circumstances India alone actively represents the aspirations and promptings of the disinherited and dispossessed of the Earth. India's fight for freedom is at once imperialist (and therefore also anti-fascist, fur imperialism is the parent of fascism) and a drive to end the war through the intervention of the common man. Neither allied nor axis victory is our aim, nor do we pin our hope on either. We work for the defeat both of imperialism and fascism by the common people of the world and by our struggle we show the way to the ending of wars and the liberation of the black, white and yellow.

VII

I have taken too much of your time and must conclude now. I have tried to show above that the only course open to us to follow with profit is to continue to fight. How should we fight?

I have already pointed out that the present is a stage at which primarily determined fighters have to play their role.

The first thing these fighters must do is to maintain and strengthen and widen their organisation. Without organisation no army not even a non-violent one - can fight. Mass actions are generally spontaneous and the resultant of social forces, but there must be an organisation of a revolutionary elite to give shape and decision to them. The spontaneity of mass actions is also often the cumulative product of organised work among the masses by such an elite. In the recent history of our struggle there has been a marked indifference shown by leaders of the struggle to problems

of organisation. The leaders, upon their arrest, have always left too much to the spontaneity of the people. No doubt, the relation of secrecy to non-violent action has been at the bottom of this indifference to organisation. Non-violence does not permit secret functioning. Yet during a struggle organisation must be sacred. I do not pretend to have found a solution of this dilemma. All that I can say is that till the authentic technicians of non-violence discover a solution, it is essential in the interest of work for even those who strictly believe in non-violence to deliberately compromise with their principle to the extent of admitting secret organisation, liven Mahatma Gandhi makes such compromises. By merely condemning secrecy and extolling open work we do not solve the difficulty, nor advance our cause.

Urbanisation then is the first item in the programme of our struggle. It is the basic guarantee of a struggle. In regard to this item. I must emphasise the prime necessity of keeping alive, and in trim, the illegal Congress organisations. These organisations are the sole unifying principle of our struggle. It is true they have no constitutional basis, but it is only through them that the Congress can function today and reach the people and fight the enemy. In several provinces those organisations are not functioning properly. The cause of such organisational weakness is rarely the lack of workers. More often it is inadequate funds and the absence of capable organisers. Neither of these is' irremediable. The Central Directorate of the I.N.C. has been trying to provide the provinces with at least their minimum requirements, and its attempts have not altogether been a failure. This is not the occasion nor the time to examine the role that India's wealthy have played in the present revolution. Mere it is enough to comment upon the entire absence of perspective or vision in them. If they could see but a little way ahead they should easily realise that if the national movement were crushed. British capitalism, harassed as it would be by the post-war world, would give them no quarter whatever. Sheer self-interest, therefore, dictated that they should invest whole-heartedly in the National Revolution. But they have proved to be not only extremely selfish but also exceedingly small men.

However, the requirements for funds must he met somehow and all those who can help should. In some provinces, such as

the United Province some of the ex-Ministers (Congress) are out of jail. If they and other prominent Congressmen who have recently been released in various provinces do not do anything else they should at least see that the financial requirements of their provinces are fulfilled. As far as the Central organisation is concerned, financing of the provinces must remain its most important job. To send out programmes and instructions without the withdrawal to carry them into practice can be no more than perfunctory and unreal fulfilment of duty.

The absence of capable organisers and leaders, who can create work and take work out of others, is more difficult to remedy. However, a partial reedy is that those few who are left should tour around, meet the other workers and discuss with them their practical problems and give them such advice and training as may be possible. Where by fortuitous circumstance there happen to be more capable men than necessary, some of them may be sent away to places where there are none or too few. New workers should be recruited, particularly from among students, and those who are being released from prison should be drawn hack into the ranks.

With funds, recruitment and training, and wise use of available talent and experience, it should be possible to tackle our organisational problems.

To hold our organisation together in the face of repression is a part of the fight - but only a part. Every unit of our organisation must be in touch with the people. The link between the lighters and the people should not be allowed to snap. The link in one word is propaganda - spoken and written propaganda: leaflets, pamphlets, posters, radio broadcasts, mobile columns of fighters touring in the countryside, meeting and talking to the people. Distribution of literature is as important as its writing and production and equal care should be devoted to each task Spheres of propaganda should also he carefully studied. Apart form sections of the public students, labour, shopkeepers, peasants - we should see that our voice reaches the services, particularly the lower ranks of the Police and the Army.

Foreign propaganda should also form a part of our job.

Propaganda is not only propaganda but also a form of our light: for to work a radio centre, to issue an 'illegal' leaflet, to hold a meeting where no meetings are allowed, to say things which are "illegal"- all this is defiance of the usurper power -and a part of the fight against it.

What more can we do? I believe, and I do not mind saying so publicly, that unless there is a shift in the international situation, a Russo-German pact, a Sino-Japanese peace, a major reverse of British aims, war on Indian soil - we cannot do anything big. I want fighters to be under no delusion. Only those who fight on without hope of immediate results will win victory Others will fall out of the ranks, will prattle wise words and pose as statesmen, but history will know them as deserters, as men of poor faith and poorer courage, who forsook duty in the face of suffering. Many friends are depressed by the thought that resistance on the scale that we can offer today -either in the form of Satyagraha and strike as acts of dislocation is ineffective. True, It is in the sense that its volume is not large enough to bring British rule to a standstill. But, it is effective in another, no less necessary, sense - it is effective propaganda, it keeps up the morale of the people, it keeps alive the hope of bigger action, it gives training to fighters, it keeps up the visible forms of the struggle and impresses upon the enemy that all his repression has been in vain. It is effective in the sense that it is a preparation for ultimate effective resistance. Therefore, we must continue to otter resistance to the British power in every shape or form possible, in accordance with whatever creed or programme we believe in.

I would call this our minimum programme for the present: organisation, propaganda, overt resistance. In addition to this we have the whole wide field of preparation: our work among students and labour must continue, our contacts with the Army and the services must be maintained and developed our preparations for dislocation must go on. A rising of the nature of that of the 9 August, but on a bigger scale and better organised and directed, should be our coal. Our every effort should take us a step nearer that goal.

A word about the food situation. I need not say anything about its seriousness. That is well known and well understood. What is not well understood is that the only real solution of the food problem is a Swaraj government. The British partly by their incompetence and partly by design, have created this problem, and so long as they are here there is no alternative to starvation. Therefore, the fight for freedom if the real fight for food. But to say this is not enough. We must also have a fight for food as a part of the fight for freedom. At the present moment the only public reaction to the food situation is charity. Charily has its own place in *a* class society, and much as I hate it as a socialist. I readily acknowledge the humanitarian motive of those who have hastened to rescue the Starving from death. It is a commendable public effort. But charity is not enough. It will not solve the problem lighters have therefore the job their most important job is the circumstances - to create feelings of resentment and anger in the needy and starving and to turn those feelings against the foreign power which is at bottom responsible for all this misery. Let the hungry create a situation in which normal British administration becomes impossible. Let us tell them -not only tell but help them to do it to seize food where they can get it. In the rural areas we should prevent grains from being sent out and distribute stocks through village punchayat or similar agencies (taking care to keep away from Government or pro-Government bodies). Fighters, organised as guerrillas, should seize grain from Government depots and similar placed and distribute them among the needy. Forcible seizure by Government of crops should be resisted. In the cities and towns too the passivity and despair of the hungry and needy should be turned into resentment and anger and given concrete, active shape of demonstration and direct action. Fighters often ask me for a programme. Here is a vital programme which tackled with imagination and courage can convert the country into a seething cauldron in which the Empire can soon be boiled to death.

Speaking of organisation, I have referred only to the Congress. Those, however, who wish to go beyond the creedal limitations of the Congress naturally require a separate organisation to carry on their special activities. I have suggested a guerrilla form of organisation for this purpose, and some progress has already been made in developing a guerrilla movement. In the very nature of things I cannot be expected to say more about this matter here except perhaps this that my views in this regard have no difficulty in reaching the proper quarters and those interested in this work cannot have much difficulty in putting themselves in touch with the organisation that has been set up.

With these words, comrades. I close. I have analysed the present position without passion and laid my views before you without rhetoric or embellishment. It is for you to decide what is worthy of acceptance in them. You will ever find me at your command. 'Do or die' remains my guiding star as it is yours. Let us therefore do or die.

Somewhere in India Jayaprakash Narayan

1 September 1943.

Letter No. 3

9 August 1946

Friends,

Soon after my release when I sent you my greetings through *Janata*, I had promised that later I would place before you my views on the present situation and explain to you our present tasks. I regret that there has been so much delay in doing this. The delay was unavoidable, because it was necessary to meet colleagues and consult with them. All this has been done, and it is possible now to place before you something in a definite shape.

Before this, through various statements jointly or severally issued, my colleagues and I have attempted to place our views before you on important questions as they arose. You have been acquainted with our stand in the last A.I.C.C. Below I attempt more systematically and fully to express my views, and I hope also the views of my colleagues, on the present situation and indicate the tasks that face us and the methods we should adopt to accomplish them.

The present situation is one of transition and rapid change. The A.I.C.C. has agreed that Congressmen should go to the British sponsored Constituent Assembly. An interim government under the British Viceroy might soon be functioning. This government whenever it may come into being cannot be a free government of a free country till the Viceroy and British armed forces and other British personnel quit India. To beg that this government he allowed to function as a free government is to beg the question.

Those who have the power to hand over power at their pleasure, have also the power to take it back at their pleasure. Therefore, let us not be duped by the talk of an interim government being "in effect" the govern men I of a free India.

Could then the so-called Constituent Assembly bring us freedom? In other words, could that Assembly declare India and independent republic and enforce that declaration? Could it, for instance, appoint a provisional government and force the Viceroy to hand over all power to it and quit India? Could the Provisional Government pack off all British soldiers and military and civil officers to Britain? Could that government tear up the strangle-hold of British finance over this country? Could the Constituent Assembly dissolve itself and empower the free Provisional Government, after the British had quit, to convene a real Constituent Assembly elected by the people on the basis of unrestricted adult suffrage? Could the proposed Constituent Assembly take all these steps, everyone of which is essential to lead India to full freedom and democracy? It would be a grave folly to suppose that in the existing circumstances and with the present corelation of forces it could ever be possible for the proposed Constituent Assembly to take any of these steps and achieve any of these objectives. But even if we were to suppose for a moment that the Assembly could make this attempt, the British would be certain to bar its way. Then if the Assembly were sincere and honest to bar its way. Then if the Assembly were sincere and honest it would have to accept the British challenge and invoke its mass sanctions in order to enforce its will. The Viceroy who would have called the Assembly to begin with would then step in and order its dissolution. Thus an all-out war of independence would ensue, out of which should emerge a real Constituent Assembly of the people and free democratic and united Republic of India.

The Constituent Assembly, however, is not very likely to follow these steps. Aware of what President Nehru has described as "the Compulsion of facts", i.e., aware of the limitations of its sovereignly, aware of its weaknesses, aware of the British stooges and enemies of freedom and democracy in its ranks, aware of the presence of the British Army and the British Viceroy - aware of all this and more, the Constituent Assembly might choose to tread what I am sure is going to be described as the path of realism. In other words, the Assembly in might decide to make compromise after compromise, producing in the end neither freedom, nor democracy, nor national unity So, the nation, thwarted an disillusioned, would have to turn once again to the path from which it is being misled today - the path of revolutionary action, the path of resistance and struggle the straight but difficult path of freedom.

Thus we see that in either case, i.e. whether the Constituent Assembly "succeeds" or whether fights and "fails," a struggle for freedom is inevitable. Any one who has a correct appreciation of the present corelation of forces in this country should not find it difficult to accept this conclusion. Today, it is still possible for British imperialism to face us with the "compulsion of facts." Till this compulsion is removed by revolutionary action, freedom would be an illusion. Nor can any one expect to change the facts of the present situation by argument concession and diplomatic finesse.

We therefore reach the conclusion - and it will bear repetition - that the struggle for freedom does not cease with the acceptance of the British constitutional proposals. That struggle will continue. In fact, the character and scope of that struggle will become deeper and wider. To the Struggle for liberty will he added the struggle for national unity and bread.

8

Golden Words of J. P.

- As a way out of the faults and failures of the party system, I toyed for some time with the idea of a cooperative, rather than a competitive, system of parties, I realised, however, that in the first place, there was no climate for such a political experiment, and in the second place, the experiment could not succeed within the given framework of struggle for power and the system of parliamentary democracy, except for limited purposes and limited periods. I still believe, however, that given the psychological climate for it, such a political experiment might yet be made.
- The hold of politics on the minds of people is such, and its alternative is in such an incipient state yet, that I shall not probably be able to persuade many of those who may read the statements, but I do hope there will be more mutual understanding and also a quickening of interest in the ideas therein propounded.
- Freedom still remained the unchanging goal, but the Marxian science of revolution seemed to offer a surer and quicker road to it than Gandhiji's technique of civil disobedience and non-cooperation. The thrilling success of the great Lenin, accounts of which we consumed with

unsatiated hunger, seemed to establish beyond doubt the supremacy of the Marxian way to revolution.

- The Russian revolution had started as a people's revolution that had the active support of the broad masses of Czarist Russia, but Lenin converted it into a minority revolution, when he forcibly dissolved the Constituent Assembly, in which he was in a small minority and seized power with the help of rebel soldiers and the urban working class. The subsequent miscarriage of the revolution and distortion of socialism to my mind was the direct result of the forcible seizure of power by a minority.

- Since Asia regained her political freedom from Europe. European socialists have been visiting us and giving us all manner of advice. All this advice and friendship are welcome but there is one little matter which the European socialists must not forget. If European communism has failed, European socialism has been no conspicuous success either.

- European socialism, both Marxian and non-Marxian, is, among other things, the picture of an industrialised society. Socialism, according to Marx as much as to other European socialist thinkers, was a stage of society that came after the maturing of capitalism. In Asia, industrial capitalist development is in its infancy and Asian countries are overwhelmingly rural and agrarian communities. The task of building up socialism in such an environment is not familiar to European socialists, so there is little guidance that can be obtained from their experience.

- If man and his consciousness and the society and culture, which he has built up are mere manifestations of matter — howsoever dialectically active — I can see no reason why in such a society, anyone should try to be good, that is, be generous, kind, unselfish. Why should then one feel sympathy with those who are weak, poor or sick? So, what incentive can there be for moral behaviour? Lust for power or wealth, or desire to win the acclaim of the people or the regard of one's peers, may be an incentive to action. But such an incentive can have no concern with valuations of right or wrong.

- Ethical ideas have no doubt a history and a social origin, but when the individual begins to question his inherited standards of conduct and asks himself; why he should act ethically, materialism offers him no answer. A person may have grown up with the ideals of social service, sacrifice, freedom, equality and the rest. But if he begins later to ask himself why he should subscribe to those ideals at all and put himself to trouble and loss on their account, the philosophy of materialism, dialectical or otherwise, would not be able to give him any satisfactory answer. I am not suggesting that among philosophical materialists, there have not been examples of great sacrifice for noble causes. What I am suggesting is that their action was not consistent with their philosophy.
- Disciplining of the bodily appetites is essential for a moral life and growth of the human personality and the blossoming of all human qualities and values. This is true particularly of socialist values. The socialist way of life is a way of sharing together the good things that common endeavour may make available. The more willingly this sharing is practised the less tension and coercion in society and the more of socialism.
- The bourgeois state had monopoly of political power. The socialist state threatens to add to that the monopoly of economic power. Such a great concentration of power would require equal, if not greater, power to control and keep it in check. There would be no such power at hand in a socialist society. Paper Constitutions could hardly be expected to guarantee freedom and sovereignty to the citizen. The economic and political bureaucracy would be entirely at its mercy.
- The emergence of Mahatma Gandhi changed the face of National Congress organisation. He made Congress a revolutionary organisation. He invited the people of India to Indian liberation movement and paralysed the British government with the instrument of non-cooperation and Satyagraha. He charged a new life in Indian people. Through Mahatma Gandhi, the meek and docile Indian people became hungry-hearted fighters.

- Generally the youth constitutes the revolutionary force in India. But to me working class has no significant rote to play. As a matter of fact, I consider it more or less a part of the petty-bourgeoisie. But the landless are a real revolutionary force. To arouse and organise them is a tremendous task. They have been suppressed due to caste and economic reasons.
- If there were a Total Revolution of my concept, the individual would also undergo a revolutionary change. So it is the totality that undergoes the change, including the individual. I think the specific nature of a total revolution at any particular time would be governed or determined by the needs of the time, the situation that obtained in the country arid the forces that were contending for power. So at different times a total revolution might take different forms, even different meanings, in the sense that its contents might also be different.
- A violent revolution is generally considered to be swift and sure. It is neither. It takes a long time, sometimes centuries, for a violent revolution to succeed, and when it does, the aims of the revolution are thrust into the distant future to be achieved no one knows when.
- Violence has not proved to be the saviour that the oppressed and exploited are led to believe. To alter slightly Tolstoy's famous remark, the revolutionaries have done everything for the people but get off their backs.
- Change might be either revolutionary or reactionary The motive force for changes of the former kind naturally comes from the deprived and unprivileged sections of society. The task of revolutionary leadership is to channelise the revolutionary urges of the people and to give them direction, an objective and an ideal.

9

Great Life at a Glance

Oct. 11, 1902: Jayaprakash Narayan was born in Sitabdiara village, in Chhapra district of Bihar. Jayaprakash's father was Baba Harsu Dayal, and his mother was Phul Rani.

Oct., 1920: Jayaprakash Narayan joined Bihar Vidyapeeth founded by Dr. Rajendra Prasad for motivating young meritorious youths and was among the first students of eminent Gandhian Dr. Anugrah Narayan Sinha, a close colleague of M.K. Gandhi, who later became first Deputy Chief Minister cum Finance Minister of Bihar.

1921: The stage was set for the return to politics of Jayaprakash Narayan. *J. P.*, as he was called, rose to prominence in *1921*, during Gandhi's first great satyagraha campaign.

1922: He went on to complete his BA and MA in political science and sociology from the United States in *1922*.

1929: He moved to the UK and became active in protest against colonial movements. Amidst such rebellious international students were Jawaharlal Nehru, Jayaprakash Narayan, and Krishna Menon of India, Jomo Kenyatta of Kenya, Tan Malaka of Malaya, Jose Vasconcelos of Mexico, and Sir Seewoosagur Ramgoolam of Mauritius. All of them were J.P's contemporaries, who later became prominent leaders in latter years in their respective countries.

1932: Jayaprakash Narayan protested at Bihar congress putting a ban on the Kisan Sabha.

Dec., 1933: Many a young leader joined the Congress Socialist party led by Jayaprakash Narayan, among them were. Jawaharlal Nehru and Subhas Chandra Bose.

1934: Bihar Socialist Party was merged into All India Congress Socialist Party, led by Acharya Narendra Dev and Jayaprakash Narayan.

1937: In *1937*, he moved to Pune and joined the Deccan Gymkhana Club as a Yoga instructor.

Oct., 1939: J. P. tried to stretch out an olive branch to Anushilan Marxists.

1942: Accused by the Congress Party of forsaking the precepts of Non-violence, Sahajananda was expelled and, out of sympathy for him, Jayaprakash Narayan resigned from the Congress Working Committee. During the Quit India Movement, Bhavabhushan's men disrupted, under the leadership of Jayaprakash Narayan and Ramanand Mishra all means of communication.

Feb., 1943: Heroic demonstrators were shot for trying to raise the Indian flag. In October some freedom fighters led by Jayaprakash Narayan went underground, but their violent revolutionary efforts faded away soon.

May, 1944: Lohia and J. P. were captured in May 1944, in Bombay. Lohia was taken to a notorious prison in Lahore. Under Gandhiji's pressure the Government released Lohia and Jayaprakash Narayan.

Oct., 1951: The Socialist Party, led by Ram Manohar Lohia and Jayaprakash Narayan was founded.

May 5, 1954: Gram Nirman Mandal was found by Loknayak Jayaprakash Narayan.

1955: Jayaprakash Narayan joined the bhoodan movement. In Bihar the movement collected considerable amounts.

Oct. 4, 1958: Jayaprakash Narayan returned from Europe and began to campaign for a new form of "partyless democracy."

Dec. 2, 1961: Bhoodan workers led by Jayaprakash Narayan greeted the President of India, Dr. Rajendra Prasad at Rashtrapati Bhavan on his birthday and presented him with 6000 acres of land in New Delhi.

1966: Following a drought in Bihar, a Free Kitchen was run by the Bihar Relief Committee, under J. P.'s Chairmanship.

Oct. 1968: Sheikh Abdullah, as leader of the Plebiscite Front convened J&K State People's Convention to discuss the future of the state. It was inaugurated by Jayaprakash Narayan.

1975-76: Jayaprakash Narayan led a campain against emergency.

1977: Elections were held and the first non-congress government at the centre was established. J. P. emerged as the grand oldman of the Indian polity.

Oct. 8, 1979: Jayaprakash Narayan passed away.

Bibliography

Ajit, Bhattacharyajea: *Jayaprakash Narayan: A Political Biography*, Vikas Publications, New Delhi, 1975.

Allan and Wendy Scarfe: *J.P :His Biography*, Orient Longmans, New Delhi 1975.

B. Vivekanandan: *India Looks Ahead: Jayaprakash Narayan Memorial Lectures 1990-2001*, Lancer's Books, 2002.

Banaszak, Ronald: *Fair Trial Rights of the Accused: A Documentary History*, Westport, Conn. Greenwood, 2002.

Beebe, Rose Marie and Robert M. Senkewicz: *Lands of Promise and Despair*, Heyday Books, Berkeley, 2001.

Bhagwan, V.: *Indian Freedom Movement and Constitutional Acts*, Atma Ram, 1999.

Bhargava and Phadnis: *Towards Revolution*, Arnold-Heinemann, New Delhi, 1975.

Bhattacharya, B. K.: *India's Freedom Movement: Legacy of Bipin Chandra Pal*, Deep and Deep, New Delhi, 2007.

Bhola, Chatterji: *J. P,:Profile of a non-conformist*, Minerva Associates, Calcutta, 1979.

Bimal, Prasad: *A Revolutionary's Quest: Selected Writings of Jayaprakash Narayan*, Oxford University Press, Delhi, 1980.

Brahmanand: *Communitarian Society and Panchayti Raj*, Navchetna Prakashan, Varansi, 1970.

Burg, B. R.: *Gay Warriors: A Documentary History from the Ancient World to the Present*, New York University Press, New York, 2002.

Chakravarty, Shachi: *Quit India Movement: A Study*, New Century Publication, 2002.

Chandra, Bipan: *India's Struggle For Independence*, Penguin Books India (P) Ltd., New Delhi, 1989.

Chandra, Shailesh: *90 Years of India's Struggle for Independence: 1857-1947*, Alfa Pub, 2008.

Das, Sandip: *Jayaprakash Narayan : A Centenary Volume*, Mittal, 2005.

Devahuti, D.: *Society and Panchayti Raj*, Oxford University Press, New York, 2001.

Dr. Kawaljeet: *J.P.'s Total Revolution and Humanism*, Buddhiwadi Foundation, Patna, 2002.

Dr. Ramendra: *Jayaprakash Vichar Sankalan*, Rajendra Prakashan, Patna, 1986.

Early, Jubal A.: *A Memoir of the Last Year of the War for Independence in the Confederate States of America*, University of South Carolina Press, Columbia, 2001.

Ernst, Nolte: *Fascism and Communism*, University of Nebraska Press, Lincoln, 2001.

Evans, David: *Ramdom Acts of Kindness*, Broadfoot Publishing, Wilimington, N.C. 2001.

Farooq, Argali: *Loknayak Jayaprakash Narayan*, Janata Pocket Books, Delhi, 1977.

Ferguson, John Hill: *On to Atlanta: The Civil War Diaries of John Hill Ferguson*, University of Nebraska Press, Lincoln, 2001.

Franklin, Benjamin: *J.P.'s Total Revolution and Humanism*, Yale University Press, New Haven, 2001.

G. S. Bhargava: *J.P.'s Jail Life: A Collection of Personal Letters*, Arnold-Heinemann, New Delhi, 1977.

Ganjoo, S.: *Muslim Freedom Fighters of India*, Anmol Publication, New Delhi, 2002.

Ghosh, Ratna: *Netaji Subhas Chandra Bose and Indian Freedom Struggle (2 Vols-Set)*, Deep and Deep, 2006.

Goyal, P. K.: *Battle of India's Freedom Movement*, Vista International, 2005.

Gunnar: *Indian Family Correspondence*, The Norwegian-American Historical Association, Minn., 2001.

Gupta, Shantinath: *Great Freedom Fighters of India*, Anmol, 2006.

H. L. Singh: *Red Fugitive:Jayaprakash Narayan*, Dewans Publications, Lahore. 1946.

Hari Hara Das: *The History of Freedom Movement in India (1857-1947)*, National, 1998.

Indu Dave: *Indian Personality in Its Developmental Background*, Himanshu, 1991.

Iyengar, A. S.: *Role of Press and Indian Freedom Struggle: All through the Gandhian Era*, APH, 2001.

J. S. Bright: *Life and Time of Jayaprakash Narayan*, Dewans Publications, Lahore, 1946.

Kailash Khanna: *History of Indian Freedom Struggle*, Commonwealth Publication, 2004.

Kaushik, A. S.: *Great Freedom Fighters of India*, Indian Publication, 2007.

Khairul Anam, Md.: *Indian Freedom Movement and Murshidabad District 1905-1947*, Bagchi, K. P., 2008.

Khan, Syed Ahmed: *The Causes of the Indian Revolt*, Oxford University Press, New York, 2000.

Krishan Mohan: *Encyclopaedic History of Indian Freedom Movement (4 Vols-Set)*, Book Enclave, 1999.

Kumar, Prafulla Pattanaik: *The First Indian War of Independence: Freedom Movement in Orissa, 1804-1825*, APH, 2005.

Kumar, Raj: *Essays on Indian Freedom Movement*, History and Culture Series, Discovery, 2003.

Kumar, Ravindra: *Champaran to Quit India Movement*, Mittal, 2002.

Kumar, Sirisa Shadangi: *The Prisons of South Orissa and the Freedom Fighters in Incarceration, 1900 - 1947*, Punthi Pustak, 2005.

Kumar, Virendra Verma: *Life and Legacy of Jayaprakash Narayan*, Radha, 2002.

Lafont, Jean-Marie: *Chitra: Cities and Monuments of Eighteenth-Century India from French Archives*, Oxford University Press, New York, New Delhi, 2001.

Lakshmi, Narayan Lal: *Jayaprakash:Rebel Extraordinary*, Indian Book Company, New Delhi, 1975.

Lion Agrawal, M. G.: *Freedom Fighters of India (4 Vols-Set)*, Isha Books, 2008.

Madhu, Dandavate: *Jayaprakash Narayan : Struggle With Values: A Centenary Tribute*, Allied, 2002.

Majumdar, R. C.: *History of the Freedom Movement in India (3 Vols-Set)*, Firma KLM, 1997.

Malhotra, Sumiti: *Thoughts of Great Personalities in 20 Century*, Raj Publishing, 2003.

Manju Verma: *The Role of Women in the Freedom Movement in Punjab (1919-1947)*, Abhijeet, 2003.

Maulana Syed Mohammad Mian: *The Prisoners of Malta (Asira'n-E-Malta): The Heart-Rending Tale of Muslim Freedom Fighters in British Period*, Manak, 2005.

Mazhar Kibriya: *Gandhi and Indian Freedom Struggle*, APH, 1999.

Meilinger, Phillip S.: *Airmen and Air Theory: A Review of the Sources*, Air University Press, Ala., 2001.

Muthaiah, S.: *Women Freedom Fighters*, The Hindu, 2004.

Nanda, S. P.: *Freedom Movement and Constitutional Development in India*, Dominant, 2004.

Napier, W. F. F.: *Life of Jayaprakash Narayan*, Oxford University Press, New York, 2001.

Narain, Jai Prakash: *Jayaprakash Narayan, Essential Writings, 1929-1979: A Centenary Volume, 1902–2002*, Konark Publishers, 2002.

Narayan, J.: *Jayaprakash Narayan: Selected Works; 1936–1939*, Nehru Memorial Museum and Library, New Delhi, 2001.

Om Prakash: *Encyclopaedic History of Indian Freedom Movement (12 to 21 Vols)*, Anmol, 2003.

Omesh Saigal: *Shaheed Bhagat Singh: Unique Martyr in Freedom Movement*, Gyan Publication, 2002.

Parashar, Parmanand: *Kashmir and the Freedom Movement*, Sarup, 2004.

Pearce, Roger: *Once a Happy Valley: Memoirs of an ICS Officer in Sindh, 1938–1948*, Oxford University Press, New York, 2001.

Pradhan, K. B.: *Freedom Movement in India*, Arise Pub, 2007.

R. M. Pal and Meera Verma, *Power to the People : The Political Thought of M.K. Gandhi, M.N. Roy and Jayaprakash Narayan*, Gyan, 2007.

Rafiya, Nisar: *Shaikh-Ul-Hind Maulana Mahmud Hasan and Indian Freedom Movement*, Manak Pub, 2008.

Ram Sharma, S.: *Education of Women and Freedom Movement*, Discovery, 1996.

Ram, S. and Kumar, R.: *Encyclopaedia of Indian Freedom Struggle (10 Vols-Set)*, Commonwealth Pub, 2008.

Ram, S. and Kumar, R.: *Quit India Movement: 1942-1945*, Commonwealth Pub, 2008.

Ramanathan, K. V.: *The Satyamurti Letters, Vol. II: The Indian Freedom Struggle Through the Eyes of a Parliamentarian*, Dorling Kindersley for Pearson Longman an Imprint of Pearson Education, 2008.

Ramu, P. S.: *Azad Hind Fauj (I.N.A.) and The Freedom Movement*, Freedom Movement Memorial Comm, 1998.

Ratan, Das: *Jayaprakash Narayan : His Life and Mission*, Sarup, 2007.

Rikhye, Indar Jit: *Trumpets and Tumults: The Memoirs of a Peacekeeper*, Manohar, New Delhi, 2002.

S.R. Sharma: *Life and Works of Jayaprakash Narayan*, Sublime, 2008.

Sharma, S. K.: *Eminent Indian Freedom Fighters (2 Vols-Set)*, Anmol Publication, New Delhi, 2004.

Slover, James Anderson: *Minister to the Cherokees: A Civil War Autobiography*, University of Nebraska Press, Lincoln, 2001.

Sundaram, V.: *Great Crusader for Women's Emancipation*, News Today, 2005.

Sundararaja, Saroja: *March to Freedom in Madras Presidency, 1916-1947*, Lalitha Publication, Chennai, 1989.

Suresh, Ram: *Loknayak Jayaprakash Narayan*, MacMillan Co. Delhi, 1974.

Taneja, Anup: *Gandhi, Women and the National Movement, 1920-47*, Har-Anand Publications, Delhi, 2005.

Yusuf, Meherally: *India Struggle for Freedom, Political, Social and Economic : Jayaprakash Narayan*, Hope India Pub, 2006.

Yusuf, Meherally: *J.P: Towards Struggle*, Padma Publications, Bombay 1946.

Index

❑❑❑